… if only all business executives were to read and comprehend *Learning to Read the Signs*, the world would be a dramatically better place, and corporations would be far more resilient and better prepared to manage present and future challenges.
Georg Kell, Executive Director, UN Global Compact

The challenges confronting executives in the 21st century include business complexity, environmental uncertainty, turbulent change processes, and unimaginable quantities of data presented in every imaginable technological form. The truth can be very elusive in the modern world. To make sense of it, leaders need a sharp mind, discerning judgment, and a reliable thought process for analyzing, assessing, and shaping one's options.

Ron Nahser brings experience, knowledge, and wisdom to this challenge in his new book, *Learning to Read the Signs*. As a successful businessman and as a student of business, society, history, and philosophy, Nahser has grappled with the numerous puzzles and traps that challenge the thinking executive. Unlike most of us, however, he has also formalized the thought process that has served him so well, creating what he calls a "path finder" methodology that has been tested and found useful by leaders in a wide variety of organizations.

His stated goal is deceptively simple: To learn how to be more "pragmatic" and to continually read what he calls "the signs of the times." This purpose opens the door to a subtle and nuanced understanding of how to "uncover the truth we do not yet know, leading to action we have yet to take."

The facts and events that bombard us daily are "signs" that need to be interpreted as they relate to what we already know. To be effective interpreters we need a process to help separate insight from opinion, truth from fallacy. Pragmatism, a philosophical school with deep American roots, provides the answer by showing us how to build a narrative of what is happening by using our detective skills in an iterative process of listening, questioning, and learning. Far from the common "do whatever works" thinking often attributed to the pragmatic thinker, Nahser shows us how to become true pragmatists – path finders – devising our own process of inquiry. The truth, we may discover, lies less in *the* answer and more in the *journey* by which we arrive at that answer.
James E. Post, JD, PhD, The John F. Smith, Jr. Professor of Management, Boston University

What people said about *Learning to Read the Signs* 1st edition:

This idea of pragmatism goes far beyond the conventional uses of today, but is a historically enduring principle that harnesses the deep intuition of our own perceptions and experiences and integrates it with the rapidly changing currents that surround us. Ron Nahser's remarkable effort to resurrect this profound philosophy in the business world is a bold and noble move and, when applied effectively, will bring forth better, more significant decisions that will enhance both our physical and our spiritual well-being.
Dr. Stephen R. Covey, author, *Seven Habits of Highly Effective People*

In today's competitive business environment, working hard is just the price of entry. Working smart is what keeps you miles ahead of the competition. And as you no doubt know, it's easier said than done. *Learning to Read the Signs and* the Path-Finder Pragmatic Inquiry will help you successfully navigate your own personal trail. It has worked hard and smart for me. I urge you to try it.
Jack Haire, Publisher, *Time* magazine

Ron Nahser has given us a brilliantly insightful look at how beautifully pragmatism can work in meeting today's global challenges. *Learning to Read the Signs* is a practical yet deeply moral book that should be required reading in the business schools and boardrooms of America.
Charles Osgood, Anchor, CBS Sunday Morning News

Nahser's unique qualifications – practical experience, business success, philosophical sophistication, and spiritual insight– make *Learning to Read the Signs* one of those rare, comprehensive books that addresses a wide audience. I will be surprised if it does not altogether change the way Americans of the 21st century understand the place of business in American culture.
Kenneth L. Woodward, Senior Writer, *Newsweek* magazine

If every business manager would read and take to heart Ron Nahser's new book, *Learning to Read the Signs*, this world would be a better place. To see business as a vocation that involves not only practical skills but also a character nurtured by ethical and spiritual wisdom is Nahser's great contribution. If you read only one book on business this year, read this one.
Rev. Theodore M. Hesburgh, C.S.C., President Emeritus, University of Notre Dame

In this time of intense scrutiny of not only the traditional ethics of business practice but the very nature of decisions we have taken for granted – reorganization, downsizing, the implicit employment contract – Nahser's thoughtful and compassionate analysis provides a guide for all thinking business people.
Roxanne Decyk, VP, Shell Corporation

A well-written, provocative discussion of pragmatism and how its novel application can contribute to both corporate and personal success.
James B. Klint, MD, Team Physician, San Francisco 49ers

Reflection leads to insight, which drives innovation – the imperative for business success. *Learning to Read the Signs* is a wonderful guide to this process.
Philip A. Marineau, CEO, Levi Strauss & Co.

Before you analyze, re-engineer, or downsize your company, here's the reality of how to successfully understand and improve your business for the long haul without doing irreversible damage in the process.
Robert J. Sunko, President & CEO, Spectrum Sports

Ron Nahser has created an insightful book at the dynamics of corporate messaging and pathfinding as we face an era where information will be ubiquitous and increasingly complex.
John Puerner, President and Publisher, *Los Angeles Times*

This book is a breakthrough, providing rich insight for our times and a perspective that generates creativity: both a philosophy and a guide for action steeped in the real world.
Dr. Michael Ray, Stanford University

Learning to Read the Signs afforded me the options to dive deep and explore the purpose of my business journey. The signs have always been there and this book offers us the vision and method by which to move forward.
Frank Smola, President, Merlin Corporation

Pragmatism is doing what is in your own self-interest, and doing the right thing at home or at work is a pragmatic course of action. Ron Nahser's great contribution is to point out that pragmatism and doing the right thing are not mutually exclusive.
Rance Crain, Editor in Chief, *Advertising Age*

Ron Nahser is philosopher, sociologist, scientist, theologian, but also a very practical businessman. He has applied his broad range of experience to the philosophy of Charles Peirce and developed a simple but practical approach to address the many pressing problems of business we face today. Accurate perception … a mutually reinforcing communication with others … a detective's mind – ideas that sound simple and yet are deep. It is Ron's great gift to us to have developed a very useful and workable approach to using these ideas to help us each day in our business lives.
Philip L. Engel, President, CNA Insurance companies

This is a book for those who are interested in doing the right thing, as well as doing things right.
C. William Pollard, Chairman, The ServiceMaster Company

This book attempts to build a model and foundation of Judeo-Christian ethics system to propel us into the next century … and it succeeds.
Rabbi Yechiel Eckstein, Founder and President,
The International Fellowship of Christians and Jews

Nahser's book supports the use of intuition in business but gives a way to test it. Or, in other words, don't believe your own (PR) bull*#$%.
David Sanguinetti, President, Retail Division, Florsheim Shoe Company

Ron Nahser really made me think. His idea that "everyone holds a piece of the truth" reinforces the importance of listening and working hard to understand the many (and often conflicting) pieces of information that come from our customers, vendors, and even our own management. Perhaps most important, Mr. Nahser reminded me of one of the most critical roles I have as a business leader – to make a difference with our communities and employees.
Barbara Allen, Executive Vice President, International Food Products,
The Quaker Oats Company

What struck me most is Nahser's interweaving of business practice, the philosophy behind it, and spirituality. He has hit upon an important connection.
Bother David Stendl-Rast, Esalen Institute

Ron Nahser has guided us through a series of enlightening stories, to a place of truth in business. Through his vision we can feel a sense of balance in the workplace that comes from a combination of good business practice, ethics and spirituality.
George E. McCown, Managing Partner, McCown DeLeeuw Corporation

Learning to Read the Signs succeeds in doing three things: it provides a method of articulating the often unexpressed assumptions that underlie human attitudes and behavior, it suggests a program for corporate renewal, and it provides a way of reconciling corporate and social goals at a time of tectonic change and hyper competition.
Padmanabha Gopinath, Executive Director, World Business Academy

To me one of the most striking sections of the book is Nahser's reinterpretation of the Benedictine monastic vows so as to make them applicable to our very secular society. He finds spirituality no more incompatible with business practice than is ethics. On the contrary, business practice will be immeasurably enriched if it can be seen as part of a spiritual and ethical discipline.
Robert N. Bellah, from the Foreword

In decidedly secular and delightfully communicative language, Nahser expands traditional understandings of ecclesiology into corporations, boardrooms, and other business settings. This book reimages long-held, limiting, and separated definitions and descriptions both of the business world and of the church world.
Dr. Peter Gilmour, Professor of Pastoral Studies, Loyola University-Chicago

Ron Nahser has succeeded admirably in thinking and writing about the theoretical and practical in the world of business. Would that there were others like him who could weave words and thoughts so easily and persuasively.
Daniel T. Carroll, Chairman and President, The Carroll Group, Inc.

For those who want to know how to prosper while practicing corporate soul-craft in the age of brutal markets, this is must reading.
Elmer Johnson, Kirkland & Ellis

Hurrah, Hurrah! Finally, a book that really talks about what is going on today. *Learning to Read the Signs* touches very carefully on many truths that must be understood by those responsible for any business if they are to be successful, both in making profits and in serving the community.
Ben. A. Mancini, President and CEO, Institute of Transpersonal Psychology

I enjoyed the book very much indeed. I hope and expect that it has the impact that it deserves.
Alasdair MacIntyre, Professor, University of Notre Dame

Ethics, shmethics. This book rocks!
Tom Bedecarre, President & CEO, AKQA, Inc.

Learning to Read the Signs
Reclaiming Pragmatism for the Practice of
Sustainable Management

LEARNING TO READ THE SIGNS

Reclaiming Pragmatism for the Practice of Sustainable Management

2nd Edition — Updated & Expanded
Including *PathFinder* Field Notebook®

F. Byron (Ron) Nahser

PRME Principles for Responsible Management Education

Greenleaf Publishing/PRME Book Series –
For Responsibility in Management Education

Greenleaf
PUBLISHING

© 2013 Greenleaf Publishing Limited

Published by Greenleaf Publishing Limited
Aizlewood's Mill
Nursery Street
Sheffield S3 8GG
UK
www.greenleaf-publishing.com

First edition: Butterworth-Heinemann, 1997

Printed in the UK on environmentally friendly, acid-free paper
from managed forests by CPI Group (UK) Ltd, Croydon

British Library Cataloguing in Publication Data:
  A catalogue record for this book is available from the British Library.

  ISBN-13: 978-1-906093-79-2 [paperback]
  ISBN-13: 978-1-907643-90-3 [hardback]
  ISBN-13: 978-1-909493-08-7 [PDF eBook]
  ISBN-13: 978-1-907643-79-8 [ePub eBook]

CORPORANTES is the *PathFinder* that helps us
uncover the truth we do not yet know,
leading to the action we have yet to take.

This essay is dedicated to everyone in organizations (and preparing for a career),
searching for better ways they and their organizations can profitably fulfill their
central social role of sustainably improving all of our lives.

The organization role is based on this proposition:

> "Marketing serves as the link between society's needs and its
> patterns of industrial response. It must be put
> at the heart of strategy."
> *Philip Kotler, Kellogg School of Management,*
> *Northwestern University*

PRME Principles for Responsible
Management Education

Greenleaf Publishing/PRME Book Series –
For Responsibility in Management Education

The Greenleaf Publishing/Principles for Responsible Management Education (PRME) book series aims to highlight the important work of PRME, a United Nations supported initiative. The series will provide tools and inspiration for all those working to make management education fit for purpose in creating a new generation of enlightened leaders for the 21st century.

Contents

Foreword to the Second Edition

Georg Kell
Executive Director, United Nations Global Compact

I first met Ron Nahser at the University of Notre Dame in 2002 when the UN Global Compact was first introduced to executives of U.S. corporations. We had a brief encounter, but one that had a lasting impact. Ron gave me a copy of the first edition of *Learning to Read the Signs*. On my way during a long trip, I started to read the manuscript with an enormous sense of appreciation. But in the hustle and bustle, I inadvertently abandoned the manuscript at one of the airports, not having finished reading it. Yet, during the following years, Ron's insights into the importance of values and pragmatic inquiry resonated with my own reflections, and I frequently used his terminology to make the case for corporate responsibility in this era of global interdependence.

Almost exactly ten years later, I saw Ron again at a conference at the University of Notre Dame. It was an enormous privilege to exchange views on the same subject, and I couldn't help but think that, if only all business executives were to read and comprehend *Learning to Read the Signs*, how dramatically a better place the world would be, and corporations would be far more resilient and better prepared to manage present and future challenges.

This book is also a critical resource for educators who are engaged with the Principles for Responsible Management Education (PRME), an initiative sponsored by the UN Global Compact that seeks to establish a process of continuous improvement among institutions of management education in order to develop a new generation of business leaders capable of managing the complex challenges faced by business and society in the 21st century.

Jonas Haertle, head of the UN-supported PRME Secretariat, tells the story in the Epilogue about how we have begun to incorporate Pragmatic Inquiry in our work to further sustainable development —"The Future We Want"—the most pressing task facing us today. We are working hard to make principled pragmatism—as described in these pages—a transformative force.

Foreword to the First Edition

Robert N. Bellah
Coauthor, *Habits of the Heart*

Learning to Read the Signs is a remarkable book: a philosophically sophisticated look at the place of business in American society today but one that comes from the desk of an actively engaged businessperson, not an academic viewing business from the outside. Taking as his point of departure that most American of philosophies—Pragmatism—Nahser reclaims it from the too easy idea that it means "whatever works" in order to show it as a disciplined mode of inquiry capable of helping us overcome the filters that limit our perspective so that we can discover "what's really going on." He starts from the most fundamental question of all: What is business for? Or, more bluntly, Why does your company exist? Once we take that question seriously we realize that profit, indispensable though it is, cannot be the only answer, for business is involved with the whole of society; it meets basic social needs and it has basic social obligations. A healthy business economy is only possible if it is part of a healthy society. Business needs a skilled and ethically reliable workforce that only good families, schools, and religious associations can produce. It needs a cultural climate that is encouraging and supportive of enterprise but at the same time maintains high standards of ethical behavior and responsibility. Individual character or cultural attitudes that encourage or even accept shoddy work or ethically questionable practice cannot in the long run be good for business. When character and culture support the ideal of a business vocation that "thinks greatly of its function" then the business life is both individually fulfilling and socially healthy. These, of course are widely shared ideals, though often honored in the breach.

But, while it does not directly address these broader social issues, the virtue of Nahser's book is that it shows through numerous stories, including his own, how these ideals can become practical and realistic. In Nahser's case, for example it led him to recast the industry requirement of "truth in advertising" to the more challenging standard of "advertising that tells the truth."

Nor is *Learning to Read the Signs* a how-to book in the sense that it provides ten easy answers to everyday business problems. The help it gives is much more profound. This book outlines a mode of inquiry that can be used to solve cognitive as well as ethical questions. Drawing on the deepest resources of philosophical pragmatism, Nahser shows us that often we do not even know the right question to ask, that we must start by trusting our doubts and seeing where they lead, so that we can even begin to ask the right questions. He brings philosophy down to earth by showing that a practical philosophy can call into question our outworn assumptions, open up new lines in inquiry, and lead to conclusions we never imagined at the beginning of the process, conclusions not just about what to do next, but about our larger purposes, those frameworks that give us meaning and direction.

Perhaps inevitably Nahser makes what is to many American business practitioners a problematic and unnecessary next step: After integrating the ethical and the practical, he moves to integrate the spiritual as well. Surprisingly, he chooses the analogy of Benedictine monasticism to make his point: Spirituality and work, spirituality and practical effectiveness, go hand in hand. When we were discussing this aspect of the book I reminded Ron that Max Weber, one of the founding fathers of sociology made this point long ago. Ron then promptly faxed me the reference: "From an economic viewpoint, the monastic communities of the Occident were the first rationally administered manors and later the first rational work communities in agriculture and the crafts." (*Economy and Society,* vol. 2: 1169). In other words, the famous Protestant ethic did not have to wait for the Reformation but was there deep in Western spirituality from quite early times. To me one of the most striking sections of Nahser's book is his reinterpretation of the Benedictine monastic vows so as to make them applicable to our secular society. I will not attempt to summarize the argument here but will leave it to the reader to discover the riches that Nahser has uncovered. Suffice it to say that he finds spirituality no more incompatible with business practice than is ethics. On the contrary, business practice will be immeasurably enriched if it can be seen as part of a spiritual and ethical discipline.

Learning to Read the Signs is not a difficult book to read—indeed it is both readable and enjoyable. Yet in these uncertain times, many may be skeptical as to whether there is a thoughtful and receptive audience for the book. Based on the response to my two coauthored books, *Habits of the Heart* and *The Good Society,* I am convinced that there is. I am also convinced that Ron Nahser's book will nurture and strengthen that community of thoughtful businesspeople who know that their careers and their firms will be at their best when the interests of business and society merge and they contribute to a larger ethical and spiritual design. I look forward to a long life for this book and its successors.

Note: Robert N. Bellah is Ford Professor of Sociology and Comparative Studies, University of California, Berkeley. The best-selling *Habits of the Heart* by Robert N. Bellah and coauthored by Richard Madsen, William M. Sullivan, Ann Swindler, and Steven M. Tipton has the subtitle "Individualism and Commitment in American Life." It was followed by *The Good Society,* coauthored by the same team.

Here is the story Dr. Bellah tells of how he and Nahser met:

> A few months after the publication of *Habits of the Heart,* I received a phone call from Ron Nahser, previously unknown to me, saying that he was the head of a Chicago advertising agency and that he would like me to autograph some copies of the book. Shortly thereafter, he arrived on my doorstep with an armload of books, telling me that the intended to give them to his clients. Although I knew *Habits* had a wide readership to the business world, I was still impressed that the book had received a careful reading from an advertising executive and that he wanted to share what he had learned with his clients. That was the beginning of a continuing friendship during which I have come to respect and admire Ron Nahser for his ethical convictions, his intellectual curiosity about American society, and, above all, his commitment to bringing out the ethical and even spiritual dimension of the business vocation.

Note from Dr. Bellah for the Second Edition:

> "I have reread my Foreword to *Learning to Read the Signs* and found it remarkably contemporary. I don't think I would want to change it at all ..."

Preface to the Second Edition: Nearly a generation later

It has been 18 years—nearly a generation—since *Learning to Read the Signs* was first completed. In that time, we have seen one of the great expansions and then implosions of our financial markets (now better known as "bubbles"), which threatened another Great Depression—our Great Recession. We continue to see alarming ecological deterioration—every ecosystem is under attack. Major shifts in the geopolitical landscape driven by financial growth ("Chindia" and BRIC have entered our vocabulary) and the desire for democracy are driven by issues of unfair representation and growing income inequality (witness the "Arab Spring" and the "Occupy Wall Street" movement). Some of these trends are in the paper every day. Very few people saw other dramatic changes coming, even though there were signs that a handful of keen observers—we might say pragmatists—read and took appropriate action. Those who did, and do, are our most effective and courageous leaders. They are the ones changing the direction and language and inspire others to take action.

In studying these events, and working with several thousand more executives and students all over the world in all kinds of organizations since 1995, I have seen increasing evidence of how we can and must develop strategies to address these issues, based on—and driven by—our values and vision. Therefore, this updated edition is aimed at helping all of us to be *more pragmatic* and learn to *continually* read the signs.

The reason why I have entitled this new preface "Nearly a generation later" is because, while the underlying concerns and trends that were evident in 1995 continue, a major generational change has been the explosion of information due to the Internet and the ubiquitous search engines.

As I tell in the first chapter, what initially triggered my interest in pragmatism over 25 years ago was becoming aware of certain facts that surprised me and forced me to challenge basic assumptions about U.S. business practices I had long held. And

I thought the way to change business was to expose other business practitioners to "surprising facts" to challenge their assumptions.

In working over the past 18 years, at first I was mightily encouraged by the access we all have to this tsunami of information. Surely some facts would catch the attention of other business practitioners and cause them to change course/strategies, as certain facts had seized me. But in working with groups, it has become clear that the problem is that there is *too much* information and, as a result, we either ignore the data or choose those pieces of data that fit into our preconceived ideas—the focus of Chapter 2. (This is not a new phenomenon of the human condition, however.)

So, in going back to the roots of pragmatism, I have come to see the foundational importance of the stance of a learner—being open to challenging our assumptions. From this stance we can be aware, first, of the **continuum** of our learning from data: the trends; and second, to better **interpret** the data as part of a larger system: the context. With this essential combination of perspectives—time and space— we can then better interpret the data to make better decisions to build better and broader models and systems, and vocabularies to articulate them. The result would be decisions and action that are more inclusive and organic than the narrower, reductionist, machine-like perspectives so often used in framing the conversation, discussions, and debates today.

To take a leading example concerning trends, consider the report entitled *Keeping Track of Our Changing Environment* published by the UN Environment Programme Secretariat in preparation for the UN Conference on Sustainable Development— Rio+20 Earth Summit—in 2012.[1] It compares key indicators presented at the first Rio Earth Summit with statistics today, and the news, while there are some bright spots, is still well short of "The Future We Want," appropriately enough the theme of Rio+20. (See Chapter 1 for several of the trends they identify.)

This 20-year comparison makes clear that we need to be much better at **connecting** the data. We intend *Learning to Read the Signs* to be a companion book to this 20-year summary of data, offering pragmatism as a method to think about how to interpret the signs.

Clearly, the original premise and intent of writing this book—to "resurrect this profound philosophy in the business world" (Stephen Covey quote—back cover)— continues to be both necessary and timely.

Three major changes

While the basic argument of the original edition remains unchanged, based on experiences and testing the method of Pragmatic Inquiry in workshops and lectures over the past 15 years with thousands of executives in organizational, academic, and personal contexts, our understanding of the methodology outlined in the 1997 edition has been revised in three significant ways.

The first change was to revise substantially chapters 7 and 8 to reflect the learning in structuring inquiries and including a dozen more case histories to show the way Pragmatic Inquiry actually works and leads to action. We have come to see even more clearly the role of **values,** which we define as **a belief, principle, or virtue held so deeply (either consciously or unconsciously) that it guides behavior, decisions, and actions.** The work of Jim Collins, beginning with *Beyond Entrepreneurship* and continuing through *Built to Last* and *Good to Great*, has focused attention on the importance of "values, core purpose, and goals."[2] We have seen that the best way to uncover the values is to see them in the evidence of experience as told through a narrative of self-reflection. This follows what Collins has identified as "Level 5 Leadership"—based on the paradoxical combination of "humility and fierce resolve." He knew this level was vital but was unsure how to help executives get to that level. (It took the right conditions "such as self-reflection, or a profoundly transformative event, such as a life-threatening illness.")[3]

We have found that the Pragmatic Inquiry is the way for executives to reach insight; to help executives find better, and in some cases dramatically different, solutions to a particular challenge they faced. But, more importantly, they found, after their humble openness to challenge their assumptions during the inquiry, to find sources of fierce resolve or *courage*—in their own words—to launch into action and face the inevitable barriers and obstacles they would encounter. So a large part of our learning is to see just how important the various steps in the inquiry are, in terms of engaging different mindsets: doubt, analysis, imagination, determination, and courage; and we have added appropriate adverbs for each step in the inquiry: Begin *Attentively*, Explore *Openly*, Interpret *Imaginatively*, Decide *Responsibly* and Act *Courageously*. (For an overview, also see our website: www.pragmaticinquiry.org.)

Second, from 2004 to 2008 I had the unique opportunity, as Provost (now Provost Emeritus), to help develop the first accredited MBA in sustainable management at Presidio School of Management (now Presidio Graduate School). During that time I was able to work with a remarkable group of scholars, educators, concerned businesspeople, and dedicated students in the area of environmental sustainability and social justice. I became familiar with the long history of environmental engagement and the development of such fields and ideas as bio-regions, bio-mimicry, "cradle to cradle," natural capitalism, the local living economy movement, B Corps, ecological economics, complex systems, conservation versus restoration, product and life-cycle analysis/assessment, integrated bottom-line accounting, and so on.

I especially realized the astoundingly simple fact that *all* organizations—commercial, civic and governmental—are in the business of serving the needs of society. To reflect this broader practice of management, we changed the subtitle of the book from *Reclaiming Pragmatism in Business* to *Reclaiming Pragmatism for the Practice of Sustainable Management*. **So, in the pages ahead, when you read "business or corporation," think "organization"; "business person," think "manager"; "society", think "society and the environment." You get the picture: We're all in this together.**

Some of these were questions I had long been engaged with, and describe in this book as well as in my book *Journeys to Oxford*,[4] a compilation of ten lectures given over 17 years at Department of Educational Studies, Oxford's Centre for the Study of Values in Education and Business. Particularly when working with Hunter Lovins, a leading environmental voice, we would often make the simple point that Hunter would say **what to think about** and I would present the case for pragmatic inquiry as a **way to think about it**. This experience heightened my belief and concern that the way to address these issues is not through more information, but in better thinking, reflection and conversation about them, that is, be more pragmatic. And given my career in advertising, it will come as no surprise that I came to see the central importance of rhetoric—the ability to express the results of pragmatic inquiries persuasively.

The third change was to better understand exactly what was going on as people inquired and reflected as I read more deeply the works of John Dewey and William James, secondary figures to Charles Sanders Peirce and Josiah Royce in the first edition, as well as modern feminist pragmatists, such as Susan Haack and Charlene Haddock Seigfried (see Bibliography for references). Two other scholars whose work I discovered in the last several years who have been very important in understanding what is happening during inquiries are George Lakoff, the cognitive linguist and professor of linguistics at the University of California, Berkeley, and Bernard Lonergan, the Jesuit philosopher-theologian. Their work and insights support and clarify the basic inquiry methodology of Peirce, Royce, and Progoff who were the main sources of understanding and presenting the *PathFinder* Pragmatic Inquiry methodology in the first edition.

Several of the stories are now dated (e.g. Florida Power and Light) and major recent stories are not included (e.g. the drama in the financial community from Enron to Lehman Bros.). The reason is that the basic ideas of—and need for—Pragmatic Inquiry are timeless and the stories could be updated every day as we read the ongoing headlines in the business press.

As the evidence of our learning, Chapter 7 "A *PathFinder* for organizations" has been substantially revised. (And the *PathFinder* Field Notebook is included in Appendix III. The Field Notebook is an introductory version of the Lab Journal, a more in-depth inquiry practice.)

The promise of pragmatism, it should be noted, is not accuracy of forecast, but constant scanning of the horizon with the goal to be resilient, always moving to better understand and act on our values and vision in changing circumstances.

Lastly, a note on philosophical content. *Learning to Read the Signs* was originally written in a style to be a "popular" version of a doctoral dissertation in philosophy accessible and engaging for our target audience: the "thoughtful business practitioner." (We weren't sure how big a market segment it was, but were pleased that the first edition sold out in short order, making it, in the words of one clever publisher, the "Harry Potter" of dissertations in moral philosophy.)

After the defense of the dissertation, and in preparation for publication, since we assumed our "target audience" was not too interested in all the philosophical reasoning, and at the urging of my able editor, Susan Speerstra, we considerably shortened heavy philosophical sections and eliminated *all* 115 footnotes. For the most part, our assessment of our audience's limited tolerance for close philosophical reading was right. However, we have been pleasantly surprised that many serious readers wanted a fuller explanation of the philosophy.[5] Therefore, we have reintroduced some more extensive explanation about pragmatism with source material, quotes, and endnotes.

I would like to thank the many scholars and executives, many of whom you will read about in Chapter 8, and my associates at CORPORANTES, Presidio Graduate School, and DePaul University who have helped in making the *PathFinder* more useful in reflecting and inquiring to "uncover the truth we do not yet know, leading to the action we have yet to take."

Preface to the First Edition

How do you lead an organization that needs to innovate—change/improve—in responding to changing market conditions?

As a practitioner of advertising communication and marketing strategy for over forty years, I have participated in developing communication programs for the entire spectrum of goods and services in American industry, from consumer packaged and apparel goods and services, hotels and shoe stores and toys and bicycles, to financial services, insurance, office furniture, machine tools and industrial chemicals. Our over 60 year old communications firm has represented companies of every kind—large ones, small ones, entrepreneurial ones, sterling successes, failures, companies in bankruptcy, steady performers, family companies. We have seen fads, staples and cutthroat competition. We have worked with some of the best talents in business and all types of personalities.

I wondered what explained the successes and failures I had seen. What seemed to be needed in virtually every conversation was a larger or at least a different context in which to think about the business issues. Then one day an item in the *Wall Street Journal* caught my eye: The US share of the Gross World Product in 1950 riding the post WWII economic boom was 52% but that by the early 90s our share had declined to about 20%. That surprising fact caused me to doubt the infallibility and superiority of our American management philosophy when it comes to innovation. Clearly, managers in other cultures had some successful ideas of their own that we could learn from. Or maybe we were overlooking something in our own culture; perhaps ideas these managers had learned from us. I decided to investigate. Inspired by Alexis de Tocqueville, who visited the United States in the nineteenth century to learn our ways of freedom, I took a three-month sabbatical in 1988 to travel overseas, meeting with Asian and European executives to study their business practices and beliefs. Then I sought out sociologists, anthropologists, and the best researchers in our business of marketing, to study our society's beliefs and practices. This in turn finally led me to study philosophy and theology as they illuminate our basic beliefs and habits of thought in America.

What I saw and learned surprised me. I discovered that it is not **what we know** but **how we learn** that is important. We seem to be simply gathering more facts, easily done in this Information Age, and piling them on top of what we already know. But learning starts when we see and interpret the information in a new way.

Therefore the purpose of this essay is to introduce you to a method that can help you evaluate and apply ideas and facts to your business and personal life by exposing the often subconscious or even unconscious assumptions and habits that underlie your current method of thinking and learning. Through the inquiry process described here, you will challenge assumptions, or **filters**, as I have called them, abandoning some old habits, keeping others, and adapting new ones.

This tale of the evolution of our American business philosophy and some ideas about how to improve it is also a personal story, a reading of the signs of my own career, in an attempt to live my profession as a vocation. I see the advertiser as a symbol-maker in our society. Those of us in advertising are like the totem-carvers and storytellers in other societies, those who attempt to give meaning to things. At the center of my own search for meaning in my life in advertising, I discovered the value of reclaiming pragmatism. On the way, I discovered a method to help others determine the meaning in their lives, to help them discover their business philosophy by which to guide their actions, careers and lives.

So I invite you to think along with me and share my story of the education of a business executive working alongside associates, clients and the consumer society influenced by our work. Examine my explanation of what's going on. Look at the discoveries I have made to lead us to a method of thinking which is intuitively obvious, but needs to be made explicit and part of the way we conduct business. This method has special significance for me in advertising because it deals with the reading of signs of activity in the marketplace, determining how to respond to those signs which suggest a business response and then the creating and communicating symbols or signs giving meaning and benefit to products and services for the marketplace.

> What are the signs telling us?
> Why are things going the way they are?
> Why and how should we respond?
> Where are we headed and why?
> What is our purpose?
> What seems to be calling us?

Do these questions and answers apply to your business practice and your life?

A place for businesspeople to find a model where pragmatism has been practiced for thousands of years is the monastery. "The *monastery*?" you say. Read on before you dismiss this instructive and very successful (read that to also mean "profitable") predecessor of the modern corporation.

My search resembles a detective story. The clues are there, and have been there for the last hundred years in our tradition. They point the way to still older truths:

to the story of pragmatism, a uniquely American philosophical movement. But we have misunderstood and corrupted it. Now is the time, I believe, for American business practitioners to reclaim it. If you do, you will improve your chances for success—in every sense of the word.

The method

The method of pragmatism, as you will see, is simple and the book will follow the method. The first section of one chapter sets forth the problem or issue to be addressed. The next three chapters lay out my Exploration of current American business thinking and practices and their origins. The third section of three chapters presents my Hypothesis about how to help solve current business problems through a method of applying pragmatism. The third section of two chapters shows how our method of pragmatism can address these problems through Action. The final section of one chapter dealing with Testing returns to the big questions raised above to illustrate how a reclaimed practice of pragmatism as a method of learning (or "inquiry," or "interpretation," as it was earlier called) can help businesspeople discover their vocation and find meaning, purpose and direction for their lives.

Chapter 1 will outline the need for Pragmatic Inquiry to begin with a doubt, or some recognition that we need to learn more about some situation to determine what action to taken next. The purpose is to change something, do something different, go in a different direction. Or, as I said at the beginning, to innovate. To see how we usually attempt to do that, we will consider in Chapter 2 what's going on in corporate America, and what filters we commonly use in business today to view reality. In Chapter 3 we will look at some attempts by contemporary thinkers and commentators to develop new filters as a way to help us see reality more accurately. Chapter 4 will show how certain patterns of thought which form our filters have been developed over centuries and are deeply held, often unconsciously, making it difficult for us to achieve the change called for by the challenges of our times. In Chapters 5 and 6, I trace the development of pragmatism from its founding by Charles Sanders Peirce over a hundred years ago to its evolution into something quite different from what Peirce intended. I also show how reclaiming Peirce's version lays the groundwork for a more successful and creative way of thinking, interpreting and doing business. Chapter 7 develops an actual method of inquiry and interpretation specifically directed to fostering business success. Applications of pragmatism in real-life personal and business settings are the subject of Chapters 8 and 9. Chapter 10 presents a summary of the ultimate way to practice pragmatism.

As Charles S. Peirce, considered by some as America's greatest philosopher and our central figure, has said, "This activity of thought (pragmatism) by which we are carried, not where we wish, but to a foreordained goal, is like the operation of destiny." Others describe this activity as participating in an unfolding story. Here is mine.

Acknowledgments: First Edition

One doesn't complete a book that has been brewing for over twenty years—while running a business—without a lot of help from associates, family, friends, clients, and scholars.

I want to thank first of all the people mentioned in the book because, as you will see, they have been pivotal in the development of my work. Without them there would be no story.

In addition to the people mentioned in the book, I need to thank my direct support team of Maeve Kanaley, who transcribed hours of discussions; Susan and Pauline Mehrtens; and Florence Agosto, all of whom endured the endless editing, rewrites and the thousands of details and without whom the telling of this story would have been impossible. Susan, our research associate, was instrumental in developing Chapter I as part of a marketing project for The Nahser Agency. Willis Harman, Maya Porter, and Karen Speerstra also collaborated at crucial moments in the editing.

I have had the benefit of being encouraged and challenged to put the ideas you will read about into practice by past and present associates and clients during my forty years at The Nahser Agency which has now evolved into CORPORANTES, Inc. in our marketing and advertising work. I want to thank all my associates over these years who have helped to test and practice our pragmatic inquiry method.

Next, I want to thank my teachers and mentors at the University of Notre Dame, the Northwestern University Kellogg Graduate School of Management, Shimer College, the Mundelein College Graduate Religious Studies department, and especially my friends at DePaul University, who, over the last fifteen years, gave me the opportunity to teach, study, and write: first and foremost, Brother Leo V. Ryan, CSV and his legion of scholar-friends to whom he introduced me, Fr. Thomas Munson, Stephen Houlgate, Kenneth Alpern, and especially Manfred Frings, who, along with Daryl Koehn and Dennis McCann, guided the development of the argument. And thanks to my DePaul students who, during my dozen years as Executive-in-Residence at the Kellstadt Graduate School of Business, proved the truth: "If you want to learn something, teach it."

Through Dr. Samuel Natale, organizer of the International Conference on Social Values, I was invited to present and discuss key parts of this material through a series of three lectures at Cambridge and Oxford Universities. Through Graham Turner I was invited to Worcester College, Oxford, to be Visiting Writer during the summer of 1994 when much of the organizing and writing of the book was accomplished.

Many friends have helped, criticized and prodded over the years, especially Philip Engel, members of the A-Team, Deb Kelly, Deb Kirby, Eileen Thompson, Rabbi Yechiel Eckstein, Rev. James Gorman, Ron Miller, Sr. Joyce Kemp, Steven Priest, Michael Cohen, Fr. Oliver Williams, Patrick Murphy, James Stuart, William Locander, Michael Bowen, Alan Gustafson, Kenan Heise, Willis Harman and the members of the World Business Academy, William Porter and members of the International Communications Forum, and Joseph Sullivan and members of Business Executives for Economic Justice.

I want to acknowledge the enormous debt I owe to my family: daughters Maeve, Katherine, Heidi and Heather who have inspired and instructed me over these past thirty years.

Most important, I want to thank my wife, Mary, who has watched in amazement, alarm, admiration, concern, but always in support and love over the last thirty-three years. She has been essential to the completion of this work.

I will continue the practice of pragmatic inquiry with organizations and individuals in business, and those planning careers in business, in repayment of their efforts and trust in order to help profit and non-profit organizations fill their role in providing the goods and services we need to help people develop and thereby contribute to profitably building a just and compassionate society.

Part I
Begin

1

Why reclaim pragmatism for organizations?

If the need of every organization is to generate new ideas for innovation, efficiency, and purpose, then pragmatism has a valuable contribution to make to managements' strategic thinking. In other words, it is the premise of this book that we in business need to be *more* pragmatic in practicing the logic of creativity on which pragmatism is based. That is because a pragmatic stance helps to overcome the narrow perspectives that too often guide organization decisions.

To see why this is so, one has only to understand that we all look at the world from our own perspective, defined by our beliefs and assumptions about how the world works. These perspectives act much like **filters**, leading us to see and understand, or ignore, or misinterpret events and facts around us. Often these filters are unconscious, deeply embedded in ourselves and in the culture. For business, they can mean missing market shifts in some crucial ways.

Examples abound of companies and organizations that have failed to "read the signs." Go no further than two archetypical industries that have defined capitalism in the United States: the automobile and the financial services industries. The troubles in these two well-known examples—both victims of their own success and excess—have come to serve as shorthand for the problems facing U.S. management. Doing business successfully in the 21st century means becoming aware of the filters that modify and limit business vision in our culture. Without this awareness, many businesses will continue to fall into short-term reactive thinking.

Consider the story of Ray Anderson and his "epiphany." As chief executive officer of Interface Carpet Co., the largest carpet company in the world, he had been asked by his sales force to give a presentation on Interface's position on the environment. His initial response was that they complied with the law. But as he read the literature in the field, especially Paul Hawken's *The Ecology of Commerce,* he got to Chapter 2, "The Death of Birth", which gave the statistics of species extinction in the context of "our wholesale plunder of the ecosystem."[6]

> "'I was running a company that was plundering the earth," he realized. "I thought, 'Damn, some day people like me will be put in jail!' "It was a spear in the chest."[7]

And we will begin with the facts similar to those that hit Ray.

As you read the list of facts below, which cover indications of social, environmental, and economic trends, see which ones hit you. Many are dated—we could update the list daily (check particularly the UN Environment Programme and WorldWatch Institute websites for latest statistics[8])—but you get the point. Maybe there is one that, while not a "spear in the chest," *might* spark a thought or concern. That is the start of pragmatic inquiry. But to state again: the important effort is to connect the dots and see the system driving these statistics and trends. And then develop and implement strategies to **change the data**.

Signs of change

Environment

- The current species extinction rate is estimated to be between 1,000 and 10,000 times higher than the natural or "background" rate[9]

- Some 20% of mammal species, 12% of birds and 31% of amphibian species were classified as "threatened with extinction" in 2006, according to the World Conservation Union[10]

- Since the start of the Industrial Revolution, carbon dioxide (CO_2) in the atmosphere has risen from 277 parts per million to 387 parts per million[11]

- Wind-energy generating capacity was up 26% in 2006 over 2005—the 16th consecutive year of double-digit growth.[12] The growth curve for solar panels is virtually the same

- Paul Hawken estimates that 99% of the original materials used in the production of, or contained within, the goods made in the United States become waste within six weeks[13]

- Soil erosion is second only to population growth as the biggest environmental problem the world faces. The vast majority—99.7%—of human food comes from cropland, which is shrinking by more than 10 million hectares (almost 37,000 square miles, the size of the state of Indiana) a year due to soil erosion. As a result of erosion over the past 40 years, 30% of the world's arable land has become unproductive[14]

- When spring run-off pollution is at its highest, more than 7.8 million pounds of fertilizer nitrate flow down the Mississippi River to the Gulf of Mexico every day. This causes a seasonal "dead zone" at the mouth of the Mississippi the size of the state of New Jersey[15]

Social

- While close to 1 billion people worry whether they will be able to eat, another 1.6 billion worry about eating too much[16]

- Americans don't just have more guns that anyone else (270 million privately held firearms—approximately 50% of the guns in the world). They also have the highest gun ownership per capita rate in the world, with an average of about nine guns for every ten Americans[17]

- World bicycle production, averaging 94 million per year from 1990 to 2002, climbed to 130 million in 2007, far outstripping automobile production of 70 million. China, with 430 million bikes, has the largest fleet, but ownership rates are higher in Europe.[18] The Netherlands has more than one bike per person, while Denmark and Germany have just under one bike per person

- Since 1992, the world's population has increased from around 5,500 million to close to 7,000 million, a 26% increase. While the rate of increase is slowing, the estimate is for a world population of 10 billion by 2100[19]

- Of the food consumed by citizens of Illinois, 4% is grown in Illinois, the so-called "breadbasket of the country"[20]

- For the $5.00 price of a 1 liter bottle of Fiji water, Paw Paw, Michigan consumers can get over 5,000 liters of water of water delivered to their faucets at home[21]

- Global consumption of bottled water more than doubled between 1997 and 2005, reaching a total of 164.5 billion liters, or 25.5 liters per person[22]

- The number of "megacities"—with at least 10 million inhabitants— has more than doubled from 10 in 1992 to 21 in 2010[23]

- India has 35 cities with populations of 1 million or more. The number is expected to reach 70 cities by 2026[24]

- In 1992, 2,400 million lived in urban areas. Now 3,500 million people do— more than half the world's population. And they account for 75% of global energy consumption[25]

- The adult literacy rate, worldwide, has jumped from 56% in 1950 to 82% in 2004[26]

- If current trends continue, the 6,900 languages in the world (down from 12,000 ten thousand years ago) will shrink to 2,500 over the next 100 years[27]

- The prevalence of obesity in the United States doubled between 1990 and 2005 to 40% of the population[28]

- The U.S. workforce (generally ages 25 to 64) is in the midst of a sweeping demographic transformation. From 1980 to 2020, the white working-age population is projected to decline from 82% to 63%. During the same period, the minorities portion of the workforce is projected to double (from 18% to 37%), and the Hispanic/Latino portion is projected to almost triple (from 6% to 17%)[29]

- The share of people living in poverty ($1.25 or less per day) was 1.4 billion in 2005, but 1.9 billion in 1981; from 52% in the developing world to 26%. But the decline is unevenly distributed around the world[30]

Economic

- Global consumption of bottled water doubled between 1997 and 2005, and is now the world's fastest growing commercial beverage[31]

- The top earning 1% of households gained about 275% after federal taxes and income transfers over a period between 1979 and 2007, compared to a gain of just under 40% for the 60% in the middle of America's income distribution, and 18% for the bottom 20%[32]

- In 1960, CEOs' income on average was 40 times the average factory worker's. By 2005, the average CEO was paid $10,982,000 a year, or 262 times that of an average worker ($41,861)[33]

- Socially responsible investment (SRI) is growing rapidly worldwide. SRI funds increased more than threefold in the United States between 1995 and 2005, more than eightfold in Canada between 2004 and 2006, and some 36-fold in Australia between 2000 and 2006[34]

- Informal employment is conservatively estimated to account for half to three-quarters of all non-agricultural employment in developing countries[35]

- China's annual automobile production grew from 320,000 in 1995 to 2.6 million in 2005. China could overtake Japan and the United States, each of which produces about 8 million cars annually, to become the world's largest auto producer by 2015[36]

- In 2005, China used 26% of the world's crude steel, 32% of the rice, 37% of the cotton, and 47% of the cement[37]

- If Chinese grain consumption per person continues to climb and reaches the European level, some 40% of the world's grain will be needed in China[38]

- The number of cell phone subscribers in China leaped from just 7 million in 1996 and 350 million—double the U.S. level—in 2005[39]

- In 1982, banks were lending out 80 cents for investments for every $1 they were lending for consumption. By 2011, they lent only 30 cents to fund investments for every $1 of consumption[40]

- If you had to summarize the U.S. focus on consumption, the demand side of the equation, consider the astounding growth of US household debt as a percentage of disposable income and GDP shown in Figure 1.1. One source funding this consumer debt was the growth of subprime debt. Credit default swaps grew unregulated and now comprise $683 trillion of contracts,[41] while real global production measures only the $62 trillion of global GDP[42]

Figure 1.1 **The growth of U.S. consumer debt**

Source: U.S. Federal Reserve[43]

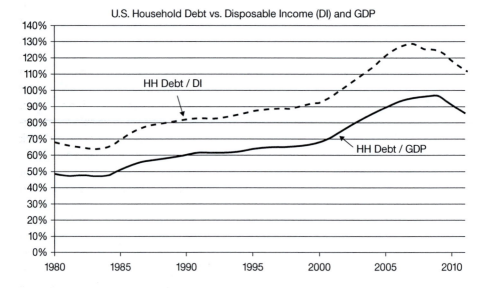

Rethinking our assumptions

What do these collections of facts mean? Do they connect so observers can see patterns and trends? How substantial are they? Will they pass with the latest fad in fashion and taste in music? Or are they signs of deeper changes?

Every day of our lives we are confronted with facts and trends like these that often compel us to act, or more precisely, *react*. When faced with new or potentially threatening evidence, we tend to interpret it to support what we already know and believe about the world. We usually fit facts into our already-determined patterns of thought: "Oh yes, that just goes to prove what I have been thinking all along." And if the facts don't fit our assumptions, we ignore or minimize them. These assumptions are often so long established and deeply absorbed that we may no longer even be aware of them. Yet they determine the way businesspeople make decisions, which are often instinctive or gut reactions. We therefore need to be aware of our philosophy because we see and interpret facts in light of our underlying assumptions.

Psychologists have long noted that in the process of exploration we filter what we see, accepting, changing, or equally important, ignoring facts and evidence in order to support our beliefs. Neuroscientists have found that these beliefs can be so deeply seated in the amygdala (the primitive part of the brain) that they trigger reactive, almost survival-like responses. In that sense our philosophy becomes almost hard-wired to determine our perception. We often say, "Perception is reality." In some psychological sense this can mean "whatever works for you," but this is not the same as a philosophical insight into reality, which often has a disturbing way of showing us that our perceptions are *not* reality.

I have seen the lone manager, because he stays at the level of his opinion, miss key trends in the marketplace because he doesn't "see" them and dismisses them as unimportant because they don't fit his picture of reality. The results can be disastrous, such as in the cases of the financial services and automobile sectors mentioned earlier. But this happens every day with all kinds of company. Take, for example, the Schwinn bicycle company, once the dominant brand and now virtually defunct, which hung on to its popular Varsity model and moved years too late into mountain bikes, even though Gary Fisher, one of the sport's originators, showed up at their door with an early mountain bike—built on an old Schwinn frame. And many fashion companies who missed the move to more casual dress, such as Florsheim with men's black wingtip dress shoes and Hanes with pantyhose, saw disastrous declines in sales.

Even in groups, managers and their associates do no better because they are not clear about their own or others' preconceptions. Little wonder that most group efforts result in wrangling and compromise with everyone fitting the facts into their preconceptions. Pragmatism can get us out of this box.

But occasionally along comes some fact or incident that forces us to stop and rethink our assumptions. We may have to adjust our thinking a little, or, in those few times in our lives when something profound happens (such as the loss of market share, a job, or even a company) we have to change our lives. In our rapidly changing world, such surprising facts and disturbing disruptions make us begin to doubt, not just react. We are not very good at this because often we are not even aware of the assumptions being challenged. This is where pragmatism can play a valuable role.

What does pragmatism really mean?

As businesspeople we think of ourselves as people of decision and action. We say, "Don't overthink it." "Keep it simple." "Let's move on with it." "This isn't brain surgery." "Ready, shoot, aim." "If it ain't broke, don't fix it." "If it ain't broke, break it." We like to think of ourselves as practical, or "pragmatic," as we say in American business.

Pragmatism is the subject of this book, but not pragmatism as it is often understood. In my discussions with business executives over the years about their business philosophy, they have often mentioned pragmatism. When I ask what it means to them, or ask them to describe someone who is pragmatic, they usually answer something like: realistic; sensible; basic; utilitarian; practical; willing to compromise to get the job done and to do whatever works for them. All these definitions center on the idea that action should not be guided or constrained by ideology or principle. All assume the individualistic principle that you should do whatever works for you, whatever it takes, or, as Nike proclaims in its advertising, "Just do it."

The *Oxford English Dictionary* defines "pragmatic" as "skilled in business, active, business-like, versed in affairs, relating to matters of fact, also a man of business or action." Many businesspeople see being "pragmatic" as the antithesis of being "philosophical." The businessperson, they think, is a doer fixed on quantitative results, while the philosopher is contemplative, abstract, qualitative, and theoretical, living outside the world of action. Yet, in reality, we all have a philosophy—an idea of how the world works. If an executive looks on reality in a quantitative, results-oriented way, he may not realize that this is within the philosophical framework of looking at all reality. We are often unaware that we are **interpreting** what we see. And to make matters worse, we assume that what we see and conclude is plain for everyone else to see and think as well.

Philosophy: the love of wisdom

As the French political thinker Alexis de Tocqueville, justly famous for his insightful observations about American society and mores, said over 150 years ago, "Less attention, I suppose, is paid to philosophy in the United States than in any other country in the civilized world."[44] I believe he is right. However, one of the most important activities in life and, we are coming to realize, in business as well, is to become aware of what our philosophy is, because this view, these beliefs, guide our actions. It is common today to equate philosophy with having an opinion about the truth of some abstract thought. But philosophy is not that. It is about the pursuit of truth; about having an **insight** into something outside ourselves.[45] We need to be aware of our philosophy because we see and interpret facts in the light of our underlying assumptions.

Pragmatism, in the philosophy developed by Charles S. Peirce, is a method of interpretation, or "inquiry" as Peirce calls it, which offers to the thoughtful business practitioner:

- A way to better understand the reality in which we operate

- A way to think critically about how we think and what we believe, especially the values that drive our behavior, decisions, and actions

- A way to improve how we think—to think more creatively

- A way for businesspeople to think together to make the best use of all our perspectives and talents

Pragmatism, in a word, gives us, as businesspeople, a way to see more accurately the reality of the world we live and work in, and to develop more appropriate action.

Peirce realized that what we see as facts and events are actually **signs** that must be interpreted. By accepting the need to **move from opinion** about what is going on **to insight**, we will improve our decision-making in business. That is the promise and method of pragmatism. Hence the title of this book, *Learning to Read the Signs: Reclaiming Pragmatism for the Practice of Sustainable Management.*

By learning to read the signs and being open to doubting our own assumptions, using the original pragmatic method, businesspeople can become aware of their blind spots and assumptions, see reality more accurately, and make better decisions that lead to better action.

The best business practitioners interpret reality and see patterns and connections better than others, and this helps them see where things are heading. Yes, we can impact events by imposing our ideas and strategies to a degree, and so shape our destiny. But we must learn to do this more in the form of an accurate response to our reading of the reality we face, much as pioneers venture into new territory, map in hand, and correct the map as they confront the reality of the terrain.[46] They are practicing pragmatism. Later they can bridge a river and blast a road through mountains to shape reality to conform to their perceptions. But it starts with engaging with the reality of the territory.

To help us interpret reality more accurately and act more effectively, I am proposing that we reclaim the method of logic that has been with us for centuries, in the form in which a series of American philosophers restated it at the turn of the century—pragmatism. These philosophers, Charles Sanders Peirce, William James, and John Dewey, are main characters in the first part of our story. Later, a Jungian psychologist, Ira Progoff, brings another dimension to the pragmatists. But first we must see the importance of the effort and why we need pragmatism as a method of inquiry in business today.

As we search for better, more efficient ways to engage the hearts and minds of employees and to market products and services, philosophy as a business activity is becoming more acceptable. While statements of corporate philosophies have appeared in everything from Jaguar and Saturn automobile ads to Victoria's Secret catalogs as a way of expressing those companies' visions and reassuring customers, I knew U.S. business practitioners were ready to read about philosophy when I saw on the side of that most typical U.S. package, a six-pack of beer from Pikes Place Brewery in Seattle, the opening sentence of a longer sales pitch: "Micro-Brew is a philosophy."

Asking the big questions

Times are changing. The reality of our lives is changing. Peter Drucker, Tom Peters, Michael Porter, Jim Collins, W. Edwards Deming, and other leading business thinkers have long and consistently remarked how important it is for a company to have a philosophy or a vision, as it is often called. And it is time to reclaim the original, uncorrupted pragmatism to help us adapt and answer the big questions facing us now. Questions such as:

- What business are we really in (versus the business we think we are in)?

- What can we be better at than anyone else in the world?

- What are the facts and trends that most impact our business?

- Whom do we serve and what do they really need?

- What practices and strategies are in our best long-term interest?

- How are we to think about the operation, successes, and failures of organizations and their impact in building a fair and just society and a thriving environment?

- How can we run our organizations better—to be sustainable—in the face of the changing environment?

- What happened to the sense of vocation in our work lives and how important is this?

- What are our goals and purposes?

- What are our values—the **beliefs, principles or virtues** held so deeply (either consciously or unconsciously) that they guide our behaviors, decisions and actions?

Pragmatism as a method of inquiry, in its original meaning, can help us with these questions. Chapter 2 will describe what is going on in corporate America and what filters we commonly use in business today to view reality. Pragmatism, and the journey to discover our destiny, begins with a doubt, as we shall see in the strange case of John Hudiberg.

Reading the signs

- How would you have defined the term "pragmatism" before you read this chapter?

- What are your favorite examples of organizations either missing long-term trends or following trends that turned out to be short-lived?

- How has missing trends, following trends, or anticipating tends affected your organization?

- Does your organization traditionally overreact to trends and events or remain product focused for too long?

- What are your favorite examples of companies that have caught trends that matched and strengthened their core competencies? What present trends is your company watching and responding to?

- What are your favorite facts indicating trends and changes?

Part II
Explore

2

The filtered view from the corporate tower

We all look at the world through filters. Usually we are not aware of our filters, but sometimes events force us to see them and consider their usefulness. One business executive told how his filters were dramatically changed, with momentous consequences for both himself and his company. The businessman is John Hudiberg, former Chief Executive Officer (CEO) of Florida Power & Light (FPL), the first American company ever to win, in 1989, the prestigious Deming Prize given by the Union of Japanese Scientists and Engineers to honor outstanding corporate quality.

Hudiberg told his story during a presentation to members and guests of the Harris Bank in Chicago. His subject was the issue of quality and how he implemented a Total Quality Management (TQM) program in his company. I followed his tale closely because I knew the Deming Prize was even more difficult to earn than the U.S. Baldrige Quality Award.

Hudiberg's tale

Hudiberg made his key point bluntly:

> Let's face it, most companies operate under the premise that the average employee is lazy, poorly educated, and in need of strict supervision by a better-educated, more experienced supervisor. I am sure that most of you manage your employees this way, using discipline to make sure that they do their work. In retrospect, I certainly did.

He was equally forceful in his conclusion:

> The most important element of a successful Total Quality Management Program is choosing your philosophy about managing people. If you leave today with only one idea, this is the most important one: your TQM Program will fail if you do not develop a new management paradigm that is based upon job satisfaction.[47]

As a student of Peirce's pragmatism, I was struck by this statement. It sounded to me like a great example of pragmatism at work: a dramatic change in assumptions about work, which led to equally dramatic action and results.

"But what caused this dramatic change?" I asked him. "What got you to begin to doubt the wisdom of your usual way of doing business?"

His is a classic example of the surprising fact giving rise to doubt, leading to an insight that changes assumptions about reality. Hudiberg recalled that one Sunday morning, as he was reading the paper and having a leisurely breakfast, he heard commotion and shouting in front of his house. He looked out of the window and was shocked to see people carrying signs, picketing his home. He recognized some of the people as his neighbors. Their signs said things like, "Florida Power & Light service stinks!" and "Down with Florida Power & Light."

But the one that hit him between the eyes was, "Hang Hudiberg!"

Doubt, exploration, change

He knew there were problems and that service had to be improved, particularly as deregulation loomed, but that demonstration was the clincher. The next day he began an investigation to determine the extent of the problem. As he expected, he found that FPL's service, measured by hours of power outage, did not compare favorably with the top-ranked utilities around the country.

But he was totally unprepared for what he found when he visited Japanese utilities. Their performance in everything from accuracy of bills to minimal number of hours of power outages was vastly superior to that of his or any other U.S. utility. That began his three-year effort to reinvent the company and, guided by their criteria, win the Deming Prize. He pulled the entire company apart, measured everything imaginable, and instituted a quality program that succeeded in winning the award for FPL. The Japanese inspectors questioned employees and customers during a grueling two-week examination period and found their answers up to Japanese methods and standards. (As we shall see, the Japanese learned all this from the United States after World War II.)

He was awarded the Deming Prize. But Hudiberg, I propose, made one critical mistake, which will play an important part in our story later. (Hint: his associates at FPL didn't see the problem in the same way.) For our purposes here, the tale of John Hudiberg shows how a pragmatic method of inquiry works, beginning with a doubt leading to investigation, and then to a change in the way one sees reality through new filters.

What happened to Mr. Hudiberg was not unique. All of us in business are looking to make changes in the face of greater foreign competition and rapidly changing market conditions. We often look where Hudiberg did.

The quest for the Holy Grail: efficiency and innovation

In our search for efficiency, we have had to look at how our businesses go about planning, revealing what we hold important. In a time of downsizing, rightsizing, and restructuring to the virtual, flat, horizontal, reengineered corporate structure, management rightly worries about the motivation of employees to contribute their best efforts and ideas. At the same time, the call for quality has produced a need for workers to have a larger understanding of the operation and a coherent vision of the corporation and its place in society. In this age of the knowledge and information worker, many commentators see that workers need to be motivated by more than money; they must believe in the purpose of their organization. They need to see the larger picture and their role in it.

Employees also need to be treated like human beings rather than as impersonal functions in a hierarchical, command-and-control structure. We are recognizing that people cannot be moved around like cogs in a machine. Treated that way, people feel like commodities and develop little loyalty or inspiration to give their best. We are seeing that we cannot just make changes as if we were tinkering with a machine—a twist here, a replacement part there. Rather, businesses are looking more like living things, which should not surprise us, since we call them "corporations" (from the Latin *corpus*, body) and "organizations" (that is, organisms, living things).

Zero-sum thinking

The machine model that has served so well for so many years in our thinking about business is looking increasingly inadequate, because it has fostered our tendency toward dualistic thinking: the yes/no, us/them, zero-sum trade-offs way of seeing the world. As a result, we lose the recognition of shades of gray, and even more, of paradoxes, those apparent inconsistencies that can spark philosophical scrutiny and explication.[48]

One business paradox is the fact that individuals in business always operate in the context of some community. It is generally believed, especially in the United States, that each person has the right to his or her own opinion. But of course each person's opinion exists alongside the opinions of others.

Other members of society are urging us, working in all kinds of organization, to look at the larger ethical context, the ecological and social impact, and the psychological climate prevailing in our organizations, especially during these difficult economic times.

We need to ask: What do our decisions look like, where are they leading us as an organization, whom do these actions serve, and whom do they affect? To help find the answers to these questions is the task and promise of pragmatism.

We need to find a way to get to the heart and meaning of facts and information and to discuss our interpretations with others—a way to change the filters of the machine model, dualism, individualism, and ethical expediency that have marred the view from the corporate tower. The better we become at interpreting reality more accurately, the more successful our businesses and organizations will be. To see why this is so, let us consider each filter more closely.

The machine model

In the current model, business is often seen as a machine that needs to be reengineered. Workers have become tools or cogs in the machine, to be moved and fixed, commanded and controlled, doing their part with no sense of the big picture, or opportunity for personal fulfillment. The personal quality and uniqueness of each individual is overlooked.

We tend to break things down into parts, as we would treat a machine, to see how things actually work. By doing this, we miss the interaction between the elements; we miss seeing the organization as a whole. This limits our perception and provides fewer clues as to what is going on. We often refer to corporate "silos," with each department or function considering only its own needs. And business often considers itself a silo with little connection to society, much less seeing our connections with our physical/natural environment.

The machine model leads easily to a preoccupation with quantification, analysis, and other specialized tools for profit maximization, which focus businesses' attention on the bottom line while failing to consider such larger, life-giving issues as vision and mission. Business schools strive zealously to turn people into number crunchers and teach managers that their focus is to be on the quantifiable aspects of business. Thomas Piper, Dean of Harvard Business School, recognized this when he said,

> Business schools, in responding to the needs of the marketplace, were focusing on the numbers side of the business ... MBA education seems to have failed in its most important responsibility: to generate excitement about careers and the opportunity for making a difference ... Without realizing it, we gradually reduced our attention to issues of responsibility and purpose.[49]

Financial and corporate employers have been looking for keen-eyed analysts who can determine the "true" value of corporations, meaning the financial value, and use this to ratchet up debt levels for the financing of destructive leveraged buyouts and takeovers. With such a fixed and narrow financial focus, businesspeople ignore the culture and core competences unique to the corporation.

Our traditional model of business as machine is coming up short. We are beginning to recognize that we cannot claim that we can be solely "scientific" or "quantifiable" or "measurable" about business. The basis of science, of course, is the ability to develop theories that deal objectively with time and space and consistently predict outcomes. We clearly have lost any claim to that ability in business, and, with this loss, the machine model is severely weakened.

Business perceptions: a dualistic way of thinking

Our machine model is supported by the habit, deeply ingrained in U.S. business thinking, of seeing issues in dualistic, yes/no, black/white terms. In defining the goal of the business enterprise we have set up a dualism that measures success in terms of profit maximization alone, to the exclusion of other measures of success in the enterprise. We reduce complex issues to trade-offs. One of the most common is the perceived trade-off between the short term and the long term. The two are seen as opposites: the "investment" strategy versus the "harvest" strategy, or "margin" versus "volume", for a product or brand. Another is the trade-off between serving the customer and serving the shareholders.

Nordstrom, the Seattle-based retailer, is renowned for its attention to its customers' needs. The Wall Street investment community frequently criticizes Nordstrom, and other service-oriented organizations, for suboptimum quarterly earnings. The typical complaint is that these organizations put too much emphasis on customer service and value, putting the customer ahead of the shareholders.

We have many other dualities in our thinking; for example, we see the business person's task as either to make money or to "do good."[50] At work we are one way and at home, another. Telling people what to do is set against letting them do what they want. None of these dichotomies is more significant than the way in which, especially in the United States, we tend to see the tension between the individual and the group, the star and team, and the freedom of the citizen and the needs of society.[51]

We are coming to realize that people have many different intelligences. Because people process information differently, we need diversity within a working group— diversity not only of race and gender and age, but also of emotional and intellectual intelligences. In his book *Emotional Intelligence*, Daniel Goleman points out that among other things, emotional intelligence includes self-control, zeal, persistence, and the ability to motivate oneself.[52] We find that by being respectful of these differences in people, we dramatically increase the ability to generate better solutions by thinking pragmatically. We all see different sides and shades of the same picture and everyone is determined to view the correct interpretation of reality. The quickest way to abort the pragmatic search is to fall into the trap of dualistic either/or, right/wrong, you/me thinking.

Individualism and the business community

This tension between the individual and the group is an effect of one of our most common and pernicious filters: our belief in the concept of individualism. We see individual self-interest as one of the basic motivators of our activities. That is why in U.S. business we have difficulty operating in the groups or teams that employers look to today as a way to gain worker involvement. Rather than fostering teamwork, the penchant for individualism creates business bureaucracies that pit individuals against other individuals in win–lose operations. Look at how we handle the central issue of top management succession. Businesses often structure themselves so that just one of several senior executives has a shot at the top job. When one succeeds, the others leave. (We will tell the classic story of management succession at Apple Computer later.)

The filter of individualism blinds us to the opportunity and power of bringing different voices together for the benefit of the whole company. The assumption driving this exaggerated individualism is our belief in the importance of one individual or star. How else can we explain the continued escalation in the salaries of CEOs?

Another side to our fascination with individualism is the way it hampers a feeling of community, both within the corporation and in U.S. society as a whole. Robert Bellah, a leading sociologist, casts the argument here in terms of what he calls the "therapeutic model," referring to the general practice in psychotherapy of insisting that clients must decide for themselves what to do. In this individualistic model, there is no room for someone to consider the interests of other human beings. Bellah and other astute analysts of our social reality show how in the United States business has lost the language of the republican tradition on which the country was founded. We have trouble with sustained moral discourse because our conversation quickly breaks down into "That's your opinion," or "Everyone is entitled to his or her opinion." We have come to a point where our "habits of the heart"[53] have led to our losing the larger perspective of community. In a business setting, this translates into problems of getting people to enter into sustained conversation and come to action, which will be central to our discussion of pragmatism.

Ethical expediency

Closely related to our obsessively dualistic thinking and individualism are the ethical crises that appear in the newspapers every day. It is abundantly clear that most major corporations want managers who will conduct business with the sole purpose of increasing financial rewards, or, in Milton Friedman's words, "maximize return to shareholders, staying within the rules of the game."[54] The result is that business pushes the limits of questionable activity, relying on federal regulators for ethical oversight. In this logic, defining business as a game (or more seriously as war) absolves businesspeople from wrestling with moral dilemmas.

Given our image of business as machine, we have no larger view of corporate purpose than maximizing profits. Such a narrow focus provides us little with which to gauge the morality of our actions. We can see this lack of ethical concern in the question of violence and sex in the entertainment media. With the proliferation of cable television, and the need to improve ratings and return on investment in blockbuster movies, producers often turn to the fail-safe formula of sex and violence. How do we decide which market segments need to be protected, and from what, and how? What is the responsibility of the producers and regulators or do we simply let the market decide?

Another area of ethical concern is the question of advertising messages. How should we, if at all, advertise such products as beer and cigarettes, especially given the impact on so-called entry-level consumers (i.e., teenagers)? What about exaggerated or misleading claims about performance, nutrition, and environmental impact? Ethical breaches in the structuring of financial dealings and in the marketing of financial services continue to be in the news.

Applications for our strategy and communications group

When people ask me if I have a secret strategy for advertising, I think of the mentors I have had, including scholars, theologians, and, not least of all, my father, who founded our company back in 1939, and I think about the campaigns we have run for our clients. I keep coming back to the fact that being a student of values is central to my work. In my firm, we believe that, if you touch fundamental beliefs both in clients and in markets, campaigns will have a longer life because they will ring true with consumers and employees. Even though business changes very fast, we know there are deeper values to be touched. We believe there are certain products and things that we really want to promote. As an example, while we resigned a veal client because of animal rights issues, we were thrilled to be working with Pritikin, the low-fat diet, exercise, and stress reduction people. Would we take a traditional, high-cholesterol fast food account? I doubt it. We feel very strongly about creating advertising that respects people. Some advertisers say, "Take this and you'll be terrific!" We're apt to say, "You're already terrific, but this may be of some use in helping you express yourself and share who you are with others."

It is clear that we need a model of marketing built not on a machine-like exchange alone, but on the principle of extended relationships based on dialogue and interpretation with customers and employees existing within the larger society and natural environment. Using this filter, products and services take on a meaning far beyond their utility and importance in how they relate to personal being. When advertising employs powerful psychological ploys to feed on fears and insecurities by treating the individual as a consuming entity that needs advertising and products for self-definition, to be happy, and to feel fulfilled, the advertising plays into the machine model. In the words of one researcher, "we have to be psychic archaeologists to peel back the layers to get to the dark places people don't know they have" and find the right button to push.[55] Anyone can become an overnight expert in analyzing advertising by using the common parlance industry formula that every advertising beginner learns:

1. Who is the advertising aimed at?

2. What do they think now?

3. What we want them to think?

We believe there is a much larger truth—that people buy and consume products to aid their own personal development, to express and reveal parts of themselves to others, and, finally, to contribute in the development of their own lives and the lives of their community. Our ethical stance, therefore, uses the twin standards of societal context and respect for the individual. We consider the products we sell in terms of how they are consumed and whether they and their advertising—the visible sign of the product—help to foster a fuller sense of what it means to be human. We follow the example of Bill Bernbach, a legendary leader in the advertising industry: "All of us who professionally use the mass media are the shapers of society. We can vulgarize that society. We can brutalize it. Or we can help lift it onto a higher level"[56]

The relationship model of developing a better society also can stimulate our work in developing creative ideas. Dualistic thinking in terms of either/or has led us away from one of the most useful sources of fostering creativity: tension.

By looking at opposing ideas as being in a relationship, this fosters the energy to solve the tension or dilemma the clients are facing. We look to other opinions and differences, not as winners or losers, but as starting points to develop other ideas. Therefore, instead of framing issues in either/or mechanical models, we do the opposite in that we focus on and frame the organic, evolving points of tension.

Due to the pervasive influence of (1) The business-as-machine model, (2) Dualistic thinking, (3) Individualism, and (4) Expediency in ethics, corporate executives generally see reality through these filters. How do we change our filters? Some insightful business leaders and observers offer us answers to this question, as we shall see in Chapter 3.

Reading the signs

- Do you agree that corporate executives generally see reality through these four filters and can you think of examples?

    - The machine model

    - Business perceptions: a dualistic way of thinking

    - Individualism and business community

    - Ethical expediency

- Do you see other filters? What are your filters?

- Does your company have a prevailing filter?

- What roles do your company's products and services play in people's lives? How are you now promoting those roles?

- Have you had any similar awakening to Hudiberg's? If so, what was it and what were the results?

- Are there facts and events that challenge your personal and business thoughts?

- Are there tensions or paradoxes your corporation wrestles with or needs to wrestle with?

3

The purpose and nature of business

Is it time to change our view?

The problems we outlined in the last chapter triggered the pursuit of quality and efficiency that led John Hudiberg to revamp Florida Power & Light. Hudiberg's "upending moment" had a parallel at the Business School of the University of Chicago. The first *Business Week* survey of business schools in 1988 revealed that Northwestern University's Kellogg Graduate School of Management was rated as number one by employers, outranking Chicago, Harvard, Stanford and other traditional leading business schools. Previously, all rankings had been made by the business school professionals themselves. But when employers, graduates, and students were polled, Northwestern shot to the top. Why? The other top business school graduates were perceived by employers as number-crunchers, while the Northwestern graduates seemed to acclimate more readily and work better within the business organization.[57]

Stung by being displaced by its cross-town rival, the business faculty at the University of Chicago began to examine its curriculum to see how they could include a more human touch. In one of the more innovative efforts, a two-and-a-half-day conference was held in 1991 to explore the process of community building. The conference was led by the Foundation for Community Encouragement, established by M. Scott Peck, a psychiatrist present at the conference, to foster community development. As the conference concluded, the dean and assistant dean, in a deservedly congratulatory mood, hugged each other in the lobby of the Business School building. That moment made me realize how far we had come in thinking about some of these problems, especially the narrow focus on quantification we have already noted.

The pursuit of quality and efficiency

In Chapter 2, we called this pursuit the "Quest for the Holy Grail." Indeed it seems this is still the pursuit around which much business activity turns. Mention quality and efficiency these days and many people immediately think of Japan, as if these attributes were something we had to learn from them. In fact, it was quite the reverse. Historically, what the Japanese know of efficiency and quality they learned from U.S. business techniques and ideas.

Shortly after the end of World War II, at General Douglas MacArthur's order and direction, a course entitled CCS: Industrial Management was developed and taught by two U.S. business school professors, Charles Protzman and Homer Sarasohn, to train future Japanese business leaders.[58] At the time, many U.S. leaders feared Japan would be taken over by socialist forces. MacArthur and the professors felt the way to stabilize Japanese society was to create a strong manufacturing system based on methods of statistical quality control developed in the United States. So Protzman and Sarasohn taught the future leaders of Japanese manufacturing everything they knew about basing manufacturing on the principles of total quality management, and judging from the evidence many decades later, the Japanese learned their lessons well. These leaders now claim that, of course, statistical quality control is important, but more important are the vision and purpose of the organization, as Protzman and Sarasohn taught them.

Recent efforts by U.S. business school professors helping Russian managers to develop a market economy began with finance-focused lectures on the "art of the deal," reflecting U.S. preeminence in this field of finance. Protzman and Sarasohn started with a more basic task: to clarify the mission and purpose of the business corporation. They asked a fundamental question: Why does any company exist? Many people, they acknowledged, would probably answer that the purpose is to make a profit. But this is a one-sided answer:

It ignores entirely the sociological aspects that should be part of a company's thinking. A business enterprise should be based on its responsibility to the public, on service to its customers, and on the realization that it can and does exert some influence on the life of the community in which it is located.[59]

The Japanese took these words to heart, with major consequences for their ideas of quality.

A few years after Protzman and Sarasohn, Dr. W. Edwards Deming arrived in Japan to teach the Japanese about quality and productivity. One of his first lessons was on how to conduct a fact-gathering survey, for he realized that the business process starts with customers and their needs. By contrast, U.S. management often looks within itself to attempt to define quality, while the major definer of quality is, in fact, the customer. Recognizing this has led us to look outward to the market to gain a clearer sense of the purpose of our businesses.

As Peter Drucker says,

> the rhetoric of 'profit maximization' and 'profit motive' are not only anti-social. They are immoral … It is the purpose of an organization, and therefore the grounds of management authority *to make human strength productive*. Organization is the means through which man, as an individual and as a member of the community, finds both contribution and achievement.[60]

Drucker here echoes Adam Smith when he states that "personal strengths make social benefits."[61] Drucker draws the important distinction between the organization as a tool by which society accomplishes its tasks, and specialization of individual labor (man as a cog in the machine) as a way of increasing efficiency. This distinction brings us back to the filters through which business practitioners too often view their organizations.

Dismantling Taylorism. Should we?

In a cover story in *Fortune* in 1993, Senior Editor Thomas Stewart wondered just how revolutionary the changes going on in business were, and concluded that we faced "a basic shift in the organization of work." He explained this by quoting Stephen Gage, a manufacturing executive: "I doubt if there's a company around here that isn't experimenting with something having to do with dismantling Taylorism."[62]

This refers to Frederick Winslow Taylor (1856–1915), whose work was misunderstood over 70 years ago but who offered the first clues on the real way to increase efficiency. Taylor still gets stuck with the time-and-motion-studies label that many people now regard as one of the worst examples of reducing workers to machines: engineers in white coats with stopwatches studying the movement of workers, looking for ways to wring more efficiency out of their unwilling bodies. Taylor, however, spoke out for something much more profound and basic.

Like John Hudiberg, Taylor saw the real revolution was not about efficiency but about changes in managerial attitudes toward workers. In his era, managers focused only on Taylor's use of time-and-motion studies. If we do not understand what Taylor was really trying to say to management, we will repeat the same mistakes, only searching for ways to squeeze more productivity out of the minds and hearts of today's knowledge workers. In our time, as Stewart pointed out, we focus on workers' access to information.

We have known about the power of the division of labor since Adam Smith. He pointed out that the basis of the "wealth of nations" was not superior trading ability, nor gold, nor material resources, but labor, and specifically the specialization or division of labor. Aware of this, Taylor explained during remarkable testimony before a Special House Committee in 1912 that "scientific management"[63] (a label he coined) was not about any efficiency device or method, but "involves a complete mental revolution on the part of the worker, and most importantly, management."

Why this need for a mental revolution? Taylor realized from his studies of U.S. businesses that workers had little incentive to be more efficient. If they were, two things would happen, both bad for the worker:

- Efficiency would be increased and workers would be laid off. This is a reverse of our downsizing, where people are laid off in the belief that the remaining workers will be more efficient. The result in decreased morale is the same

- Increased profits ("surplus," to use Taylor's term, echoing Marx) would go to the owners, not the workers

Taylor saw that the workers understood better than management how to improve work, how to become more efficient, and how to change the work process so the organization might be more "agile," which Stewart regarded as the core benefit of the current revolution. In Taylor's own words, "It is through those suggestions from the workmen that nine-tenths of our progress is made"[64] and not through the suggestions of management. The actions of management actually held up the implementation of change for the simple reason that the workers saw no benefit for themselves in the change. The issue still facing us today (some consider this the most important issue)[65] is the same one Taylor spent his life studying: how to motivate the worker to make improvements.

In his studies, Taylor found maybe one company in a hundred that had successfully implemented scientific management. All one hundred companies used the techniques, just as we do today. But the key for the one successful company, Taylor found, was to treat the workers "justly." This may seem an old-fashioned, almost Biblical-sounding word to business ears today, but justice was the basis of Taylor's mental revolution for managers: "Unless this condition of seeking to do absolute justice to the workman exists, scientific management does not exist. It is the very essence of scientific management."[66]

The Chairman of the House Committee pressed Taylor as to how this could come about, since management was hired to pursue its own interests. He asked Taylor, "[You have said that] scientific management cannot exist unless there is a complete change of mind ... Now, do you conceive that it is possible to have a complete change of mind when a man is engaged in business for profit?" Taylor responded: "I do."[67]

Taylor felt this was possible for the same reason many of us think and hope so today: we see concrete evidence in thousands of U.S. corporations that managers believe in showing employees how to work better together to improve the efficiency, quality, and innovation of the product. Each of these corporate endeavors reflects how the leaders have changed their view of the business process, shifting away from the machine image, toward a more living, dynamic, interrelated, organismic model.[68]

New findings in science, such as the chaos theory, quantum physics and its uncertainty, systems theory with its feedback loops, all support this move to a larger, more vital view of human behavior.

Dualism and dialogue

Peter Senge, Director of the Center for Organizational Learning at MIT, founding chair of Society for Organizational Management, and currently a senior lecturer at MIT, calls this emerging model the "learning organization."[69] It shifts us from the machine model to a model based on dialogue. This gets us away from the false dualistic filter of yes or no, one versus another.

He argues that people must become observers of the habits of their own thinking. Corporations, to be learning organizations, must encourage workers to be open to new facts that will create doubts and questions that challenge how they think about the world and how business works. As we shall see in Chapter 4, Senge sounds a lot like the pragmatist-at-work in Charles Peirce's original vision and Josiah Royce's development of it.

Drawing on the work of physicist David Bohm, Senge argues that we can no longer see the world as one against the other or as this versus that. This kind of thinking leads to the danger that competition can crush an idea and close down thinking if people see themselves only as winners or losers. In effect, Senge is challenging a basic assumption of U.S. society: someone has to be right or wrong.

Senge would move the corporation away from dualism to foster conversation with others. He argues that the best managers need to handle and deal with opposing truths or points of view. This will be a key subject in Chapter 4, when we develop a pragmatic method of building on different points of view to determine what is really going on, and then take action from this view of reality.

Senge's call to managers to foster conversation and encourage dialogue is part of a wider transition in U.S. business, away from a militaristic model with its war-like images and languages, to one more human and relational. The discipline of marketing reflects this shift well. Marketers often speak of "campaigns," "delivering advertising against a market," and "marketing warfare." We also structure markets to fit computer models in which various factors can be manipulated to see the results in the outcome. Working in limited markets where market share can be captured only by raiding a competitor's turf leads to playing confrontational win/lose, zero-sum games.

Christopher Lasch, a leading observer of the American scene, remarked that "the anxious person is the ideal consumer."[70] By being anxious, consumers become more likely to buy product X, hoping to feel good about themselves. In this old marketing model, if we considered the consumer as a person, we often thought of him or her as incomplete or sick, and the product as medicine. We conducted market research by looking for the "hot button" to push. This led to a manipulative model that assumed the sole function of marketing was to set up an exchange between producer and consumer, which missed an important element.

Now, as Senge and Tom Peters and other insightful analysts recognize, this is beginning to change. We are coming to realize that customers are not so much machines with buttons to push, as people with whom the successful company creates a long-term relationship. This switch has been clearly articulated in the recent literature. Professor Philip Kotler of the Kellogg Graduate School of Management at Northwestern University has noticed that marketing's focus has shifted: "What I think we are witnessing today is a movement away from a focus on exchange ... in the narrow sense of transaction and toward a focus on building value-laden relationships and marketing networks."[71] Kotler defines marketing as the management of the relationship between the customer and the company.[72] He is also calling our attention to the fact that we no longer look on the consumer as someone to be manipulated. He has taken the view that values must be an important part of the brand.

Managing relationships precludes the competitive mindset of dualism, calling for new values, such as dialogue, and measurement parameters, such as corporate social responsibility, as well as an end to isolating the individual as a consumer from the community.

Individualism versus community

We noted at the beginning of this chapter how the University of Chicago brought in M. Scott Peck to lead a conference on community building. When I had first heard of this conference, I was intrigued. Why would the University of Chicago Business School, the home of more Nobel Prize economists than any other institution in the world, decide to bring in a psychiatrist to instruct their students, staff, and alumni in how to build community? Did they see this as a critical component for the successful management of people?

I was so intrigued by such questions that I headed south from downtown to attend the conference. It was not the lofty "ivory tower" discussion that academic conferences usually are. We were divided into small groups and given a problem to solve as a group. But we had to work within the confines of some strict rules. No one who had the floor could be interrupted or corrected. If you wished to challenge a person, you could only say, "I hear you saying ... ." Only when the other person was satisfied that you had heard and understood could you then respond. Unless one has tried conversing with others this way, one can't imagine the difficulty and frustration.

The point of the whole endeavor was to solve the assigned problem by using the sense of teamwork that arose from being in a community. Like the process of conversing, this sounds easier than it was. Peck began by pointing out the four stages we went through to form our groups into communities: pseudo-community, chaos, emptiness, and genuine community.[73] The first two of these are familiar to those of us in business, since U.S. corporations operate at the pseudo-community level, with its strained conviviality, role-playing, and saying what's expected, rather than one's true feelings. And we all know what happens if people really speak their minds. Chaos.

Peck's facilitators called on us to be honest, to say what we were really feeling. We did, and there was chaos. As you might imagine, at that point a strong impulse swept over us fast-acting, no-nonsense business types to bolt for the door. But we were assured this chaos was just a transitional stage. If we held on, we would open the possibility of genuine community.

We stayed put, wondering what Milton Friedman would make of all this. In time, our group moved into the third stage, emptiness, a time of giving up old assumptions, beliefs, and fears. We turned within. We revealed ourselves. We began to share our truths on a deeper level, and we listened and really heard each other. By the end of the third day we had moved into real community. How did we know? We all felt a deep connection that translated into dynamic teamwork that made solving the problem we had been given in the beginning an easy process.

My experience at this conference has lingered over the years as an inspiration and a vivid illustration of the potential U.S. business, if only we could change our filters from individualism to seeing the possibility of creating genuine connections between people. Just as Peck started his career within the psychiatric "therapeutic expressive individualism" model and moved beyond it to work with groups to create community, so, I think, must businesspeople work to overcome the "grenade-over-the-wall" way businesses are usually run today.

This phrase always gets knowing nods. It is the business process that occurs when researchers come up with an idea for a product. They throw it over the wall to designers to create a working model, who throw it over the wall to the product development people, saying "Shape it up!" They throw it over the wall to the manufacturing people, saying "Make it!" They make it and throw it over the wall to the sales people, saying "Sell it!" Research people don't know what will sell. Design people don't know what will be easy to manufacture, and the folks in sales, those closest to the customer, have little or no input. Where's the close teamwork and sense of community here?

Corporations aware of the challenge of global competition, such as Motorola with its Participative Management Program, realize the limitations in this individualistic approach and are reorganizing to foster more effective teamwork. What might this look like? From my experience, and from my reading of observers and commentators such as Peter Senge, Peter Drucker, Scott Peck and Robert Bellah, I can paint a general picture of what appears when the individualism filter comes off in a business.

People begin Stage 1 in what Peck calls "pseudo-community." They begin to say what they feel, which leads to Stage 2, which he calls "chaos." Rather than trying to clamp down to restore order and the pseudo-community, managers need to react by saying, "Now we are getting somewhere," or, as one of my associates has observed, when some people get emotional, don't cut them off. You will hear what they are really thinking. For many of us not comfortable with the "touchy-feely" side of human nature, especially in business, this is difficult. But Stage 2 is even more difficult. We usually deal with chaos by sorting through the ideas, shutting off some and favoring others. We try to fit ideas into our own patterns of thought and choose those that reinforce our assumptions or give reasons for what we want to do.

To enter Stage 3, which Peck calls "emptiness," we have to empty ourselves and be willing to put our assumptions and hypotheses aside and listen to others. At the conference I attended, Peck forced us to do this by not allowing us to respond to the other person until we had restated correctly what he or she had said.

Do all of this and you still won't get to community unless you confront the issue of decision-making. I see a continuum in the ways decisions are made. In the most traditional companies, it is tyrannical: "I am the boss and I will tell you what to do." Bosses who are a bit more progressive will say, "I am the boss and want your input before I make the decision," or "I am the boss, but I want you to make a recommendation, which I may or may not accept." More enlightened managers seek to empower their staff: "I am the boss but give you the power to make the decision." In some unusual companies, decisions are made by majority rule, or by consensus, with everyone agreeing with, or, at least on the surface, accepting the decision.

But for the company that has moved into Stage 4, "community," decisions arise naturally from the teamwork process, with no one individual identified as the decision-maker. For this to take place, people—from the CEO to associates—have to let go of their power and let themselves be vulnerable. Each person adds ideas, insights, or "a piece of the truth," building toward the decision and the action. In this setting there is no place for the rugged individualist.

Peck, with his community-building process, and Senge, with his stress on dialogue, open the way for U.S. businesses to remove the filter of individualism to come to better group decisions. Clearly, their way of thinking, talking, acting, and relating goes far beyond the machine model and dualism to unlock the creative potential of the corporation. Getting beyond individualism also has ethical implications, which brings us to our final filter.

Reexamining our ethical filter

Moved by images of leading businesspeople (often educated at our leading business schools) going off to jail for insider trading and other ethical violations, business schools and corporations are once again making major efforts to incorporate ethics into the curricula. This problem of ethical violations is partly a consequence of our thinking of business as a machine that operates in dualistic win/lose, me/them, "look out for No. 1", maximize-return-to-shareholders behavior patterns. As we break free of the tyranny of dualistic thinking, see the corporation as more than just a profit-maximizing machine, and respect the individual within a context of community and the environment, we can begin to see ethics in a new way.

Being in community allows us to consider behavior in terms of its impact on all stakeholders. Where business once operated to maximize profits while staying within the rules of the game, such an ethical stance is no longer adequate. Increasingly we are demanding that corporations be socially responsible, that they consider their impact on society. Business can no longer consider its activities only in terms of the balance sheet, or shareholder demands. Now it must have a larger awareness and deeper ethical sensitivities. For example, we now expect that companies will consider their impact on the towns where they have factories. We call on the entertainment industry to question whether its movies are contributing to the violence in our society. We challenge marketers to consider the impact of their messages on impressionable market segments. We require engineers to consider the impact of their products on the environment, in terms of composition, use, and disposability.

All this is evidence that our ethical filters are changing, as more managers come to think in the larger context, in the community within which their companies operate.

We see signs of a major shift in the way business managers are looking at their actions and purpose. Some call this a paradigm shift. But how great a shift is it? I believe what looks like a focus on quality or products and services in light of strong competitive action and changing social trends really is evidence of a much deeper shift in the way we think. Up to now we have been driven by very old models and ideas, the basis for the filters of which we have spoken. In order to break free of these filters and see the world through new ones and read the signs more accurately, we need to recognize where our filters came from and how long we have held our assumptions about how the world works. So, in Chapter 4, we turn to the historical roots of our often hidden assumptions to see how great the shift must be and how deep are the roots of our current filters.

Reading the signs

- What does "quality" mean in your organization?
- Why does your organization exist?
- Think about the word "justice." How does it manifest itself in your workplace?
- Would you call your organization a learning organization?
- How has your organization attempted to work in teams?
- Why are some teams more productive than others?
- How do you share what *you* know with your colleagues?
- How do *you* learn at work?
- Does your organization look at its relationship with and impact on all stakeholders, including the environment?

4

How our filters came to be

The journey to the point where I recognized and was able to name what I call "filters" demanded study in areas such philosophy, theology, anthropology, and sociology, where businesspeople rarely tread. Along the way, I sought out and had memorable encounters with professors, especially those taking unusual approaches to teaching courses of study in business schools.

One such course was Conceptual Foundations of Business, ("Confounds" as it came to be known) at the Business School of Columbia University in New York. In this course, first developed in the 1930s, students read a wide range of texts, many of them dealing with the legal, theoretical, and historical framework that gave structure to U.S. business regulations and laws.

The philosophical habit

As I approached Uris Hall on Columbia's Upper West Side Manhattan campus to visit Professor James Kuhn, who had taken over teaching the course, I saw an inscription: "A great society is one in which their men of business think greatly of their function."[74] This quotation was carved in huge letters across the top of the hall. Many years earlier, when I had first found this passage in the writings of the philosopher Alfred North Whitehead, it had set my thinking about the purpose of business in a whole new direction. The belief that had sustained me during frequent discussions with skeptical associates about such matters as the larger and greater role of business in society—there it was in big letters, across the top of one of the United States' best business schools!

When I met Professor Kuhn, I mentioned this to him and he suggested that I reread the essay "Foresight," from which the words were taken. Whitehead had originally given this as a speech at an anniversary celebration at Harvard Business School. The essay paints a picture of businesspeople as those in a society who greatly consider the consequences of their actions, and who must always look to the future of society. Whitehead, in the sentence just before the one above said: "The behavior of the community is largely dominated by the business mind." He saw clearly that the logic of business sets society's priorities, agendas, and values. And he saw that, therefore, the business mind must be capable of reasoning for the good of society; that it has to think like the philosopher: that is, in terms of the essence of what is being done. The business mind must be able to "survey society from the standpoint of generality … philosophy is an attempt to clarify the fundamental beliefs which finally determine the emphasis of attention that lies at the base of character."[75]

I call this way of thinking a philosophical habit or discipline. It is the ability to compare possibilities and actualities; it means being able to hold two opposing ideas, to see the truth of seemingly conflicting ideas, and see where they lead; to move between theory and action, constantly testing and learning. In other words, the philosophical habit requires us to hold paradoxes of fact and theory, short term and long term, general and concrete, critique and direct intuition. We are to hold in mind simultaneously the paradoxes of "the fact, the theory, the alternatives, and the ideal" and see their implications and consequences. But further, this habit or discipline attempts to uncover the values which, building on Whitehead, we define as **any belief, principle or virtue held so deeply—consciously or unconsciously— that it drives our behavior, decisions and actions**. We will see later how this habit of examining and developing values is critical to addressing my original question of how to lead an organization in need of change.

Kuhn's "Confounds" course changed with the times. He described it as a sinking ship where he was forced to throw overboard those readings the students liked least. By the time I arrived on the scene, Aristotle and Plato were long gone. Hume and Locke had followed. Only Adam Smith's *Wealth of Nations* hung on as a "suggested" reading. Several years later, the entire course was dropped, replaced by a negotiation course.

When I visited Professor Kuhn again several years later, I noticed a new wing had been added to the front of Uris Hall, covering up the quotation. I looked around expecting to see that it had been recarved in some other prominent place. When I told Professor Kuhn I couldn't find it, he informed me that, from all the money made on Wall Street, the Business School had been given some substantial donations to build the new wing; but when Kuhn had suggested the quotation be recarved, the money couldn't be found! To further show business school administration and faculty indecisiveness of the importance and way of teaching ethics, consider this story. A year earlier, in 1987, John Shad gave Harvard Business School $30 million for the study of ethics. After much debate, it was decided instead to build Shad Hall, a fitness and recreational facility at the Business School.[76]

This story reveals the ethical orientation of our time, and our inability to see the larger context in which we do business. We very often "hurl bits and shards of the past at one another without knowing when they were spoken nor the context in which they once made sense," as the moral philosopher Alasdair MacIntyre put it.

> Modern moral utterances and practice can only be understood as a series of fragmented survivors from an older past and … the insoluble problems which they have generated for modern moral theorists will remain insoluble until this is well understood.[77]

As a result, we are apt to lose the larger perspective.

Certainly the people who decided not to recarve the Whitehead quotation did not think in the larger context of business activity. Few people could attribute the words to Whitehead, or had even heard of him. It sounded good, but what did those words really mean? Perhaps someone objected to the reference to men of business. As MacIntyre might say, it appeared to be some "shard" from the past that had been hurled against a wall. MacIntyre's image of hurling bits and shards struck me; we lack an understanding of the original framework of ideas and values in which they made sense. Many shards have been mentioned in earlier chapters—competition, the machine model of business, dualism and individualism—shards that shape our views and standards of business behavior, but without a context in which we can understand their meaning and apply them today.

A deepening understanding

It became increasingly clear to me that I needed to deepen my understanding of the Western philosophical tradition. I was able to begin, in part, under the guidance of a remarkable professor at DePaul University, Robert Faulhaber. Like Kuhn at Columbia, Faulhaber took responsibility for broadening the business students' minds. Most business schools have at least one person assigned to this lofty but usually unappreciated task. They are tolerated by their associates from the more quantitative disciplines, but Faulhaber was in the unusual position of being held in great respect because of his ability to engage students by using the Great Books— those by Plato, Lucretius, Hobbes, Locke, Hume, Tocqueville, Mill, Bentham—in the seminar method.

Faulhaber had seen the syllabus of the course I was teaching at DePaul, "Marketing in a Changing Social Environment", designed to help business students look to a larger purpose for their careers. He asked me to teach his course with him. Regrettably, before I had the nerve to accept his offer and combine our courses, he died. A month or two after his death, I had a call from one of his associates, the chairman of the Economics Department, asking if I would like to inherit his files of readings and lecture notes, including those from his nine-month undergraduate "Great Books" class. I was honored and jumped at the offer, hoping to make some sort of amends.

So it was that I would grab a couple of the files, stuff them in a bag, and spend my vacations over the next several years immersed in readings from Descartes, Plotinus, and the Federalist Papers. As I continued reading, every so often I would hit something that resonated with business conversations I had had. Or I would come upon an idea, a shard that fit exactly how people I knew (myself included) saw business and the world in general. I became a Great Books fan, and through them began to see the wider, deeper historical context in which we live, think, and do business. I came to see that contemporary business ideas are nothing but assumptions, not eternal, infallible laws[78] gathered from the writings of other times and places addressing the conditions and questions of those times.

What follows is not a history of Western thought, but an attempt to consider the roots of our culture and the origins of the filters we spoke of in chapters 2 and 3, to provide some sense of why these filters are so common and so difficult to change. As Whitehead said, the business mind dominates society, and it is most important for us, as businesspeople, to rethink our basic models and assumptions. Many of us do not know how deep they go, and how long we have been used to thinking with these filters. In fact, we do not consider them assumptions at all, but models of how the world actually works.

Descartes' machine

The idea of using the machine as a model for how the world and business work has a history hundreds of years in the making. Ultimately, it goes back to Descartes' notion that the body is a very complicated machine. The scientific revolution of the 17th and 18th centuries gave rise to insights such as the laws of motion and of gases, which suggested that the universe was as predictable as a machine. Building on the earlier work of Vesalius, Paracelsus, and other anatomists, William Harvey described the circulation of the blood by likening the heart to a pump. The French physiologist Julien de La Mettrie even took to speaking of "man, the machine." Newton saw the universe as clock-like. By developing the steam engine, James Watt made possible large-scale mechanization of the means of production, which led in turn to the conception of the worker as a component in a machine.

By the middle of the 18th century, the machine model had become so pervasive that it was garnering critics as diverse as the poet William Blake (with his lamentation of the rise of "dark Satanic mills") and Adam Smith, often considered the father of modern capitalism. Smith noted the dangerous consequences of the mechanistic model of economic organization. In his most famous work, *The Wealth of Nations*, Smith wrote:

> In the progress of the division of labour, the employment of the far greater part of those who live by labour, that is, of the great body of the people, comes to be confined to a few very simple operations, frequently to one or two ... He naturally loses, therefore, the habit of such exertion, and generally becomes as stupid and ignorant as it is possible for a human creature to become. The torpor of his mind renders him not only incapable of relishing or bearing a part in any rational conversation, but of conceiving any generous, noble, or tender sentiment, and consequently of forming any just judgment concerning many even of the ordinary duties of private life.[79]

Moral philosopher that he was, Smith realized that people become what they do. Given stupid, mind-numbing, repetitive tasks in a work environment that regards him as little more than a robot, a worker is dehumanized, losing the capacity to reason, to feel nobly, and to make sound judgments, until he sinks to become the character so well satirized by Charlie Chaplin in the classic movie *Modern Times*.

Smith's insight was echoed 72 years later, but used for a considerably different purpose, by Karl Marx, when the factory system had become common all over the industrial world: "Owing to the extensive use of machinery, and to division of labor, the work of the proletarians has lost all individual character and, consequently, all charm for the workman. He becomes an appendage of the machine."[80]

Not only laborers but the whole of society was, and has continued to be, caught up in a mechanistic view of reality, now dominated by modern technology, organizational behavior, and marketing. Only as discoveries in quantum physics and new sciences such as ecology and chaos theory become dominant are we beginning to trade in the machine image for a more valid view of organizations as living systems, and business transactions as ongoing, multifaceted relationships, rather than as polarizing exchanges between owner and worker, buyer and seller.

Beyond the battles of dualism

Dualistic thinking goes back to the ancient Greeks, notably to Heraclitus with his theory of "opposites in unity." Aristotle exemplified the logic of dualistic thinking in his argument on the principle of contradiction, when he posited that something cannot be A and non-A at the same time. In the context of his scientific studies, Aristotle found such dichotomies very useful, even obvious. Since the rediscovery of Greek thought in the Renaissance, science has built on this dualistic view of the world, especially on the dualism between "substance" and "accident," "form" and "matter."

Aristotle formulated the concept of "objectivity," foreshadowing the scientific observer as outside of and distinct from the experiment. The 17th-century French mathematician and philosopher René Descartes carried dualism even further in his insistence on dividing the universe into two substances: matter and mind. His insight, which he stated in his famous Latin phrase *Cogito ergo sum* (I think, therefore I am), freed the mind from outside authority such as the Church, opening the way for the tremendous creativity of the age of enlightenment and the age of scientific discovery. Aside from the persisting body/mind dualism, we are still reaping the technical, financial, and physical rewards of that transformative time.

Descartes' creed also led us to believe that by going into our minds, we would find truth: *Cogito ergo est*—I think, therefore it is. While we know positive thoughts and attitudes have great benefit, the slippery slope is that we have come to look inward for infallible knowledge of ourselves and of our world. As Tocqueville observed in *Democracy in America*, America was the one country where the "precepts of Descartes were least studied and best followed." He saw that "in most mental operations each American relies on individual effort and judgment." This reliance has led us to believe that "perception is reality." We are like the Queen of Hearts in Lewis Carroll's *Through the Looking Glass*. Situations, facts, and even events can mean whatever we choose them to mean. It's a free country, we say, and we are each entitled to our opinion.

With the sanction of science and some two thousand years of logic behind us, we took dualism to extremes in what the semanticist S.I. Hayakawa called "bipolar thinking": good/bad, black/white, right/wrong, win/lose. Our debating methods, adversarial approaches in legal issues, and even our sports reflect this way of thinking: "Winner take all"; "Winning isn't everything—it's the only thing." What this has meant for business is that our whole approach to what we do has gone astray in the direction of dualism, that is, we think in terms of winners and losers, success and failure.

Unity goes beyond dualism

Since Descartes' day, scientific discoveries by people such as Niels Bohr, Werner Von Heisenberg, John Bell, Rupert Sheldrake, and Albert Einstein indicate that dualism is wrong. Einstein has shown us that time and space are inseparable. Science is forcing us to return to a view of the world that is even older than dualism: unity. As Heraclitus said, "All is one." And in one of the towering examples of the synthesis of opposites in the history of ideas, Thomas Aquinas in the 13th century combined the newly rediscovered philosophy of Aristotle, with its emphasis on the scientific view of nature, with the prevailing fundamentalist focus on Biblical revelation,[81] to create a view in which both were seen as valid approaches to reality. Philosophy and theology not only could, but must, work together, argued Aquinas. The battle—dualism—between the two continues today.

We are all in this together; we are coming to realize that we must run our businesses so that unless everyone wins, no one can win. But getting past dualism will require more than striving for win–win deals. It demands that we get beyond our American penchant for individualism.

An American point of view

None of the filters coloring our view of reality is as complex, or uniquely American, as our version of individualism. It is complex because individualism is rooted in our basic view of what it means to be human, the right of privacy and the primacy of the rights of the individual. It is especially American because no other culture in the world has been as committed to focusing on the efforts, rights, and identity of the individual person as opposed to those of the group.

As Alasdair MacIntyre says, we are in the habit of throwing fragments of old arguments around, so much of what follows may seem familiar to you. But you may be surprised, as I was, to realize that they are not eternal truths but were written in the last several centuries as we were formulating our Western ideas of freedom of the individual. As I read through Faulhaber's notes, often sitting on a quiet beach on Harbour Island in the Bahamas, I got a clearer picture of the influence of Hobbes, Locke, Smith, Hume, and Tocqueville. I came to realize how hard it is to get past our individualism and to foster a sense of community in business, and in society in general.

In the process of formulating these ideas for our society, we have, through our filters, selectively read the ancient Greeks (and medieval thinkers, as we shall see in Chapters 9 and 10). The Greeks had very different assumptions from ours. To them, people were primarily social beings, living with others in community. Any Greek who tried to go it alone was called *idios*, that is, "strange," "peculiar," "understanding only his own language," "different from those of a group." Nobody wanted to be called that, so a major determinant of behavior in the community-focused world of the ancient Greek city-state was the desire for approbation: wanting to be highly regarded by the group, to be seen as virtuous and as a good person. This concept was later restated by Smith in 1759 in the seldom-read *Theory of Moral Sentiment*.

The Greeks' social/community view disappeared slowly but steadily in the Middle Ages. When philosophy once again flourished, stimulated by the rediscovery of the Greeks, a very different image of the proper relation between person and group appeared, particularly in Thomas Hobbes' *Leviathan*, published in 1651. Hobbes analyzed society, looking for basic principles analogous to those used by the scientists of his time to describe the paths of the planets, and concluded that: "Society is a war of all against all, and only a vigorous government can keep individual hostile impulses in check."

While Hobbes was not writing about economics and business, in today's world of ruthless competition, his characterization of the nature of humans rings true. In his view of society most people have approximately equal ability and are striving for the same things, but with dire consequences: "If any two men desire the same thing, which nevertheless they cannot both enjoy, they become enemies. And in the way to their end, endeavor to destroy or subdue one another." Hobbes views humankind as having a "perpetual and restless desire of power after power that ceaseth only in death." Some want fame. Others may want ease and sensual pleasure, others, admiration or flattery for their excellence in some art or ability of mind. Competition for riches, honor, and power is what causes this battle of all against all:

> each individual in the community is driven by his passion to pursue his private purposes. Unfortunately, the object of these purposes is such that no person can ever be wholly satisfied … The result is that the City of Man remains in a chronic condition of civil war. [82]

The result, in an oft-quoted passage, is Hobbes' assessment of life in a state of Nature: "without laws, the life of man would be solitary, poor, nasty, brutish and short."[83]

For all its gloom and negativity about motivations to action, Hobbes's legacy is an important part of our society and heritage, still heard in U.S. business conversation today. Hobbes is one of the earliest spokesmen for the zero-sum game we play, with its winners and losers. We also still retain the idea of commerce as people at war with each other, cutthroat competition checked only by government rules and regulations.

Charles Darwin was popularly believed to lend Hobbes a veneer of scientific respectability, with his idea of the "survival of the fittest." Business tycoons of Darwin's day, whose success suggested they were the "fittest" of their society, were quick to pick up and apply evolutionary theory to justify their often predatory business tactics.

I turned next to John Locke, whose ideas I knew had been very influential on the Founding Fathers of the new American republic, particularly his belief that people had inalienable rights. Like Hobbes, John Locke saw people primarily as atoms, isolated individuals, standing alone against their fellows. While his view of human nature was not as bleak as Hobbes's, Locke did share Hobbes's view that virtue was not innate, and like MacIntyre he saw that we selectively hang on to bits and pieces of our past, using them as interpretations for our actions. Consider this key passage:

> Instances in keeping compacts ... that men should keep their compacts is certainly a great and undeniable rule in morality. But yet if a Christian who has a view of happiness and misery in another life be asked why a man should keep his word, he will give this as the reason: Because God who has the power of eternal life and death requires it of us. If a Hobbesian be asked why, he will answer: "Because the public requires it and the Leviathan will punish you if you do not." And if one of the old philosophers had been asked, he would have answered: "Because it is dishonest, below the dignity of a man, and opposite to virtue, the highest perfection of human nature, to do otherwise."

Locke continues with this radically pessimistic assertion:

> Virtue generally approved, not because it is innate, but because profitable ...We find that self interest and the conveniences of this life make many men own an outward profession and approbation of them [moral and eternal obligation] whose actions sufficiently prove that they very little consider the law-giver that prescribed these rules.[84]

In Locke's view, we do not do good because we want to, or like to, but because it works. It is a way to get ahead, to make money.

Adam Smith shared Locke's belief that virtue is not something people aspire to consciously. In well-known passages from *An Enquiry into the Nature and Causes of the Wealth of Nations* on the "invisible hand," Smith offers his theory on the workings of the marketplace:

> It is not from the benevolence of the butcher, the brewer, or the baker, that expect our dinner, but from their regard to their own interest[85]
>   ... he intends only his own security; and by directing that industry in such a manner as its produce may be of the greatest value, he intends only his own gain, and he is in this, as in many other cases, led by an invisible

> hand to promote an end which was no part of his intention ... By pursuing
> his own interest he frequently promotes that of the society more effectu-
> ally than when he really intends to promote it.[86]

Smith had no illusions about the business temperament. In a less familiar passage, he noted, "People of the same trade seldom meet together, even for merri-
ment and diversion, but the conversation ends in a conspiracy against the public,
or in some contrivance to raise prices."[87]

This was, of course, in the days before our antitrust laws, and the truth of Smith's
observation was the reason why such laws were later passed.

Selfish, greedy, interested only in private advancement not the public good, the
image of the typical businessperson in *Wealth of Nations* is far from positive.[88]
Smith's contemporary, David Hume, extended this image into the realm of thought
and habits of mind:

> The greater part of mankind are naturally apt to be affirmative and dog-
> matic in their opinions; and while they see objects only on one side, and
> have no idea of any counterpoising argument, they throw themselves pre-
> cipitately into the principles, to which they are inclined; nor have they
> any indulgence for those who entertain opposite sentiments. To hesitate
> or balance perplexes their understanding, checks their passion, and sus-
> pends their action. They are, therefore, impatient till they escape from a
> state, which to them is so uneasy: and they think, that they could never
> remove themselves far enough from it, by the violence of their affirma-
> tions and obstinacy of their belief ... In general, there is a degree of doubt,
> and caution, and modesty, which, in all kinds of scrutiny and decision,
> ought for ever to accompany a just reasoner.[89]

Hume found few among his contemporaries who were "just reasoners." As we shall
see in later chapters, this is what Charles Peirce and Josiah Royce wanted to help
us be.

Hobbes, Locke, Smith, and Hume left us images of human nature and motivation
very different from the ancient Greek idea of man as a social being, pursuing virtue.
The 18th-century philosophers convinced us that human instincts were not to be
trusted and that life was to be measured one individual at a time.

Nowhere did this belief become more pervasive than in America. By 1830, our
individualism had become prominent enough to attract the attention of foreign
commentators. The astute Frenchman, Alexis de Tocqueville, visiting America in
1831 to study the new democratic culture that was then so novel to Europeans,
noted:

> How it is that in ages of equality every man seeks for his opinions within
> himself ... in the same ages all his feelings are turned towards himself
> alone. Individualism is a novel expression, to which a novel idea has given
> birth. Our fathers were only acquainted with égoïsme (selfishness). Self-
> ishness is a passionate and exaggerated love of self, which leads a man to
> connect everything with himself and to prefer himself to everything in the
> world. Individualism is a mature and calm feeling, which disposes each

member of the community to sever himself from the mass of his fellows and to draw apart with his family and his friends, so that after he has thus formed a little circle of his own, he willingly leaves society at large to itself. ... individualism, at first, only saps the virtues of public life; but in the long run it attacks and destroys all others and is at length absorbed in downright selfishness.[90]

Tocqueville had recognized the baneful influence of individualism on our sense of community, encouraging people to be selfish and blind to political and social ties. He also realized, in connecting individualism with selfishness, its profound ethical implications. Given our penchant for rugged individualism, Tocqueville would not have been surprised that we have problems with ethics.

What motivates us to be good?

It took multiple vacations on the beach with Faulhaber's notes before I had pulled a satisfying answer from Western historical sources to the question "What motivates us to be good?" Hobbes said it was fear; Locke insisted it was the balance of political and social factors. Smith claimed that out of self-interest social good would come, but that if people set out to do good, they would more often than not achieve the opposite. For all these figures, ethics was a matter of individual judgment: the lone person assessing what was best for him or herself.

Tocqueville describes the ethical implications of individualism, which erodes the larger sense of concern for community. This individualism leads to a selfish rather than a moral basis for connection with people. When we think of ourselves as "optimizers of our own interests" in society, we lose the motivational basis for ethical behavior, that is, for being responsible persons for the larger good.

Work and vocation

We must not separate business from morality. If we do, the purpose of business becomes little more than providing the means of survival—mundane, material concerns. And we lose sight of the higher purpose of our work—not only to achieve success, but also to fulfill our personal existence.[91]

Several examples can help us to examine our filters of ethical expediency and look through new filters to find higher motives and potential in business. St. Benedict, the founder of Western monasticism, regarded work as a form of prayer. In the Rule (*Regula Benedicti*) he created (which became the dominant form of monastic regulation throughout medieval Europe), all monks were required to work as part of their devotion to God. We will see later how monasticism may offer further insights to reestablish the higher purpose of business.

In the 16th century, Luther applied Benedict's idea to lay life in his concept of vocation or calling. Each person has a special, unique calling for his or her life, and work should reflect this. As we perform our vocation, we are both serving God and our fellows, and meeting our ethical obligations. The importance of vocation has been dwindling in our society. Many people in business select their field of work on the basis of expediency and promised return, often ignoring their personal vocation if it does not fit in with the demands of their job. We often talk about the need to balance personal and business lives when, in fact, Luther and Benedict were calling us to see our work life as our personal vocation.

More directly influential in American history than Benedict or Luther were the Puritans, who developed Calvin's idea that work, insofar as it provided for material success, was an integral part of the spiritual life, the way to achieve outward indications that one had been "elected"—chosen by God for eternal salvation. When they emigrated to New England, the Puritans brought this belief with them, and the Puritan work ethic became deeply embedded in the American psyche.

In time this idea that work had a higher purpose became institutionalized in our legal system, but few people today are aware of this fact. Luther McKinney, chief legal counsel of the Quaker Oats Company, said that each corporation has to answer one central legal question: "Why is this corporation permitted to exist? Why was it given a charter of incorporation by the state? Every corporation must decide how it serves society." [92] McKinney's answer is all the more remarkable because he said it during the volatile so-called junk bond era of the 1980s when Quaker was a frequent take-over target. It is ironic that the original legislation in the 19th century, which led to the creation of our giant business corporations, had the purpose of organizing our work to serve the public good. How many corporations today realize that their first obligation—what they were really created to do—is to help make society better? But as the demand for increased corporate social responsibility and meaningful work intensifies, we are seeing a return to this truth, as more and more businesspeople begin, in Whitehead's words, "to think greatly of their function" (see Chapter 3).

Such diverse writers as theologian Matthew Fox and marketing educator Philip Kotler are calling for corporations and the individuals in them to do the reflective work in order to discover the values, character, purpose, and meaning of work. In a way that gains broader understanding and support, Kotler has said that the importance of the values of an organization underlie the reputation—or brand—that is the foundation of relational trust.

This chapter has described how the filters on our current perceptions—the machine model, dualism, individualism, and ethical expediency—have centuries of history behind them. Enmeshed in such tangled legacies, we face the challenge to reorient our thinking and become the "just reasoner" that David Hume described. Hume was prescient in his description of what would be necessary for the business mind of today to addresses the challenges of the future: "In general, there is a degree of doubt, and caution, and modesty, which, in all kinds of scrutiny and decision, ought for ever to accompany a just reasoner." [93] In seeing the value of doubt, Hume was a precursor of pragmatism, as we shall see in Chapter 5.

Reading the signs

- What connection do you see between the wisdom of the Great Books and contemporary business ideas?

- What does it mean for you and for your corporation to "think greatly of your function?"

- Do you slip into bipolar, either/or thinking?

- What motivates you and your organization to "be good?"

- Does your work reflect your vocation?

- Are you a "just reasoner?"

- Can you think of examples where you and your associates have been "just reasoners?"

- Does your corporation have a soul? Did it ever have one? Does it need one? What purpose would it serve?

Part III
Interpret

5
Pragmatism
A community of inquirers

David Hume was not alone in recognizing the value of doubt. The American philosopher Charles Sanders Peirce built his philosophy of pragmatism around it, and even businesspeople encounter situations in which doubt proves its worth. Take, for example, this story told by a friend of mine, Barb Allen.

An executive vice president of the Quaker Oats Company, Barb got a call one day from an associate who asked her to talk to a young woman who had some observations and concerns about Quaker. She was unsure what opportunities were really available to women within the Quaker environment. Barb said she would be happy to meet with her, having fielded discussions like this many times before. As they talked, it slowly dawned on Barb that perhaps she didn't know what was going on after all, in light of some of the observations the woman was making.

Barb decided to investigate on her own. She went around and gathered facts; in some cases they were available; in others, she had to have studies conducted to come up with data that might support or challenge the young woman's hypothesis about lack of opportunities in Quaker. Barb talked to others about it, and changed her point of view, coming to look through different filters. From that began the Quaker Women's Management Group. Women came together and more stories were told, with further clarification of both the strengths and the weaknesses of the organization and what actions the group should recommend to top management.

In this simple story we see genuine pragmatism at work. In this chapter we will see that Barb Allen was using the pragmatic method of inquiry developed by Charles Peirce to determine the truth of the situation at Quaker.

Peirce: forgotten American scientist-philosopher

Charles Sanders Peirce (1839–1914), whose name is pronounced "purse," was a multifaceted physical scientist, mathematician, and philosopher who founded the only American school of philosophy: pragmatism. It is recognized as the only original contribution this country has made to the history of philosophy. I first heard about Peirce not through an academic but through a community activist, Father Thomas Duffy. Father Duffy had been a Catholic priest working in Columbus, Ohio, on issues of poverty and community organization during the 1960s. He later became an Anglican priest and spent 12 years working with Ira Progoff, whom we will discuss later. Duffy had discovered Peircean pragmatism in his search for a method of community inquiry that would get past the polarization, name-calling, and vitriol that too often characterize political discourse. Thanks to Duffy, I joined the growing numbers of people rediscovering Peirce and his original meaning of pragmatism, in pursuit of "the truth we do not yet know."

Peirce coined the term pragmatism from the Greek word for "deed" or "act." This scientific method of inquiry was applied to philosophy and logic as well as to the hard sciences. The collective, shared pursuit of truth is central to Peirce. We must be open to other reading of the evidence.

Peirce's pragmatic method of inquiry can be summarized in three principles:

1. **Perceive accurately** what is going on; what is important is not what we think we know, but what we are willing to learn

2. Knowledge and understanding are best acquired in a mutually reinforcing communication with others that might be called a "**community of inquiry**"

3. The best way of seeking "the truth we do not yet know" is what Peirce termed "**abduction**"

His first point, **perceiving accurately**, is not such a simple matter as it may seem. We inevitably grow up and move into our management positions carrying internalized beliefs that act as filters, causing us to see what conforms with those beliefs and to fail to see what might contradict them. It is particularly difficult to catch ourselves at this because not only are the beliefs largely at an unconscious level, but the same beliefs tend to be held by many of the people around us so that we are not confronted with a need to disclose our filters. In the course of most of our lives, our filters are never challenged. One of the virtues of contact with others with sharply differing beliefs is that such challenges occur.

Creating a **community of inquiry** often involves listening to people whose views, or even personalities, we may not particularly like or feel comfortable with. It involves creating an atmosphere of mutual respect, trust, and willingness to humbly search together for the truth we do not yet know. The trust involved is in one another, in the process, and in one's "inner-knowing." In such an atmosphere the "detective mind" can flourish, unhampered by rigid preconceptions because reex-amining previously held beliefs has been made safe.

And third, **abduction** has nothing to do with UFOs. Rather, it is the middle approach between induction and deduction. Abduction is like the classic approach of a detective to solving a crime—survey the evidence, develop hypotheses, and keep on going around this circuit until a discovery or conclusion that explains the evidence emerges. We will look at this in more detail later.

Unrecognized genius

One might well wonder what happened to Peirce, that he is only now being redis-covered.[94] As the founder of the only school of philosophy recognized as uniquely American, you might expect him to be famous. But one of the major ironies of Peirce's life was that he was a genius whose brilliance earned him little fame, and even less money.[95] Furthermore, he built a philosophy around the concept of interpretation, yet was repeatedly misinterpreted throughout his life, even by his friends. Only in the last several decades has Peirce begun to come into his own, as something of an intellectual cottage industry, with its own society and quarterly journal. The celebration of his 150th birthday in 1989 attracted international atten-tion with a sesquicentennial conference and celebration at Harvard with every-thing from talks to t-shirts. But before 1970 his 80,000 handwritten pages sat in Harvard's library gathering dust.

Such a fate would not have been predicted from his family background. Peirce was born to one of America's leading intellectual families in 1839. His father, Benjamin Peirce, held an endowed chair at Harvard in astronomy. Charles's genius was recognized early in his life, to his later misfortune, because he was treated as a precocious boy and allowed to get away with far more than he should have been. Rebellious incidents marked his life, on several occasions even foreclosing his long-term success. As a college chemistry student, Peirce sawed a laboratory bench in half during class as a joke. The unamused instructor, Charles W. Eliot, went on to become president of Harvard, and never forgot Peirce, considering his an undisci-plined, wasted talent, and blocking his appointment to any teaching post. When Peirce finally got an academic post at Johns Hopkins, his defiance of convention again cost him dearly, when he was reported to be living in Baltimore with a French woman while separated but not yet divorced from his first wife. The University trustees and administrators regarded this as another example of his dissolute and undisciplined character, and even though eminent friends such as William James interceded for him, Peirce lost his job.

Thereafter he eked out a precarious living as a surveyor and mapmaker for the U.S. Coast Guard's Geodesic Survey, a position that in no way matched his bril-liance in mathematics, astronomy, chemistry, and, most of all, logic. His writing for learned journals, dictionaries, encyclopedias, and magazines provided supple-mental income, but he was chronically in debt for most of his life, at one point so much so that he hid in the attic of his barn to avoid his creditors. He was able to survive and keep writing at all only through donations from William James and others. He died, obscure and penniless, in 1914, but his followers, Josiah Royce, William James, and John Dewey went on to further his ideas of pragmatism.

What we have lost (why we have trouble reading the signs)

If Peirce's life was full of material hardship and frustration, it was even more full of intellectual frustration, as a consequence of his being misunderstood by none other than his staunchest friend and benefactor, William James. With the best of intentions, James sought to spread Peirce's ideas in the world, but in retrospect James misunderstood Peirce on certain key points and considerably narrowed Peirce's broader definition of pragmatism.

Peirce and James had been friends since their days as classmates at Harvard, and had formed a Metaphysical Club[96] in Cambridge, Massachusetts, after graduation, with Oliver Wendell Holmes, Chauncey Wright, Francis Ellingwood Abbott, and others. These clubs, popular around America in the 19th century, would meet for discussion of contemporary intellectual fads and fashions. In the 1870s, the fad of the moment was the German philosopher Georg W.F. Hegel. Hearing Peirce expound on Hegel and other philosophical issues, James recognized Peirce's genius and followed his work closely.

Peirce wrote regularly for a small, prestigious philosophical magazine, *The Monist*, and for *Popular Science Monthly*, which in the 19th century was a scholarly magazine dedicated to presenting the latest scientific thinking (rather than tips on how to do your own plumbing). These two magazines, while highly regarded in intellectual circles, had limited circulation, so Peirce remained relatively unknown. James achieved much wider fame as a psychologist and author of many books, including *The Varieties of Religious Experience*. So in the summer of 1898, to cap a year-long program dedicated to studying the work of James, the Philosophical Union of the University of California invited William James to present the keynote address. Although the Union had spent the year studying James's philosophy, James decided to turn the spotlight on Peirce by using his speech to introduce Peirce's brand of philosophy, which Peirce called "pragmatism." This speech was to have catastrophic consequences.

After a dynamic opening that displayed the reasons for James's popularity as a speaker, he stated Peirce's theory fairly well: "Beliefs, in short, are really rules for action, and the whole function of thinking is but one step in the production of habits of action."[97] Peirce and James both had as their target abstract thought. Both saw action and engagement with reality as the test for beliefs. Then James got to the point of his lecture: "This is the principle of Peirce, the principle of pragmatism. I think myself that it should be expressed more broadly than Mr. Peirce expresses it."

James' next sentence was the beginning of the end for Peirce's pragmatism:

> The ultimate test for us of what a truth means is indeed the conduct it dictates or inspires … I should prefer for our purposes this evening to express Peirce's principle by saying that the effective meaning of any philosophic

> proposition can always be brought down to some particular consequence, in our future practical experience, either active or passive; the point lying rather in the fact that the experience must be particular, than in the fact that it must be active.[98]

Or, in other words, did an idea or belief work in some particular way or experience? Later in the speech, he asserted that an idea could be tested by whether it had "cash value"—meaning observable or experienced consequences—or not.[99] Business-people certainly (mis)understood this! For it is but a step from "have an effect" to "be effective," and James has been widely understood in this sense.

In the opinion of many, James came to a major insight, either intentionally or unintentionally, by creating a new way to approach truth and knowledge. One of the oldest questions in philosophy asks how do we know the truth. Plato said that we have it already in us, in the form of innate ideas only waiting to be discovered. Followers of Aristotle said we find it by abstracting it from reality. James said that we know the truth by looking at consequences: Does the belief work? Is it effective? While this might have been insightful, it was not what Peirce meant. James had focused only on consequences, while Peirce was presenting a method of inquiry to discover the truth, or what he called "the development of concrete reasonableness."[100]

James came close to a dualistic position with his notion of an idea either working or not working, having "cash value" or not, while Peirce had focused on the active learning process of constantly testing beliefs. By focusing narrowly only on consequences, James missed this central feature of Peircean pragmatism, which is not whether an idea works, but whether it is true.[101]

The aftermath of this episode was irony upon irony: the speech was a great success, was published and widely read. James dedicated the volume in which it appeared, "To My Old Friend, Charles Sanders Peirce, to whose philosophic comradeship in old times and to whose writings in more recent years I owe more incitement and help than I can express or repay."

At first Peirce was pleased to receive some acclaim, but when he had read and absorbed what James had said, he realized that his friend had seriously misinterpreted what he meant. Over the years, Peirce became more critical of James's views, finally declaring, "I thought your *The Will to Believe* was a very exaggerated utterance, such as injures a serious man very much." And he said later, "I think James' views do much damage."[102] But by that time it was too late: "pragmatism" had gone into circulation with James's interpretation, and Peirce was left feeling his invention had been "kidnapped."

In 1905, writing of himself in the third person, Peirce announced in one of his articles in *The Monist* that:

> finding his [Peirce's] bantling "pragmatism" so promoted ... it is time to kiss his child good-by and relinquish it to its higher destiny; while to serve the precise purpose of expressing the original definition, he begs to announce the birth of the word "pragmaticism," which is ugly enough to be safe from kidnappers.[103]

But lacking James' fame, and with little talent for self-promotion, Peirce was never able to get much of a following for his original, pre-Jamesian creation. As events turned out, Peirce late in life found a follower, Josiah Royce, who did understand his ideas correctly and was able to interpret them in other contexts.

Pragmatism and business

What does the preceding discussion of Peirce and James have to do with achieving success in business? I believe that it is at just this point—where James narrowed pragmatism to focus on success—that we were set, as a culture, on the road that has led us to our present state of affairs in business.

In my experience, when a businessperson hears the word "pragmatism," he or she thinks of something different from what Peirce, Royce, and Dewey meant. It is closer to James's idea of "consequences": if something works, it is right. I mentioned earlier that many of my fellow businessmen and women use the word in this sense. Partly as a result of James's misinterpretation, U.S. business has fallen into a short-term, reactive mode in which if something does not work you just try something else. We have come to feel driven to action, even in situations where reflection and contemplation might be more appropriate, out of our fear of being accused of overthinking, leading to "paralysis by analysis."

Seven benefits

By contrast, "pragmaticism"—Peirce's original theory—offers to the thoughtful business practitioner seven reasons to engage in this philosophy

1. A way to get past the pitfalls of simplistic, dualistic thinking by providing a way constantly to test your beliefs and assumptions

2. A way to avoid rigid thinking and narrow focus in this era of increasingly rapid change, by its encouragement of doubt

3. A way for groups and teams to discover something or decide on a course of action, through its extension of the scientific method beyond the laboratory

4. A way to determine what is true, to verify your perceptions, by developing a reliable method of observing and formulating hypotheses

5. A way to get beyond what you think you know, by identifying the "truth you do not yet know"

6. A way to discover just how you go about thinking and making sense of the world, in the context of the "learning organization" mentioned in Chapter 2

7. A way to gather evidence and interpret it for the basis of a position or story that becomes the basis for explaining decisions and action to yourself and others

We shall see in Chapter 8 how Peirce's pragmatism is being adapted in business and what happens to our thinking when we return to what Peirce meant. By reclaiming his original pragmatism, we can learn to read the signs that allow us to solve many of the problems now besetting our business organizations, while at the same time changing the filters that block us from determining what is really going on.

Given his genius and the breadth of his interests, Peirce offers an immense richness to anyone delving into his writing. For our purposes, I am focusing on three aspects of his thought:

- His theory of signs

- His conception of knowledge and how it is found

- His description of the scientific method

Peirce on signs

Part of the rediscovery and recent revival of interest in Peirce is due to his role as one of the forerunners of the modern discipline of semiotics, the study of signs. Peirce saw everything as a sign. In his very broad definition, "A sign … is something which stands to somebody for something in some respect or capacity."[104] The key to handling signs, Peirce realized, was in interpreting them. Their meaning is not self-evident.

Consider the octagonal red metal sign on the street corner. An indigenous dweller in the rainforest of New Guinea, who has never had any contact with other cultures, cannot know what this sign means. He would not have the knowledge to interpret a "red octagonal street sign" as "Stop!"

Peirce realized that the interpretation of signs is usually done in accordance with our habits of thought. Some of these habits are culture-wide, as with the stop sign. Others might be more limited, like the closed door to the boss's office indicating "do not disturb." Yet others might be uniquely personal, like the orchids in our advertising agency's lobby, the meaning of which is known only to those of us who remember our founder's fondness for them as a symbol of beauty and strength. But all such habits of interpretation have in common their rote quality: over time, we tend to forget that there might be some other meaning the sign could have. Some visitors to our offices, for example, might admire a delicate hothouse flower while we are always reminded that it is a stunning, sturdy wildflower in its natural environment.

There is a danger, Peirce knew, in habitually interpreting the signs in our everyday world: there is blindness or, to use our metaphor, the wrong filters.[105] These filters mean, in line with Peirce, that we do not interpret the signs correctly; we don't see what is really going on.

An extreme example of maintaining rational interpretations of entities and events in the world is found in Nietzsche's statement: "Truth is error." He meant we live by errors of interpretation but deceive ourselves by calling them truth. Peirce, on the other hand, said there is always the truth that one is pursuing and does not yet know.

We met an example of this in Chapter 2, in John Hudiberg's story. Until his set of surprises that Sunday morning, Hudiberg had been blind to the dozens of signs that his neighbors and customers saw all too clearly, indicating deficient service by Florida Power & Light. Hudiberg's account is a good example of the learning that is possible when we get out of habitual thinking. It was after his surprising Sunday that Hudiberg went around his company looking for the signs of poor service. And in his investigation, he learned. He opened himself up to new interpretations of the signs. In one investigation, it was found that customers whose bills were consistently inaccurate (the sign) all had dogs (the hypothesis). The interpretation of the inaccuracies? The meter readers guessed at the readings when they heard barking.

In the same way, as businesspeople we confront signs—of trends, of customer needs, of supplier problems, etc.—all the time. We fit these signs into our habit patterns. We see clouds and conclude there will be rain. We see someone grimace and conclude he is in pain. We see a defective part and assume defective manufacturing. But our interpretation might not be correct, if our assumptions are not right. And since we cannot always be sure of the accuracy of our assumptions, we need to stay open to the possibility that we might be interpreting the sign incorrectly. Or even worse, we simply react to some sign or event, not understanding what it means. We need, in other words, to be open to learning how to read signs.

In the "Signs of change" in Chapter 1, I provided a list of what I called "surprising facts." Such facts are examples of Peircean signs. They ask whether one really knows what's going on, or whether assumptions about contemporary reality are wrong. (See Appendix II for a summary of our study that puts pragmatism into action.)

Knowledge: a cable not a chain

Peirce never felt that interpretation was a solo activity. Just as the meaning invested in signs is always a shared meaning, so knowledge is not something Platonically achieved in isolation, but a collective, cooperative endeavor—a cable rather than a chain. This symbol was very important for Peirce. Each person's connection with reality is seen not as a link to another person's knowledge, as in a chain, but as a thread that comes together with the threads of others' realities to form a cable with each strand, either small or large, contributing to a larger, more accurate picture of reality. With the chain model, the effort is only as strong as the weakest link. We refer to this as group effort sinking to the lowest common denominator. But not so with the cable. Each strand makes the effort stronger.

The individuals connected in this kind of mutually reinforcing communication made up Peirce's community of inquiry. His model for this cable of knowledge was science, and his characteristic community of inquiry is the community of scientists. In science, each scientist contributes ideas, findings, facts, and hypotheses that help to advance our understanding of the world. Even in Peirce's time, before "big science" created laboratories with hundreds of researchers, science was a collective enterprise, quick to share discoveries and insights, building on collaborative efforts.

It also operated under a protocol—the scientific method—that Peirce recognized as a powerful way to get beyond the major impediment to the pursuit of truth: the "fixation of belief."[106] Fixation of belief and habits are inevitable and useful in life. They arise when in the ordinary course of life the tentative hypotheses we start out with are tested by our experience and in time become fixed, often as deeply held beliefs. Without them, action and living would be very difficult and chaotic. In contrast to scientists, who in Peirce's model are aware of their filters, most of us are not aware of many of our beliefs and habits, and they filter out what we see, so that we only think we know what is going on. Peirce realized that fixation of belief when it was unconscious might be a hindrance to our seeing reality as it is. Our assumptions act as filters, leading us to fit the signs into our habitual thinking patterns, or, in some cases, to fail to see them altogether. We get stuck in habits of reasoning, or in our assumptions about the world, and the result is that the world goes on changing and we keep on failing to see new trends, opportunities, or markets. Not only do we not easily examine our assumptions but we are even more reluctant to examine how we reason. Peirce stated the fundamental problem clearly:

> Few persons care to study logic, because everybody conceives himself to be proficient enough in the art of reasoning already. But I observe that this satisfaction is limited to one's own ratiocination, and does not extend to that of other men.[107]

Peirce sought to apply the logic used in science to everyday life, and in a series of articles he described the steps to do so: "The first step toward finding out is to acknowledge you do not satisfactorily know already."[108] In much the same way that Hume urged modesty, Peirce recognized the Socratic virtue of admitting one's ignorance. But most people need some inducement to get to the point of suspecting they do not have a handle on what is going on—an inducement such as surprise: encountering some fact or situation that contradicts what you previously thought was true—your fixed beliefs. Then, Peirce felt, the surprise would give rise to doubt.

Doubt: the hero

Doubt is one of the heroes of Peirce's philosophical system, because "Doubt … stimulates us to inquiry until it is destroyed … The irritation of doubt causes a struggle to attain a state of belief. I shall term this struggle Inquiry."[109] Inquiry is the search for "the truth we do not yet know." Doubt, for Peirce, began outside, created by a clash with reality: something happens which cannot be explained by the usual assumptions; something does not fit.

In the story opening this chapter, Barb Allen heard surprising things about the condition of women at the Quaker Oats Company. This led her to doubt that she knew what was really going on, and this in turn sparked her inquiry in the form of further investigation and interviews with many people on the Quaker staff. With all these contributions and different perspectives from people in the corporation, Barb's investigation became a shared, cooperative endeavor.

Inquiry often results in discoveries that force rethinking and the sacrifice of old assumptions that turn out to be erroneous. Peirce's favorite example of this rethinking (he claimed it was the "most marvelous piece of inductive reasoning I have been able to find"[110]) is the story of Johannes Kepler's 17th-century search to determine the path of Mars. Kepler began with the assumptions about the solar system common to people of his era: the planets moved in strange orbits called "epicycles" with a stationary Earth at the center. But after repeated observations, calculations and hypotheses, Kepler could not make the accepted theory fit in with what he was seeing. Finally he was forced by his data to conclude that the orbit of Mars was elliptical, which meant that the Earth could not be at the center of the universe, nor could the planets move in epicycles around an allegedly stationary Earth. He gave up both of these beliefs and moved to new fixed beliefs. In doing so, he was challenging conventional cosmology of the time. To Peirce this illustrates the process of inquiry, which challenges the fixation of belief. As I have come to discover, this method is as useful in the corporation as it is in the laboratory. We, too, can overcome false or outdated theory by adhering to pragmatic practice and continuously challenge what we believe and investigate what goes on in our businesses.

How to find the truth we do not yet know: Peirce's scientific method

Peirce's delineation of the scientific method has one central feature that he regarded as one of his major contributions to the science of logic: abduction. This was Peirce's term for the particular way science pursues "the truth we do not yet know." It differed from deduction and induction, the two epistemological approaches more familiar than abduction, in several ways.

When we use **deduction**, we start with the general idea, truth or assumption and then apply it to the particular. Often we start with a belief or assumption—something we learned from our parents, religion, culture or school—and take it for the truth. As reality and facts in daily life confront us, we fit these facts into our reality according to our assumptions.

In **induction**, we do the opposite: we experiment, experience life, and observe facts, with no prior beliefs or assumptions, and build to the formulation of a general hypothesis to explain the facts.[111] Conventional Newtonian science insists it follows the inductive method of logic, in its claims to being "objective." Peirce realized, however, that science really progresses via **abduction**, a third way of determining the truth, in which data are collected (as in induction) and general assumptions are held in view (as in deduction). But these assumptions are treated as hypotheses. That is, they are held consciously and tentatively, until repeated testing against reality (as with induction) proves them to be correct. They then must be held as theories that must continue to be tested as new facts are gathered.

If a corporation has a general strategy and sticks with it, despite changes in the market, then it practices deduction. As an example, many companies stay with a product line too long, feeling sure they know what is going on. And if a corporation reacts to every market and competitive blip that does not fit the product line, then it practices induction. Such companies have no direction. But Peircean abduction offers a way to move from strategy to market condition and back to adjust strategy.

Examples of the use of abduction abound in business. Take market research: we create several versions of ads to express different benefits that we think (hypothesis) will appeal to consumers, and then we go out and test (inductive experimentation) these ideas to get consumer reaction. Then we decide on the best one. Another example is what Marshall Loeb, a former editor of *Fortune* magazine, called "value-added journalism." A writer gets an idea for a story (hypothesis). Then he talks with 60 or 70 people to find out what's really going on (fact-collecting/testing of hypothesis). He revises his idea, or hypothesis, for the story in light of what he learns in his interviews. The "value" added here comes from the fact that stories develop from more than one person's perspective, which is what Peirce expected when he spoke of abduction: beliefs, in the form of hypotheses, are tested in the shared, cooperative endeavor that is science.

In this process, the critical step is the setting of the hypothesis, because it determines what you will test, and also what you will observe. As Einstein once noted, the hypothesis you hold will determine what evidence you generate and what you will see. We often say: "I believe what I see." But more often we act as if "I see what I believe." If the hypothesis is too narrow or wrong, you will see different facts, not surprisingly those that support the hypothesis only if you leave out other data.

There is another element in pursuing the truth: the impact of the observer on the experiment. Science has come to recognize that the observer is actually part of the experiment, as scientists found in analyzing atomic structures. The position of the observer and the experiment itself actually affect the situation. As a result, science's claim to total objectivity is a myth. Each person intrudes him or herself on the event. Donald Hunt, former president of Harris Bank, liked to call people's attention to the fact that "you are only one data point."

Hypothesis testing can be a gradual process, a piling of facts on top of each other until a discovery or conclusion emerges, as in Barb Allen's investigation at Quaker. Or it can be sudden, as John Hudiberg experienced on that memorable Sunday morning. Modern pragmatists have often described the process as analogous to the method of Sherlock Holmes. Father Duffy, of whom more later, has often used the example of the television series *Columbo*, where the eponymous detective would gather evidence and eventually come to one little clue or fact that did not quite seem to fit the easy hypothesis. This would create a nagging doubt, and of course this one little clue turned out to be the key to piecing the real story together.

Notice how the detective mind works: survey the evidence, formulate a hypothesis, and then keep testing it against the evidence. Does it explain what happened? Does it explain the evidence? And, most importantly, are you prepared to change your hypothesis in light of new evidence or evidence that doesn't quite fit?

Peirce developed his logic within the confines of the sciences, from his training as a scientist and mathematician, but I have tried to show its wider applicability. Late in his life Peirce found a student faithful to his ideas, Josiah Royce. He applied Peirce's ideas outside science, principally to religious inquiry, extending Peirce's community of inquirers to a "beloved community," based on the model of the early Christian Church. How Royce became a vital link for me in extending pragmatism to business will be the subject of Chapter 6.

Reading the signs

- Who is your corporate "Barb Allen"? What was discovered?

- What signs do you see around your workplace? How do you interpret them? How might others interpret them?

- How do you find "truth you do not yet know"?

- Does your corporation favor induction, deduction, or abduction?

- How do you and your coworkers handle doubt?

6

Extending Peirce beyond science
Diverse voices and corporate change

The venture capitalist Don Valentine was one of the early and largest investors in Apple Computer and as a member of its Board had witnessed firsthand one of the more memorable corporate personality clashes of our time: the battle between Steven Jobs and John Sculley for control of Apple. I had watched this battle from the sidelines with fascination because it dealt so dramatically with a central problem facing all businesses: how to manage a corporation change. When I met Mr. Valentine at a wedding reception, I waited for the opportunity to get an eyewitness impression of the boardroom battle. Over the nuptial reception dining table we struck up a conversation.

"What a tragedy that they couldn't get along," I said, as the conversation turned to Apple. "Each had such a skill to complement the other: Jobs, the prophet and charismatic leader, and Sculley, the thoughtful organizational professional." Don didn't pause for a moment in his reply. "They couldn't both run the company, so one had to prevail." He implied that it had become time for Jobs to step aside. I continued, "But wouldn't it have been better if they had found some way to work it out?" With the finality of someone who had witnessed the struggle, Don said, "No. You can't have talents like that working together. Only one voice can prevail in running a successful business."

I disagree. The Apple story illustrates one of the most basic and costly problems we have in U.S. business. It shows our difficulty in bringing diverse voices together to create a learning organization. I felt so strongly about this issue that as Mr. Valentine was leaving, I made one more attempt to press my point about bringing the combined talents together to see if he harbored any doubt or wish at all. But he growled emphatically "No!" looking at me as if I were beyond hope.

I remember this conversation often when I see executives unable to communicate and work together. What a waste of talent and perspectives.

This is where Josiah Royce's extension of Peirce beyond the realm of science proved so helpful to me: Royce points to a way in which diverse perspectives can be brought together for corporate benefit. When I came upon his work, I saw how to envision Peirce's scientific inquirers as a dynamic business community of interpreters.

Josiah Royce: Peircean interpreter

Josiah Royce was one of the few people in Peirce's lifetime who Peirce felt really understood what he meant by pragmatism. Indeed, Peirce went so far as to call Royce the only true American pragmatist. While they shared an appreciation of pragmatism, Peirce and Royce were otherwise very different. Unlike Peirce, brought up in erudite privilege in Harvard and Cambridge, Royce was raised in the frontier environment of a mid-19th-century mining town near Sacramento, California. While Peirce found his academic preferment thwarted at every turn, Royce, after studying in Leipzig and Göttingen under R.H. Lotze, moved easily from Johns Hopkins, where he received his PhD in philosophy and studied with James and Peirce, to the University of California, Berkeley, and then in 1882 to Harvard, where he spent the rest of his life.

Royce was initially drawn to Peirce through his interest in how ideas are formed. Peirce's logic offered rich insights. Royce admitted years later how difficult he found Peirce's work and how long he had to struggle with Peirce's seminal articles on abduction and the fixation of belief. Their first contact, in fact, was inauspicious, as Peirce was blunt in his assessment of Royce's skill as a logician. In 1901 Royce recalled the first letter he got from Peirce in response to his sending Peirce a copy of his book *The Religious Aspect of Philosophy*:

> Some twelve years ago, just after I had printed a book on general philosophy, Mr. Charles Peirce wrote to me, in a letter of kindly acknowledgment, the words: "But, when I read you, I do wish that you would study logic. You need it so much."[112]

Royce took Peirce's advice to heart, applying himself to Peircean logic to understand how social and religious communities come to their beliefs. Unlike William James, who focused on proving the truth of beliefs by what works, Royce stayed true to Peirce's original sense of pragmatism as action guided by beliefs that have been developed through the process of interpretation. The key issue was not what consequences ideas might have, but the process by which we formed our ideas to begin with. Royce wanted to answer questions about purpose, duty, and goals, not just about whether an idea "works." So he posed questions such as: What do we live for? What is our duty? What is the true ideal of life? What is the true difference between right and wrong?

Royce devoted much of his thinking to the virtue of loyalty. His answers to these questions led him to conclude, in part, that the basis of loyalty is dedicating yourself to a cause you can believe in.[113]

He acknowledged that he owed to Peirce's "direct and indirect aid" much of the awareness and perspective he eventually reached in his central concern of loyalty. Especially useful in applying Peirce's pragmatism to business is Royce's understanding of the types of knowledge and the process of interpretation central to the CORPORANTES *PathFinder* Method for practicing pragmatism. Royce directed his inquiry into the idea of loyalty to the central question of the Christian community and how the community formed its beliefs through interpretation. He wanted to answer the apparently simple question: How do you come to beliefs to which you can be loyal? He found that the answer started with Peirce's categories of knowledge.

Perception, conception and interpretation

In *The Problem of Christianity*, published in 1913, Royce noted that two categories of knowledge, perception and conception, have dominated "a great part of the history of philosophy."[114] Perceptions are what we see, the signs or evidence around us that we take in through our senses. Conceptions are ideas, especially our beliefs, which filter what we see. Royce took from Peirce the realization that there is a third category of knowledge different from perception and conception—**interpretation**, which brings perception and conception together and compares them. In Royce's words, interpretation "surveys from above. It is an attainment of a larger unity of consciousness."[115]

Interpretation involves a triadic process: (1) An interpreter perceives an object; (2) He filters it through his ideas; and (3) He interprets it by comparing what he has seen and what he knows.

So, what is this larger unity of consciousness? Let's assume, for instance, I see a hexagonal red sign with the letters STOP. I have seen a lot of these, I know that STOP means to bring my car to a full stop and proceed only under certain conditions, and I know that these signs were erected by authorities who may or may not cause me to pay them $50 if I fail to obey. But I also believe that obedience to the law is a good idea. I interpret the stop sign according to information and values I possess and make a decision to stop or not. I filter this through my own ideas, gained from experience.

Here is another example. As a scientist, I observe the motions of the planets. I am aware of the current model about how celestial bodies move but I have consciously chosen to entertain this as a tentative hypothesis, not a fixed belief. So when I observe a discrepancy between the actual motions of the planets and the accepted model, I am able to offer a new interpretation of what I have seen.

This is what goes on all the time in our heads as well as when we talk with others. It also happens when we think. Peirce saw thinking as an interior dialogue we have with ourselves: the mind of the past discussing the issue with the mind of the future. Royce took this further, by describing interpretation as essentially a social process, applicable as much to the religious realm as to science. That is, both scientists and religious communities are communities of inquirers who seek truth, and who interpret and reinterpret signs in a shared endeavor.

Dewey and the reconstruction of experience

It is important to continue to note how misunderstood the pragmatic method of inquiry is because John Dewey, like James and Peirce before him, finally gave up on even using the word "pragmatism" in his writings.[116]

These concepts are difficult to appreciate since they challenge usual ways of thinking about creativity. But the effort to see what Peirce, Royce, James, and Dewey are trying to say is well worth the effort if we value new ideas and the consequences of those ideas for innovation.

John Dewey, like Peirce, held that inquiry begins when some event happens that disturbs the usual habits of thought. This leads to thinking differently about what we believe, which Dewey saw as being formed from our experience. Dewey, therefore, concluded that "all learning is the continuous reconstruction of experience."[117]

This aspect of continuous learning is another key element that Dewey credits to Peirce's thought: **continuum of inquiry**. We have just said that one of the key ideas of pragmatism is the reconstruction of experience. Another key word is the "continuous" reconstruction of experience. If you read Dewey's books, you will notice the lack of footnotes: Dewey usually references himself. So it is remarkable to note that in the introduction to *Logic: The Theory of Inquiry* he states: "In this connection, attention is called particularly to the principle of the continuum of inquiry, a principle whose importance, as far as I am aware, only Peirce had previously noted."[118]

Shared interpretation

Royce's categories of knowledge, and his notion of interpretation as a social process, offer businesspeople a way to think about and develop action. This way gets us past the pitfalls inherent in our customary way of deciding how to act, based either on perception, leading us to react to the trends of the moment, or on conception, clinging to our beliefs and strategies long after they have ceased to be useful. We can create much more successful business organizations if Royce's process of shared interpretation becomes the basis for developing market strategies and corporate goals.

My initial exposure to Peirce was daunting, but I had good company. Royce had to devote years to understanding what Peirce meant. James, as we have seen, misunderstood Peirce and at other times found him barely comprehensible.[119] So did I, and it was only by studying what William James, Josiah Royce, and John Dewey[120] did with Peirce, and how they addressed the logic behind American thinking, that I got a clearer idea of what pragmatism really means, as it applies to my work as a corporate executive. Thanks to Peirce and his legacy to James, Royce, and Dewey, I came to recognize that we no longer have to wrestle with competing ideas such as high quality versus low cost or centralized versus decentralized. Instead of trying to figure out which one to act on, we must deal with different ways of interpreting the piece of reality each of these ideas helps us see. With pragmatism, we can bridge the old dualism of action/contemplation, since we know we are always doing both, in a natural interaction that has positive impact on both ethics and the "bottom line"; and we can see reality not as something static (as in the machine model of business we spoke of in earlier chapters) but as ever-changing and requiring constantly new interpretations.

This is becoming increasingly obvious as U.S. business faces competitive challenges as never before. Managers such as John Hudiberg are seeing the need for dramatic change, as are a host of business consultants and other leading thinkers. For example, Peter Drucker decries the dichotomy between intellectuals and managers. He claims that intellectuals are concerned with words and ideas and managers are concerned with people and work. He predicts that "to transcend this dichotomy in a new synthesis will be a central philosophical and educational challenge for the post-capitalist society."[121]

Peter Senge advocates strongly the process of dialogue within the learning organization and describes admirably the Peircean community of inquirers and the role of interpretation through dialogue. Senge says:

> The purpose of a dialogue is to go beyond any one individual's understanding … people are no longer primarily in opposition … in dialogue a group explores complex, difficult issues from many points of view. Individuals suspend their assumptions, but they communicate their assumptions freely.[122]

He quotes David Bohm, whom many credit with revitalizing the art of dialogue today: "The purpose of dialogue is to reveal the incoherence of our thought."[123]

Gary Hamel and C.K. Prahalad describe the strategic intent of a company and its core competences. In their influential articles in the *Harvard Business Review*, they stated the need to bring core competences, or what they call the collective learning of the organization, to support the strategic intent. Strategic intent comes from foresight: a well-articulated point of view about tomorrow's opportunities and challenges.[124] This stance of foresight is reminiscent of Whitehead's philosophical stance (see Chapter 4).

Jim Collins has seen the necessity of values, core purpose, and goals in building a sustainable organization, and for leaders the necessity to hold firmly to ideas, yet the humility to challenge them. Tom Peters talks about the need for vision and for getting comfortable with paradox. M. Scott Peck's effort to create an environment of community is designed to foster the process of interpretation, as people let go of their assumptions and listen to others. Robert Bellah calls for us to rediscover the methods of civil discourse and get beyond our individual opinions. Alasdair MacIntyre wants us to get away from our use of segmented shards of assumptions and certainty, to rediscover the importance of virtue as a basis for action. Each of these analysts solicits us to join in cooperative inquiry, to get beyond our belief in the competition of ideas and in the supremacy of the individual's opinion.

But this is not easily accomplished. As businesspeople, we believe in the need for action now. We tend to cling to our narrow definition of the purpose of business—to maximize return to shareholders—which leads to a short-term focus on quarterly performance. We lack faith in group or committee thinking, which we tend to feel reduces individual ideas to the lowest common denominator (the weakest link in the chain of reasoning), and put a premium on strong, decisive leadership. Most of all, we resist changing our minds; we hate paradox and feel fearful when our most basic beliefs are challenged.[125]

Inspired by Royce and Dewey, I have extended Peirce into the realm of commerce, as we will see in the next chapter. But I needed the insights of an unlikely and remarkable person who in many significant ways is a pragmatist, although he is a Jungian holistic depth psychologist. Ira Progoff noted the principles of starting where the person was and noting the "continuum" of a person's life, what we would come to call the "path".

The decisive bridge

To cut a ten-year story short, I looked for a way to actually *practice* pragmatism. In the thousands of pages of philosophy I read, only John Dewey had several steps of inquiry in a book for school teachers: *How We Think*.[126] I found another method in the field of psychology. I worked to combine Peirce's pragmatic method of inquiry, described by Dewey, with Ira Progoff's "Intensive Journal" concept. This combination has proven to be an exceptionally powerful way for people to get in touch with the movement of their organizations' lives, to see their own lives and their work more objectively, and to discern meaning and direction of their organizations and their careers where it had been lacking before. The result is a laboratory-like notebook that I call the CORPORANTES *PathFinder* Notebook. Aware of all this, I melded the ideas of Peirce, Royce, and the practical steps of Dewey with a dialogue process I encountered, to develop a way for practicing pragmatism in business. This is the subject of Chapter 7.

Reading the signs

- What do *I* live for?
- What is *my* duty?
- What is *my* true ideal of life?
- What am *I* loyal to?
- What are *my* values?
- What conversation goes on in my mind?
- How do I characterize my thinking? Do I use deduction, induction, or abduction? Do I rely on perceptions, conceptions, or interpretation?
- Following Drucker, how do I bring ideas and work together?

Part IV
Decide — Hypothesize

7

Pragmatism from theory to practice

A *PathFinder* for organizations

The story of how this book, and the CORPORANTES *PathFinder* Pragmatic Inquiry® process, came to be goes back many years, long before I had ever heard of Charles Sanders Peirce and Josiah Royce. I had been teaching as executive-in-residence at DePaul University's Kellstadt Graduate School of Business, working with Professor Dennis McCann, chair of the Religious Studies department, when the seeds were first planted.

Dr. McCann suggested that I attend an Intensive Journal workshop led by Dr. Ira Progoff of Dialogue House. Progoff, over the course of 25 years, had developed his Intensive Journal Process into a powerful method of self-discovery used by over 250,000 people. His approach offers a way for someone to get a perspective on the "unfolding" of his or her life, using the seed analogy. Progoff believes that each life, like a seed, has the potential for development, which can be realized if we look back into our past to see what our development has been. From this perspective, the action we should take—the next steps to where our lives might go from here—becomes clear.[127]

Progoff's Intensive Journal Process

Progoff gets his workshop participants to look back on their lives through various writing exercises, held over the course of a week (the word "intensive" is not used lightly). When I learned that the workshop would take a full week, including evenings, and that the journal consisted of five main sections with 25 subsections,

I thought full-time introspection for a week was more looking at the interior movement of my life than I needed. However, I knew of the success that Progoff had had, and so I sat through the seven-day workshop, drifting in and out at times to call my office and meet with clients, never quite sure just what was going on, but slowly becoming aware that Progoff was really on to something.

As I listened to the discoveries and insights of my fellow workshop participants, I realized that Progoff had found a way for people to get in touch with the movement of their lives, to see their lives somewhat objectively, and to discern meaning where there had not seemed to be any before. Generally people end up in one of these workshops because their lives are not going well, or they are facing a tough decision, or they are stuck and feel some block or stagnation in their lives. Me? I was there because my professor had insisted I must attend. But as the week passed and I moved through the five major sections (called "Dimensions"), and 25 subsections, I kept thinking about Progoff's idea of my life having movement. It intrigued me.

Slowly it came to me that many other things I had never considered before could also have a life and movement. Dr. Progoff talks about work or a project having a life of its own. This is a familiar idea to all artists and novelists whose characters, at some point, seem to come alive, taking over the storytelling process. As an example of this, Dr. Progoff is fond of telling a story about Tolstoy when he was writing the novel *Anna Karenina*. Tolstoy came down late to dinner one evening looking shaken and awful. His family asked what was wrong. "Anna Karenina just threw herself under the wheels of the train," Tolstoy replied.

Anything that has a history can be considered to have a life—a nation, a people, a social movement—and so it can be asked: What does it wish to be?

Progoff's method was developed for individuals, but suddenly it hit me: Why not use the method for a company or any type of organization? Could we talk of an organization having a life similar to that of an individual with its stages of life: birth, growth, peak, decline, and death? A business, after all, has all the characteristics Progoff mentioned—a history, key events, relationships with others, and questions about which direction to pursue in the future. Could someone in business not keep a journal for his or her corporation, treating it like a person? This insight was the genesis of what became, in time, the CORPORANTES *PathFinder* method of inquiry.

From Intensive Journal to CORPORANTES *PathFinder* Notebook

I worked extensively with Ira Progoff to reorient parts of his Journal Process toward a business audience. Much like an individual going through Progoff's Journal Process, we created equivalent elements for the corporation: a Period Log reviewing the recent period in the business's history; Stepping Stones, where the executive became the corporation and got inside its "life," identifying with it and tracing its long-term history; and Dialogues with the people and works of the corporation. I tested this basic premise with friends and associates to see how they would respond. Everyone found the idea of a corporation having a life of its own, with its adventures, cycles, personality, and culture, to be believable and provocative.[128] This certainly was different from our more mechanistic idea of the corporation described earlier.

Duffy's Rosetta Stone

There were some problems, chiefly centering on the challenge of translating what is essentially one of the best methods of self-reflection[129] into a useful tool for business. Businesspeople, for example, are not keen on what can seem as therapy. They incline more toward action, not contemplation. Rather than look within, as the Journal Process demands, they want to look outward. Rather than relying primarily on intuition, they look to reason, rationality, and linear thinking. So I did not get too far in my task until I met Father Thomas Duffy, who led me to Peircean philosophy, which proved to be the Rosetta Stone that allowed me to translate Progoff into business.

Tom Duffy had been Progoff's training director for a dozen years, so he was familiar with the Intensive Journal Process. When I met him, he had just begun his study of Peirce and I thought, "Oh no, more wonderful but obscure and unsellable ideas." So, I could not believe my luck when Duffy told me that Peirce called his method of inquiry "pragmatism."

Pragmatism! That word so familiar and comforting to legions of U.S. business practitioners! The marketer in me knew it would be much easier to sell businesspeople on a method based on "pragmatism," which looks outward to reality, than it would one based on "holistic depth psychology," which looked inward. Yet it was through holistic depth psychology, and Progoff's application of it in his Intensive Journal Process, that I began to find a way to address the filters of the machine model of business, dualism, our penchant for individualism, and the ethical dilemmas facing business.

So, I began to study pragmatism, as Peirce originally defined it. This is much easier to say now than it was to do then. I found Peirce almost incomprehensible: big, often invented words; long, complex sentences; subtle and rigorous ideas. But the more I worked with him and with his students, James, Royce, and Dewey, who had also had to grope their way toward comprehending him, the more I came to see how Peirce complemented Progoff. The sharing of ideas with others (through dialogues, which is at the heart of Progoff's Intensive Journal Process) is akin to Peirce's gathering of evidence. As I saw more connections between Progoff and Peirce, I came to appreciate the role played by the surprising fact and the nagging doubt in opening people up to the possibility of new hypotheses and actions based on new beliefs.

We did not have to present the idea of the corporation having a life of its own as the basic premise for the process. Peirce himself carried the idea of the community of inquirers further to explain that idea. He hypothesized that you should be able to draw up an experimental test to prove that people in close enough connection can influence one another:

> Namely if this be the case, there should be something like personal consciousness in bodies of men who are in intimate and intensely sympathetic communication … esprit de corps, national sentiment, sympathy are no mere metaphors. None of us can fully realize what the minds of corporations are, any more than one of my brain cells can know what the whole brain is thinking. But the law of mind clearly points to the existence of such *personalities* [my emphasis]. And there are many ordinary observations which, if they were critically examined and supplemented by special experiments, might, as first appearances promise, give evidence of the influence of such greater persons upon individuals.[130]

Peirce offers the example of Christians coming together over the centuries to pray together in a common body. (I will consider monasteries later as a form of corporation.) We could begin instead where businesspeople felt comfortable: with a practical problem that the company needed to solve. The writing exercises, which Progoff put in a journal and we recorded in a notebook, then became a way to capture data and investigate a problem.

Then Peirce's model of the scientific method fell into place. As a community of inquirers and interpreters, we were looking for the truth of the practical situation, asking "What should we be doing?" This question leads to the earlier question of looking beyond the signs of the situation to the true meaning of what is really going on. Since the businesspeople were in a corporate setting, the emphasis was on the **we**, not I, for, true to Peircean process, our investigation was a collective endeavor.

Organization habits

We found that the most difficult task was to address the habits, the patterns, or in summary, the culture of an organization. As was said in Chapter 5, the practice of pragmatic inquiry gives teams and individuals:

1. A way to get past the pitfalls of simplistic, dualistic thinking by providing a way to constantly test your beliefs and assumptions

2. A way to avoid rigid thinking and narrow focus, in this era of increasingly rapid change, by its encouragement of doubt

3. A way for groups and teams to discover something or decide on a course of action, through its extension of the scientific method beyond the laboratory

4. A way to determine what's true, to verify your perceptions, by developing a reliable method of observing and formulating hypotheses

5. A way to get beyond what you think you know, by identifying the "truth you do not yet know"

6. A way to discover just how you go about thinking and making sense of the world, in the context of the "learning organization" mentioned in Chapter 2

7. A way to gather evidence and interpret it for the basis of a position or story which becomes the basis for explaining decisions and action to yourself and others

Branding the process

After starting with a journal program for the exploration of an individual's path of becoming, we ended up with a scientific, pragmatic method of inquiry: Begin, Explore, Interpret, Decide–Hypothesize, and Act. Then, being in advertising, I recognized the importance of naming the process. In honor of Peirce, the sometime mapmaker, we chose the name *PathFinder*, even though everything from cars to corporations shares the name and it could not be trademarked by itself. We found that people relate well to the dynamic idea that the corporation is on its way—on a journey. Businesspeople often talk about where the corporation is going, its goal, or its destination. The Quaker Oats Company, for example, uses "roadmaps" as a designation for its planning process.

To distinguish our *PathFinder* from all the rest, I cast about for some better word than "corporate" to describe our venture. I knew "corporate" came from the Latin *corpus*, meaning body. Indeed, the corporation, in the Peircean/Roycean view, is a body. Then I discovered that the present participle form of the verb *corporare*— *corporans* and its plural *corporantes*—means "forming into a body." Why not use it as a name? Our lawyer assured me that we would have *no* trouble trade marking that obscure word.

Since Latin is often falsely described as a "dead" language, I was given a lot of advice urging me to choose a different name. But *corporantes* describes perfectly what the process does. "Forming into a body" is the essence of the community of inquirers of Peirce and the beloved community of Royce. As people inquire together, discovering what action to take based on shared beliefs, they form into a body. So we incorporated our company as CORPORANTES, a wonderful if underappreciated use of the word *corpus*.

Further, we even trademarked *Pragmatic Inquiry* to highlight the difference from the usual misunderstanding of pragmatism noted earlier.

The CORPORANTES *PathFinder* Pragmatic Inquiry

After the better part of five years, we had a name, legal status, a notebook, and a process. What did it consist of? The *PathFinder* is a tool to assist individuals and organizations on their journey of inquiry—five steps to be specific. Here is a brief sketch.

When an organization embarks on the *PathFinder* process, it starts with a problem it is facing, which may be as broad as defining a corporate mission or as focused as mapping out a new marketing strategy. The process of five steps consisting of 12 exercises which, while done in order, are actually iterative in practice. (And these exercises are always followed by testing and the inevitable "Begin Again.") The key is getting people to be quiet and reflective. We will describe the five basic steps in their sequence in the loose-leaf notebook. (See Appendix III for the short version: *PathFinder* Field Notebook.)

Reflecting pragmatic inquiry as developed by Peirce, formulated by Dewey, and practiced by Progoff, the 11 exercises are divided into five parts: (1) Begin—establish a baseline question and answer to be tested; (2) Explore; (3) Interpret; (4) Decide–Hypothesize; and (5) Act—the path ahead—test the hypothesis (see Figure 7.1).

Figure 7.1 **CORPORANTES** *PathFinder* **Lab Journal© helix**

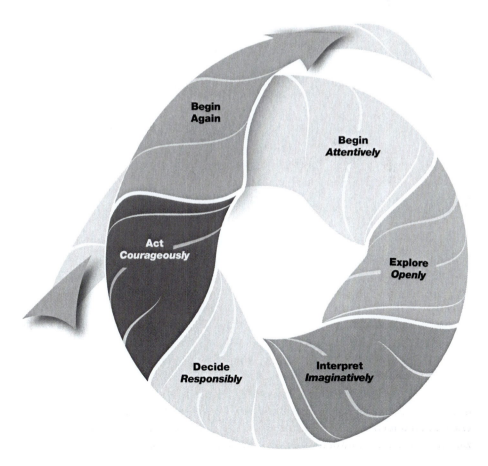

Inquiry mindsets

You will notice the helix is shaped like a rope, or cable, as Peirce suggested (see page 53) and that there are adverbs to describe the mindsets for each step of the inquiry. Research from leadership studies as well as from neuroscience, educators, psychologists, philosophers, and theologians[131] points out that we need multiple mindsets or ways of knowing to be most effective in engaging difficult situations. The successful leaders are able to move between these different ways of seeing and thinking by combining opposite mindsets of thoughtful/action-oriented, analysis/synthesis, openness/decisiveness, and so on. Jim Collins has famously characterized this highest level of leadership as being able to hold the paradox of "humility and fierce resolve."[132]

Here is a brief description of each step and the associated mindset:

Begin *attentively.* Take the stance of a questioner and learner, and be open to admitting you don't know all the answers, be ready to challenge your assumptions.

Explore *openly.* Engage many diverse points of view and opinions especially from stakeholders you might not normally talk or agree with. The concrete get the facts as well as the opinions of others.

Interpret *imaginatively.* Be creative, make connections, map the system, listen for the conversations, develop insights. What does the data collected in Explore mean?

Decide *responsibly.* Weigh the evidence, make judgments, and come to an answer that takes into account the impact of the decision on all stakeholders.

Act *courageously.* Your decision should reflect your values, which are the ultimate ground and impetus to drive your decision.

Begin again. In light of the inevitable challenges and barriers that arise, you need to be ready to ask better questions and test better ideas.

Here are the steps of the Pragmatic Inquiry, putting these mindsets into action in the flow of the arc of inquiry.

Begin attentively

Every day of our lives, we are confronted with facts, problems, situations, issues, opportunities, and challenges that demand our attention. Usually we react to this daily flood of information and events almost automatically by fitting them into our existing patterns and habits of thinking and behaving. That is because we assume we know what is going on and based on those assumptions we decide what to do.

Learning begins when some fact, incident, challenge, obstacle, or opportunity comes along that forces us to stop and begin to question or doubt what we know. And what we know comes from our experience. That is why Dewey stated that "all learning is the continuous reconstruction of experience."[133] Then we treat what we know as **an assumption to be tested.**

The inquiry begins with five questions to establish a baseline:

1. As you move forward, what market need, problem, issue, or opportunity do you see which you and your organization might address? (Why is this opportunity important to you, your organization, and those you serve?)

2. What challenges, questions, barriers, concerns, problems, and issues do you face in meeting this need? (Who else is your challenge/question important to, and why?)

3. What is your preliminary answer now?

4. What are your organizational and personal values and vision and how are they impacting your preliminary answer?

5. What actions are you planning to take or are taking now?

This establishes the baseline or "hypothesis" to be tested through the inquiry.

Explore openly

This is where people record their observations and impressions—the surprising facts or nagging doubts that spark further inquiry. This is comparable to a scientist's notebooks that record the results of lab experiments. In these sections, the "investigator as corporate *PathFinder*" accumulates the equivalent, in the form of data from life experiences.

People look at the experiences, facts, trends, and so on, from five different points of view: the personal, the organization, the market, society, and the environment (see Figure 7.2).

For each of the five perspectives, we make the distinction between the "now"—Bearings—and the "past and future"—the Path. For the Bearings, we ask participants to think about the present time, starting from a recent period, usually when the problem came about. For the Path, we ask them to reflect on how the problem came about, key turning points in the past, mistakes and learnings along the way, and where things are headed. From these two time perspectives, they gain a "snapshot" of the present and a "movie" of the past and future—the arc of the movement.

The five points of view are:

- **Personal Bearings and Path.** Since everyone starts with a personal point of view of the problem, we created a section called Personal Bearings and Path. The participants first put down their thoughts about their position within the organization in relation to the problem. The Personal Path allows individual employees to trace how they arrived at their positions with regard to the problem at hand. And we ask where the individual seems to be headed

Figure 7.2 *PathFinder* stakeholder relationships

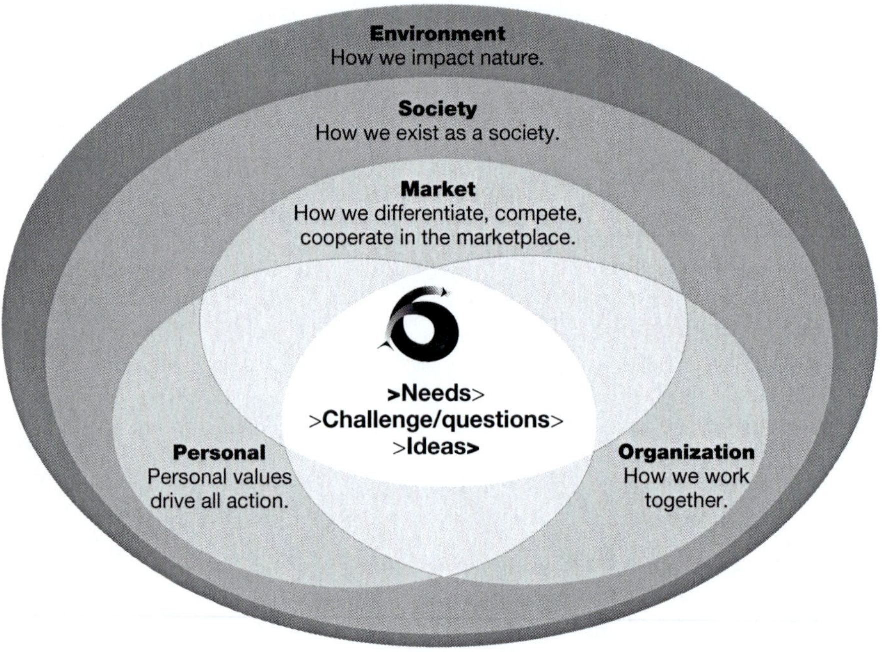

Environment
How we impact nature.

Society
How we exist as a society.

Market
How we differentiate, compete,
cooperate in the marketplace.

>Needs>
>Challenge/questions>
>Ideas>

Personal
Personal values
drive all action.

Organization
How we work
together.

Pragmatic Inquiry

Revealed Needs _____

Identified Challenge/questions |Cq| _____

Actionable Ideas _____

- **Organization Bearings and Path.** For an organization, this begins with figuring out where the corporation is now. Participants write their thoughts about organization problems and issues in the *PathFinder* to get their Organization Bearings. In the Organization Path, we ask how the corporation got to its present situation. What were the critical steps in the development of the problem that is the focus of the investigation? Where does the organization seem to be headed? (And these same questions apply to the organization's competitors.)

- **Market Bearings and Path.** We ask where the market is in relation to the issue and where it has been and where does it seem to be headed. This includes consumers, distribution, and other key stakeholders. Who else— competitors—are also engaged in serving the needs involved with your issue?

- **Society Bearings and Path.** With the increasing emphasis on social responsibility, we have added the social perspective. Where is society in terms of the issue and where has society been and where is it headed?

- **Environment Bearings and Path.** What impact is the organization having on nature? Where has the state of nature been and where is it heading? This section recognizes that ultimately we are living within and profiting from the ecosystem of nature

Interpret imaginatively

After the Explore step, we search for what the data, ideas, and experiences mean.

External conversations

We begin with listing and connecting actual conversations to capture the language and logic within and among important members of various stakeholder groups, as well as coworkers and others that the inquirer can actually contact and have a conversation with. This models the scientific community, which pursues the "truth we do not yet know" through individuals listening to and learning from each other as they present their findings or evidence.

Habits and patterns: culture

A major aspect of successful inquiry is identifying one's habits. We recognized the overpowering need to make clear the organization's habits of behavior, to permit an examination of the underlying assumptions and hypotheses. This, as I noted in Chapter 4, is one of Peirce's major insights; what he called the "fixation of belief." So often, the belief on which habit rests is the hypothesis that filters what we see and thus may hinder true understanding. This happens when companies become hardened in their approaches and systems, which makes them unresponsive to the marketplace. But it can also happen that, as companies grow, they forget the original beliefs and visions of their founders. In the section on habits, we try to spot what the corporate habits are that result from either stated or unstated beliefs, and what decision might be made based on the hypothesis to see if it is true.

Internal conversations

The next step is to engage in conversations, both with oneself and with other people, which might help to develop one's thoughts. We ask the inquirers to think of someone they would like to have a conversation with; an **imaginary conversation**. From such internal conversations, we can get other perspectives on the problem, as well as new ways to gather data. Both in my work with Progoff's Intensive Journal Process and in corporate settings, I have seen some amazing discoveries take place, as people listen to other voices—those within but in the words they think the other person might say. And the range of conversation partners is vast: from Moses,

Jesus, Plato, Lincoln, and Florence Nightingale, to founders of organizations, Peanuts, high school coaches, deceased relatives, and so on.

Maps and Images

We can now attempt to map the system that represents the way the need is being met today. Then we ask the inquirer to map what the system would be like if it were to accomplish the values purpose and goals of the organization. This was a central element of Peirce's process of inquiry. Recalling Peirce's work as a surveyor, mapmaker and mathematician, we created a section called Maps and Images, which takes the process of thinking beyond words and helps to discover connections by drawing on the power of both the rational and the intuitive parts of the mind. Examples of the power of images abound in science: for example, August Kekulé's discovery of the carbon-based benzene ring through the dream image of snakes biting their tails and rolling down a hill. The use of maps, images, equations, and diagrams appeals to businesspeople used to dealing with flow charts, outlines, and diagrams. Since everyone knows about the effectiveness of the "incubation" time in problem solving, we ask the participants to record their wake-up thoughts and dreams, which, like Kekulé's dream, can contain a key insight.

Decide responsibly

The inquirers now write their conclusion, which technically is to be treated as a hypothesis in the scientific sense that the conclusion is held as tentative. For executives, we often entitle this "Decide." The participant hunts for the deeper truth and defines a new corporate hypothesis. This is akin to what Tom Peters and other business analysts have called the mission, "passion," or heart of the corporation—its underlying purpose.

Act courageously

The final part is what U.S. businesspeople like best: action. In the *PathFinder* approach, this is presented in true Peircean form—beliefs, then action. This reflects Peirce's recognition that consistent action (rather than reaction) must be based on belief.[134] Finally, the Explore and Hypothesize steps are translated into action, The Path Ahead. We caution participants that this action must be part of the wider process of testing the hypothesis. That is, after the corporation acts, there needs to be measurement and evaluation to be sure the hypothesis holds up in reality. If it doesn't, the process must begin all over again. In any case, the process continues as reality changes, calling beliefs into question.

What have you learned?

It is then very instructive to compare your beginning questions, answers and actions to see what you have learned, or, more often, *un-learned*. Also, you will be

Figure 7.3 **Before and after comparison: "What have you learned?"**

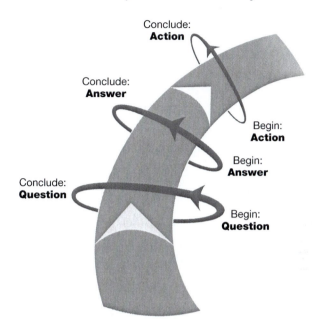

able to see your values at work, proving the pragmatic axiom that values and ideas are known by their consequences.

Measurement—begin again

The last step is, of course, to see just what has happened. As William James famously said:

> Truth HAPPENS to an idea. It BECOMES true, is MADE true by events. Its verity IS in fact an event, a process, the process namely of its verifying itself, its veriFICATION. Its validity is the process of its validATION.[135]

And that is what happens to our values, as we live, develop, and test them.

Testing the *PathFinder*

By this point, after all my years of work, study and synthesis, I was eager to see whether my hypothesis—that is, that our CORPORANTES *PathFinder* Process was a useful tool in business—held up in reality. I waited for a suitable corporate "patient" to appear—suitable in that such a corporation would recognize the need to ask big, basic questions, while being fairly small and resilient (so I could not do too much damage, if my system turned out to be flawed). Most importantly, my first patient had to be willing to experiment.

I did not have to wait long before an ideal candidate appeared. Just how my hypothesis about applying the Peircean pragmatic method of inquiry tested out, and what it has looked like in action in a variety of different businesses, is told in Chapter 8. What we learned was that all it takes to begin is to have a serious question, doubt, situation, challenge, opportunity or problem—something that creates the need and desire to "uncover the truth we do not yet know, leading to the action we have yet to take."

Reading the signs

- Here are some of the larger questions—the macro view:

- How can I, as a businessperson, get out of the short-term, reactive rut that most companies are currently stuck in?

- How do I plan more accurately for the future when things are changing so fast?

- How do I stimulate creativity, flexibility, and innovation at a time when people are concerned for their jobs?

- How do I evaluate the performance of my business in a way that goes beyond the quarterly profit and loss statements?

8
Pragmatism in business
Lessons learned

Many of the stories you will read in this chapter were in the first edition published over 15 years ago, as well as many new stories. They cover the range of organizational life and a bewildering range of challenges. We have not updated any of them since each case is intended to give you a snapshot of a specific learning context and process. After each inquiry, there was much activity as the participants put their decisions into action and tested them. Those who were most successful realized that the purpose of the inquiry was not just to come up with an answer but also to be able to reason and engage in the practice and discipline of pragmatic inquiry as they faced the future and the inevitable challenges and barriers … and the ones who succeeded, continued to "begin again."

Over the years, working with and listening to the thousands of pragmatic inquirers ranging from CEOs and executive teams down to college students, we have learned better ways to engage thoughtful practitioners in inquiry (see the Preface to the Second Edition for the highlights of the learning). So, as participants have been engaged in the process, in a sense, we have been conducting our own *Path-Finder* Pragmatic Inquiries over these many years and learning, based on the evidence of our experience.

Common Ground: The first test

Not long after I had developed a preliminary version of the CORPORANTES *Path-Finder* Notebook, I received a call from the Executive Director of Common Ground, Jim Kenney, asking me to help them resolve some strategic planning issues they faced.

Common Ground is an interfaith study center headquartered in Deerfield, Illinois, a northern suburb of Chicago. It operates a continuing education program, originally focused on Jewish/Christian dialogue but since broadened. It now considers a variety of questions dealing with science, contemporary culture, economics, and spirituality, but all from the perspective of the world's religious wisdom. I had known the two founding leaders for years and had led some of their groups in topics on business and ethics, so I knew that the organization fit my criteria for a test case well: they were small, resilient, and open to considering the deeper issues behind the surface problems.

From my initial conversation with Mr. Kenney, it was clear that they were willing to experiment. Moreover, many on their Board of Directors were familiar with the Journal Process, and introspection. Common Ground looked like the perfect first patient. "Igor, get the operating table ready," I thought in an "internal conversation." My test case was underway.

The challenge

Common Ground had been very successful for 20 years in offering a wide range of talks and workshops to the general public, mainly on the North Shore. At the board level, they had always had vigorous discussions ranging from arcane aspects of philosophy and religion to financial practicalities and long-term strategy. At the time they called me, they were facing internal conflicts and difficulties in working together. There was some confusion of roles and responsibilities. They needed restructuring to clarify the new position of Executive Director and the role of the Board. There were differing views about goals and the ideal size of the organization. The Board members had different agendas about their target audience and different opinions about what courses to offer. Clearly, they needed to get all their cards on the table to determine what was really going on.

The process

We scheduled a day together, armed with a set of general questions to help the group get to the bottom of such difficulties as: What are the responsibilities of the executive director? and "What skills should Board members have? We also considered the larger context of what decisions needed to be made concerning future direction of Common Ground.

As we worked through the exercises in the *PathFinder*, the meeting began to heat up, particularly when we got to the section on Conversations. Many of the dozen people in the meeting noticed a real shift at the point when individuals began to read the conversations they had written. Since many in the group had practiced meditation and were used to interior, reflective activities, the internal conversation process brought people's hopes, fears, and larger perspectives to the surface. By the end of the day, it was obvious that everyone had been taken to a deeper level and had achieved important insights. But it was equally clear that there had been no real resolution of the issues. I left wondering what would happen.

The result

I didn't have long to wait. Jim Kenney called me several days later to say that the *PathFinder* session had been a watershed in the life of the Board. As he put it in a letter he wrote to me later:

> Our "day" was not without stress and even had its measure of pain, but it paid off. I have to tell you that, largely as a result of the exercises you led, some major changes have taken place. The clarification of the Common Ground vision which eventuated from that day brought about a dramatic resignation from the Board, and, more important by far, several dramatic recommitments.
>
> I should also add that my own position as Executive Director has now gained some of the structure it had clearly lacked. I couldn't be more pleased, but, more to the point, it didn't turn out as I might have wished before the "Day." I learned a great deal about encounter, conversation (with self, with enterprise, with visions, and with the all-important others).

From this first experiment, I found that several of the key assumptions on which the *PathFinder* process was based were correct:

1. People realize that corporations do have a life of their own as they examine the past, key events, turning points, and twists and turns in the path the corporation has followed

2. Building on this past, it becomes easier to clarify where the organization is now and the problems and opportunities it faces

3. The future then becomes clearer, as if one were to say, "If this is our past and where we are now, from that perspective this looks like a more promising and likely path of action"

4. All participants in the process have valuable things to contribute if they present the ideas as their individual perspectives on the reality of the organization's life

5. There is a power in everyone sharing openly—what Peck calls the power of being in community, as we noted in Chapter 3

6. The process of Internal Conversation is very powerful, both for those who are used to listening to their inner voice and looking for the surprising answers that come back, and for those who have never taken the time to reflect and listen. The latter are invariably shocked to hear another voice within them that they had overlooked. (We will point this out in the dramatic story of Unity Church and Larry Clark.)

7. Once the path of the corporation becomes clear, each individual can see his or her role in the development of the corporation and can then decide whether to continue to be a part of the corporation's life of action, and if so, in what capacity

I also realized that, when dealing with this method of inquiry, one must be prepared for the unexpected: things will not necessarily turn out as anticipated.

Finally, I was gratified to see that the *PathFinder* process is a powerful way for people to change filters: the organization is seen, not as a machine, but as an organism, with a life, past, and destiny. Differences of opinion do not have to be obstacles leading to dualistic choices or compromise since the process can transcend these pitfalls. The Board members of Common Ground were able to see themselves not as individuals competing with each other, but as part of the larger reality of an organization that had a life of its own, which they were there to help develop into a reality.

Encouraged by this initial success, I felt ready to apply the *PathFinder* process to resolving problems other clients might face. As it turned out, the past years have brought a wide range of such problems to our doorstep, most dealing with the elusive issue of corporate purpose and direction, which the following dozen or so case histories will illustrate.

Pritikin Longevity Center: corporate cohesion and redefinition

A pioneer organization in programs designed to reduce the risk of heart disease via diet, exercise, and stress reduction, Pritikin was founded in 1976 by Nathan Pritikin, who had cured himself of heart disease by the regimen he later provided to the public at his Longevity Center in Santa Monica, California. This regimen involves both a medically supervised on-site program of lifestyle change, and a line of healthful prepared food products. In 1989, the Quaker Oats Company bought the rights to the Pritikin name and its products and services with the intention of taking the Pritikin program into wider distribution: to bring the message of low-fat diet, exercise, and stress reduction to the largest possible audience.

The challenge

By 1991, Pritikin was at a point of great change, with a lot of creative potential and an urgent need for coordination among its various leaders, many of whom had been brought into the organization only recently. Three groups were involved in sorting out Pritikin's future: the Longevity Center staff, based in Santa Monica; executives of Quaker, the corporate owner that addressed the marketing issues; and the R&D staff within Quaker in charge of product development and improvement. Both Quaker and its R&D were based in Chicago: Quaker executives at Quaker Tower in downtown Chicago and the R&D staff in the Barrington laboratories outside Chicago.

Having dealt with these three groups as the CEO of Pritikin's advertising agency, I knew that each group saw Pritikin differently. Different managers had different levels of understanding about the company's core beliefs and philosophy and how these had evolved over time. There was a need to balance the corporate values of the home office with those of the California founders. Most urgently, Pritikin's identity had to be clarified for the wider management team, to promote the unity and cohesion necessary for a successful marketing and advertising campaign.

The process

I began with a one-on-one meeting with Bill Trotter, Pritikin's president, to explain the CORPORANTES *PathFinder* process. Bill, a chemical engineer by training, was not inclined to spend time reflecting and writing in our notebook. But I got him to agree to give me one hour. Beginning with the Corporate Bearings section, Bill described in bullet points where the corporation stood at the moment. He mentioned how the current direction of Pritikin had changed from the original vision. Hearing that, I took him right into the Conversations section, suggesting he have a "talk" with the founder, Nathan Pritikin. Bill at first looked quizzical, but to my surprise thought it could be useful. He spent a few minutes writing and suddenly stopped: Nathan had "told" Bill to get back to the heart of his founding message, that the process of marketing the Center was being approached too rationally, overlooking the powerful emotional content and appeal of the healthy life. Bill handed me the sheet of paper, looked at his watch, pleased that he had completed the assignment in less than 20 minutes, and left. But he knew this was the insight we were all after, and Bill heard it through his Conversation. This experience also gave me a clue as to the efficiency of the *PathFinder* process. Moving to a different level and listening to a different voice can often bring dramatic insights quickly, exposing faulty hypotheses and helping to formulate new ones.

After this, our agency was able to create better advertising, with a clearer focus on Pritikin's emotional appeal. With this key achievement behind us, we went on to use the *PathFinder* process with the three Pritikin groups—the Pritikin Longevity Center, Quaker Oats corporate staff, and R&D—in a day-long workshop that was the first time they had ever met together.

The result

Getting everyone involved in the business into the same room in itself helped to provide a more complete picture of the operation. By using the *PathFinder* process, they went further, to: (1) rediscover the founder's mission, and how it still informs their business; (2) clue the newly hired staff into the core beliefs of the company; and (3) clarify for all three groups of managers what is and is not important to the success of the business.

By coming to a place where they could truly listen and hear one another, they achieved an empowering sense of community, and saw Pritikin as an organization with a life of its own. They saw how it had grown, how it learned from its mistakes and experiences, and how they were, each of them, part of this larger process. They also saw what might lie ahead, and what the key issues were that had to be addressed.

Using the *PathFinder* process with Pritikin was, for me, a great chance to observe how the method of inquiry can foster community even between groups with very different corporate cultures. It was gratifying to see the corporate/Chicago and New Age/California cultures meet, mingle and come to greater unity and cohesion, but also to see the depth of differences among the different parts of the organization. Writing Conversations during our day together once again brought dramatic insights. In one woman's Conversation with the Pritikin organization, the organization described itself as "a distant relative who had been invited to a family wedding but no one was quite sure who this relative should sit with at church, or at what table in the pecking order at the reception should they be seated." We all laughed at the insight that indeed Pritikin organization was having trouble finding its place in the Quaker family of products.

Particularly helpful was seeing how Pritikin, with its corporate vision, values, and direction, did help further the mission and values of its parent company, Quaker, and seeing what Quaker might learn from its experience with Pritikin.

Bang & Olufsen: new president meets his American team

The challenge

Bang & Olufsen (B&O) is a Danish electronics designer and manufacturer of beautiful and functional, very high-end hi-fi, television and multi-media equipment. It had been a client of ours for two years when a new president took over. He had been president of B&O in Sweden, a country of five million people, where he had built the sales up to equal sales in the United States, a country of 250 million people. (Not surprisingly, he thought there was great opportunity for growth in the United States.) He was unfamiliar with B&O's U.S. operation, unused to the degree of diversity and the backgrounds of his new staff, and had little understanding of what had been going on in the U.S. operation to bring it to its present situation.

The process

We used the *PathFinder* process to familiarize the president with the U.S. branch of the company. At the same time, we would consider related issues: How was the business evolving? How was corporate planning doing? What was the future direction of the firm?

Most revealing to the president was the use of the Corporate Trail section. He could tell by looking at the numbers where the company was in the present, but most significant for him was to hear the various members of his staff recount the key decisions and turning points in B&O's 20-odd years in the United States. His staff also learned something about him as he wrote his perception of what he had heard in Europe about B&O's development in the United States.

The result

The workshop brought together not only leaders from B&O but also some of the Frank C. Nahser Advertising agency staff, so that all of us might come away with a better sense of the company and how it might be marketed. For the new president, the *PathFinder* process provided a deeper understanding of the history within B&O's U.S. headquarters, so the present situation made more sense to him. For us as advertisers, the process gave greater clarity about the direction of the company.

Hollister, Inc.: honing a sense of corporate mission and vision

Step into any hospital in the United States and you encounter the ubiquitous Hollister product: the Ident-A-Band worn on the wrists of nearly all hospital patients. As a leading medical supply company, Hollister specializes in ostomy and wound care products. It is a multinational corporation, with facilities in the United States and five other countries.

The challenge

At the time Hollister turned to the *PathFinder* process, their CEO, Michael Winn, had been trying for seven years to develop a corporate mission statement. Despite the efforts of many committees, no one had been able to come up with something that all could buy into. I had known Michael for years and had often had discussions with him as I took courses, studying Progoff and Peirce, and building the *PathFinder* process. One day when he mentioned the frustration he was feeling about the mission statement problem, I suggested he try the *PathFinder*; perhaps it could get things moving.

The process

Michael and I spent a day together, going through parts of the *PathFinder* process. As had been the case with Bill Trotter at Pritikin, I suspected that some interesting insights might come from Michael having a Conversation with the founder of the company, John Dickinson Schneider. The results were surprising.

The results

Michael Winn had known Schneider, and it was he who had appointed Winn as president. Before Schneider's death, they had several discussions about the company and his vision for it. As Michael wrote his imagined Conversation, years after Schneider's death, memories of those meetings came back, but with Mr. Schneider becoming increasingly unhappy about many of Michael's decisions. As he read the rising diatribe, I started to laugh. Michael looked up and glowered knowingly: "This isn't funny, Ron—he's very upset!"

It became clear to Michael, as Schneider berated him during one of their Conversations, that the corporation had gone astray from the founder's intention by focusing solely on product quality. Working on the Corporate Trail section, Michael suddenly remembered an incident immediately after he had been made president when Mrs. Schneider, the founder's wife, gave him a copy of E.F. Schumacher's *Small is Beautiful* as a memento of the occasion and a reminder for the future. Michael and Schneider assured Mrs. Schneider that they had not forgotten the intimacy and family atmosphere that had, in her opinion, been a large reason for their success. However, Michael realized that, by focusing primarily on product quality during the intervening years, he had neglected the marketplace and the employees. Clearly, Hollister needed to regain the values and customer focus of the original company.

As a result of this realization, many troubling areas of the business came into focus for Michael. In one Conversation, the Hollister Corporation had a "talk" with Schneider in which he took Michael to task. Michael got what he called a bird's-eye perspective on the company and his role in it, a level of objectivity he had not had before. More to the point, he met his goal of developing the basis for the corporation's mission statement. After our meeting, he drew up a draft, circulated it among his executives, and got universal support.

The following year, Michael returned to the *PathFinder* process, this time to gain insights for creating a vision statement. While I wrote the first edition of this book, we were using the *PathFinder* process for a third time, now including the Hollister executive staff, to establish standards of excellence, "World Class Principles," supporting their vision and mission.

One of the underlying purposes of why Michael Winn embarked on the articulation of the mission and vision was that a critical decision point was coming in the life of the corporation. The founder of the company had given the stock to employees, a magnanimous gift to be sure. The stock was placed in a trust that was going to be terminated in 2001. At that time the shareholders would vote on whether to continue the trust or sell their stock and take a considerable gain in profit. Michael was concerned that if the latter happened, this would spell the end of the unique purpose, values, and goals of the corporation. When the time came, the vote was unanimous to continue the trust, which meant that the legacy of the company would continue. This meant a sacrifice on the part of the participants in the trust who could have increased their return had the company been sold, but they recognized the gift that they could pass on to the next generation.

Harris Bank: integrating diverse components into one corporate vision

Harris is one of Chicago's most venerable banks, with over $13 billion in total assets, and a solid reputation that goes back to its founder's original concern for probity: "Honesty and fair dealings." Now owned by BMO Financial Group, Harris is one of the largest banks in the Midwest of the United States. The various components of the bank deal with corporate and community banking, private banking, trust and investment management, bank card and institutional financial services.

The challenge

When we put the *PathFinder* process and method of inquiry to work for Harris, it was to deal with the problem of coordinating and integrating these various components together in a coherent or unified corporate vision. In a workshop with their top managers held at Chicago's beautiful Shedd Aquarium with the dolphins singing in the background, we guided them through the elements of the process, and set them to work writing.

The process

We have found that this period of reflection—a time of disciplined introspection and contemplation—is a key part of the process. Not only does it generate insights, it puts non-verbal types on a par with the verbally aggressive to allow everyone to be heard. By encouraging the use of images, in addition to words, the *PathFinder* process also helps visual types find the right way to see the problem and solution.

The result

The Harris team was asked to draw a picture in the Maps and Images section of what the unified bank might look like. Two members began working with circles symbolizing the two main areas at the bank, Commercial and Personal, and came up with an image—a pair of glasses—that helped them to understand the role of the bank and how its various parts related to their corporate vision of "total customer focus." They were able to articulate the vision in ways that were meaningful when applied to all the component parts of their enterprise, which gave us the basis for an advertising campaign with the theme of helping people make better financial choices. They also saw the power of the *PathFinder* process, which they have used again in departmental and small meetings.

The Harris case taught me how accessible the *PathFinder* process is, regardless of personality type or articulateness: visual people are drawn to the Maps and Images section; quiet people who normally find it hard to get a word in edgewise and those who form thoughts more slowly (but who all have their piece of the truth to offer) get heard; the vocal ones, who often dominate meetings, have the chance in the Conversations section to go within and listen to their inner voices. Perhaps most importantly, the *PathFinder* process puts everyone on an equal footing.

C.P. Morgan Company: what business are we in?

C.P. Morgan was the second largest builder/developer in Indianapolis, and the third largest home builder in Indiana. The president of the firm, Chuck Morgan, was very open to new thinking, and eager for new ideas on how to approach the market. When I was first contacted by a member of the Morgan Board, they were hoping I could give them some ideas on marketing and communications.

The challenge

Their advertising and company literature had no coherence and nothing hung together because of a deeper confusion. Finally, the management committee realized they had no agreement among themselves as to what they were doing as a company. They were having trouble asking that fundamental question, which Peter Drucker asks so often: What business are you really in?

The process

I suggested they try the *PathFinder* process to get some clarity about their business. Their management group came to Chicago for two days. The only warning I gave them was to rest their right brains!

As they were writing in the Corporate Bearings section, describing the present condition of the business, they described themselves as "home builders." I watched Chuck as he, like Bill Trotter, wrote in outline, bullet-point fashion. When we got to the Maps and Images section, they drew pictures of their company. Chuck Morgan created beautiful drawings of homes, friendly neighbors, and rich and vibrant communities. The meeting came alive as the managers responded to the warmth and enthusiasm of Chuck's vision of what the company was doing.

The result

By the end of the two-day workshop, they came to realize that they were not in the business of building houses as much as they were about creating communities. This insight changed everything: their communications, advertising and sales materials, signage and logo, displays, and even their corporate motto. Before, their motto had been "Perfecting the Building Experience." Now it became "Creating Better Environments for Living."

C.P. Morgan Company made a major shift in its thinking, from a focus on the product (homes) to a focus on the benefit (communities). Later, it widened this focus even more to include an ecological concern—saving trees, working with land contours, and incorporating environmental awareness in their building techniques. It changed its presentation from picturing individual homes to showing them in a neighborhood setting, lining a street with children playing and neighbors visiting in front of the houses. With such a compelling vision, and greater clarity about what business it was in, C.P. Morgan Company was able to create an effective advertising strategy that gave it higher recognition in their market.

Cotrugli Business Academy: the art of strategic leading

With the fall of Yugoslavia in 1991, the Balkans again reignited centuries-old battles. It took four more years of fierce fighting to secure their boarders (with the help of American military advisers). Almost immediately, the business community established the Croatia Business Association (CROMA). The long-time dream of its leader Esad Colakovic was for business to be the source of innovation and help provide stability to the war-torn country. And at the heart of this dream was the establishment of a business academy to train present and future business leaders.

The challenge

The members of the CROMA Board asked the World Business Academy, of which I am a Founding Fellow, to help them develop a new business school curriculum that would address the social as well as the business responsibilities of organizations. Specifically, we were to build on the work of the cofounder of the Academy, Willis Harman, to re-vision the purpose of business with special emphasis on values and intuition.

A one-week pilot program was developed for perspective students, investors, and board members to get an experience of the new curriculum. *PathFinder* Pragmatic Inquiry was chosen for a two-day presentation and actual experience.

The process

After the first three days in Zagreb, the capitol of Croatia, the group moved to Porec, a beautiful seaside city on the Adriatic. There we assembled for our inquiry. Although language was a bit of a problem and some simultaneous translation was required, I worked with the group through all the steps of the inquiry. It was fascinating to see because some of the issues were very broad, concerning the future of Croatia as a country, and others were very narrow, such as questions about career direction.

The results

The readings were very favorable and we were asked to incorporate *PathFinder Pragmatic Inquiry* into the curriculum of the CROMA Business Academy, subsequently named Cotrugli Business School, after one of Croatia's legendary intellectuals, Benedetto Cotrugli, often cited as being the first to develop double entry bookkeeping, among many other accomplishments.

I'll mention one specific case. Boris Cavrak, then CEO of one of the largest INA refineries in Croatia, was having trouble with the challenge of improving the quality of its crude oil. Since it had gone from State owned to publicly owned and now were in a competitive market, it had to dramatically increase its product mix and its quality. This was no trivial case because the oil industry represents over 10% of the gross domestic product of Croatia.

As you can see from his sketch in Figure 8.1, Boris approached the question rationally. Boris, with a master's in Chemical Engineering from Syracuse University,

Figure 8.1 **Rational: left brain image**

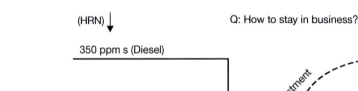

might be expected to lay out his challenge as a good engineer would. I pressed him to see if he could get some insight as to what was the real issue. Was it really just a matter of getting more investment? Boris thought for a moment and departed. The next day he asked me if I had ever read Franz Kafka's *The Castle*. I had not. He said on reflection he had realized that it was not only a simple question of increasing investment but also of determining how decisions were made within the INA organization. He concluded that it was a very difficult question and that the organization really represented Kafka's Castle, where, when you entered, you were unsure what was real and what was not (see Figure 8.2). Based on his point of view and expertise he was later promoted to be the third in command of the entire INA organization.

Figure 8.2 **Rational and emotional: whole brain image**

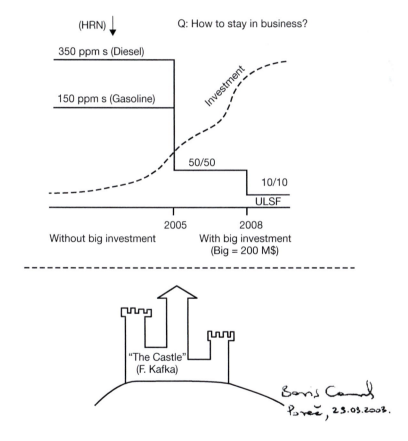

Unity Church: conflict resolution and personal transformation

With its appeal to disaffected churchgoers of many denominations, especially the younger generation, Unity Church has become one of the largest and fastest-growing congregations in Chicago. Part of its appeal lies in its innovative approach to spiritual and religious issues.

The challenge

At the time they contacted me, they belied their name: the Board and pastor were anything but unified. There was dissension among Board members, and confusion over the roles of the Board and pastor in administrative and management issues. Beneath these obvious problems there was a lack of clarity about the purpose and vision of the organization.

The process

We went through the *PathFinder* process during a weekend retreat. I will always remember this workshop for the dramatic breakthrough that arose from the Conversations exercises. The chairman of the Board had been pushing to run the church according to more businesslike principles and techniques. The pastor was resisting this. Things came to a head over the issue of the budget. I had a hunch they could get fresh perspectives on this issue by listening to different voices. So I asked everyone to have a Conversation with an important figure from whom they thought they could learn something.

The Chairman, Larry Clark, had recently read a book called *Joshua*, whose title character was modeled after Jesus, and he chose to have a Conversation with Joshua. He started by asking,

"Joshua, as you look at what's going on at Unity—the apparent struggle between the Board and the Minister—what do you think it all means?"

Joshua "answered," "Do not be fooled by appearances or quick answers. Search for what is real, for what is within your higher self. The main thing is for the congregation to be served; the money will come."

Larry pressed further. "That's comforting, but how do we know that the money will come?"

He felt Joshua answer, "You don't. You just trust that it will."

At that moment, seeing he was agitated, I wandered over and looked over his shoulder and saw Larry scribbling quickly and in large, bold script across the top of the page, "This is baloney (*sic*)! This is just me attempting to write a dialogue." But then he turned to writing again. Soon he sat bolt upright for a moment, as if he had been struck by lightning. He paused momentarily and then began to write furiously.

"You don't," (repeating what he had just written but this time with intensity), "you just trust that it will. Do what you need to do. Put out the hook and then wait."

Larry asked, with growing concern, "But what about planning for expenditures and income? What about a budget?"

Joshua answered, "Oh, that works, too. But it just depends on how you look at it and what you want to accomplish."

At this point, Larry looked exhausted, but then he came back to life, realizing that he had achieved a real breakthrough by listening to another side of himself. The rigid professional had been cracked open, and the work of faith had been made clear to him, in his own words.

The result

Internal Conversations like this helped Unity to surface their problems and understand the source of their conflict. In their discussions, they were able to be much more open with each other, and that gave them a clearer sense of their various roles and responsibilities. The long-standing tensions between the pastor and Board were healed, as the Board took on a role as the pastor's Advisory Council.

This case showed me the value of having the *PathFinder* process run over at least two days, allowing the participants to sleep on it, which is a reason why we like to schedule the *PathFinder* workshops to include an overnight stay. It is not unusual, I have discovered, for someone to return to the group on the second day having had a telling or insightful dream.

So it was here, on our second day, when I asked people to take a few minutes and write in the Maps and Images section any dreams or wake-up thoughts they had had. One woman spoke up rather tentatively because her dream did not seem like much. She had dreamed that a teenager had asked for the keys to her car, and she had had to lay down rules and regulations before she would hand them over.

We all sat still for a moment as the dream's message sank in and then we all burst out laughing at how succinctly it summed up the previous day's discussions about giving the pastor the power he wanted, within rules established by the Board. By drawing on the intuitive, the *PathFinder* process seems to unleash the problem-solving resources stored in our unconscious minds.

Quaker Oats Company: determining core competences

An American household name, Quaker has facilities in 16 states and three continents. Half of its 21,100 employees are in the United States. Besides producing cereals, snacks, sports drinks, and pet foods, Quaker owns the Pritikin Longevity Center and food service businesses. Like many major corporations, Quaker had seen the need to build on diversity of opinions through teams, but when they tried to reach consensus on what their major corporate strengths or so-called core competences were,[136] it seemed their differences brought only problems.

The challenge

By the time I arrived on the scene, an ad hoc executive group had made several unsuccessful attempts to define the corporation's core competences. They received all sorts of responses, but were unable to bring their diverse points of view together to define a future direction for the firm. They kept coming up with what seemed like contradictory, mutually exclusive ideas or things that did not fit together. Finally, they had reached the point where their diversity, with all its differences and divergences, seemed more like a liability than an asset.

The process

In the two-day workshop, we worked through a long list of questions beginning with Corporate Bearings, determining to get at the deeper issue of bringing divergent viewpoints together to the benefit of the company: What's going on? Why define core competences? Why are we having so much difficulty doing this? Where are we now? What were our core competences in the past? What skills have contributed to our success? What lack of skills has caused our failures? Are our present core competences still relevant in today's marketplace? What core competences will drive our future?

The result

Once again, Internal Conversations and the Maps and Images exercises proved very useful, as well as the section entitled Habits. The participants started to see, as they examined the Corporate Trail of Quaker, how certain behaviors repeatedly seemed to guide decisions, helpfully in some cases and harmfully in others. Using both writing and imaging, focusing on the present as well as the past, the verbal types had a chance to listen while the quiet voices were heard. As we worked through the questions, people began to feed off each other's insights and images. An excitement was generated that carried on beyond the meeting. The group came to agree on a set of core competences, but, more important, they came to appreciate their different points of view, and saw how diverse opinions can actually build on each other and be a source of strength, when handled in a supportive environment like the *PathFinder* process.

Shimer College: developing a vision

A small college in Waukegan, Illinois, Shimer College has a curriculum centered on the Great Books, one of only two such colleges in the United States. When they called me, they were having problems updating their vision and statement of purpose. There was dissension among the staff about what their collegial vision should be, with different groups of faculty having different ideas.

The challenge

Shimer didn't lack for ideas. In fact, that seemed to be part of the problem: they had too many ideas, too many visions. Initially they saw this as their problem. But their real problem, I knew, was to find the truth in their diversity of visions.

The process

We applied the *PathFinder* process, and they were quick to pick out appropriate people to have Conversations with, and wrote long and moving Internal Conversations. In the case of Shimer, not surprisingly, it sounded like an assembly of the Great Books authors. At the end of our 24-hour period, we had not one but three vision statements. At first we tried either to bring them all into one statement, or to eliminate two of the three visions in favor of just one. However, as we looked at the three vision statements written in felt-tip pen on large sheets, the group came to a different place—a place where they could see the value of a relation between all three, and how each one was well suited for a specific purpose. As with Quaker, using the *PathFinder* process brought an organization to a deeper appreciation of difference and diversity, via the Internal Conversations exercise.

The result

Shimer was the first academic setting in which I had used the *PathFinder* process, and I became convinced that there is a significant difference between, on the one hand, academics and spiritually oriented people like those at Common Ground, and businesspeople on the other: academics and spiritual practitioners are more readily articulate and comfortable with Internal Conversations in situations like seminars and prayer. But the process is the same, whatever the experience level of the individual.

Grosvenor Publications: improving the product

The challenge

Headquartered in London, Grosvenor Publications published books and magazines, including *For a Change*, a magazine that they wanted to improve. For them, the *PathFinder* process was to be a way to get new ideas on how to revamp their magazine. What actually transpired turned out to be much more.

The process

As we worked through the various parts of the process, the staff got their ideas, but they also discovered an overlooked resource in their midst: for years, at their usual meetings, the articulate verbal types had dominated, shutting out the rest of the group, one of whom had been quietly observing the scene all the while. In the *PathFinder* process setting, where everyone gets heard, this man "appeared." As we went around the table, each person read from his or her notebook entries, and we all were struck by the cogent analysis this quiet fellow had to offer.

The result

From this experience, I learned the value of using the *PathFinder* process as an equalizer for the group. I am convinced that many companies are like Grosvenor Publications: they have insightful, valuable employees in their midst, whose voices too often are not heard. We need to hear these voices for our quality and teamwork programs to succeed. We need to realize that more voices do not necessarily add to confusion but can give different perspectives on the truth we seek. Which is why I came to use the *PathFinder* process in my own company as will be seen later.

Stanford University Graduate School of Business: creativity in the classroom

The challenge

Michael Ray, John G. McCoy–BancOne Professor of Creativity and Innovation and professor of Marketing at the Stanford Business School, has long been a noted authority on using innovative classroom methods to help students explore issues of creativity and inner purpose. He had been asked to teach a course in advertising and wanted to use techniques such as journal writing as a way for students to help visionary companies communicate their uniqueness.

The advertising course was called Advertising and Communication Management, subtitled Marketing Communication for Emerging Values Oriented Companies. Michael wanted the students to explore how to best move from advertising communications that "contribute to environmental and social degradation" to something with integrity that awakens the human spirit, fosters regeneration and also contributes to profit in a way that keeps this new type of business alive. He chose the CORPORANTES *PathFinder* Notebook pragmatic method of inquiry to gather and articulate the intuitive insights and facts seen in a different light.

He saw it as the middle way between free-flow journal keeping and the tightly constrained, traditional, strategic, and creative planning models, which would be used later to organize the material that surfaced during the *PathFinder* work.

The process

I arrived before a divided classroom in the third week of the course. About half the students had studied with Michael before and were eagerly looking forward to using innovative methods to enhance the creativity necessary to create an advertising campaign for their chosen client. The other half were highly skeptical of using soft methodology such as journal writing and values analysis. During the three-hour class, I took the students through all the sections—at one point having them "become the company" through the Corporate Bearings and Corporate Trail, then "become the customer" and have a conversation between the customer and the company, using the appropriate *PathFinder* sections. They then drew pictures in Maps and Images of various aspects of the marketing relationship. The intention, of course, was to get the students inside both the customer and the company to see how a relationship might be structured and communicated. After the class, the students separated into their "agencies" to work on their clients, by all sharing their work to find insights, commonality, and differences.

I then came back to Palo Alto six weeks later toward the end of the course to see how they had further developed the ideas that surfaced during the initial exposure to the CORPORANTES *PathFinder* Notebook.

The results

At the end of the last class, one student who had been particularly skeptical finally said, "I thought this journal writing was going to be gimmicky, but it wasn't. I got four 'ahas' out of it." I asked her if that was good, and she said, "I would have been thrilled with one." The other students at the end of the course found it a worthwhile way to take different perspectives and tell the story of the corporate vision in terms of the needs of the customer for the product.

As Michael concluded, after the student "agencies" presented their campaigns developed for their "clients", he wrote this evaluation:

> The challenge of this course was to open students who needed to learn the business of advertising to a whole new context for and concept of advertising and what it could be. We did this by asking students to work with client companies that are well known as being socially responsible. Most of these companies do little or no advertising.
>
> The *PathFinder* allowed all these objectives to be met. The students, opening to different perspectives through their work with the CORPO-RANTES *PathFinder* Notebook, which allowed them to make significant breakthroughs, then applied their new knowledge of advertising and communication practice in surprisingly innovative ways.

Of course, I found this very satisfying because it was the direct application of the CORPORANTES *PathFinder* Notebook in the creation of our product—advertising.

3M: how to market an innovative product

3M is known throughout the world as an innovative company. Certainly if the purpose of this book is to answer the question, how do you run an organization that needs to be innovative? 3M would be an ideal candidate for *PathFinder* Pragmatic Inquiry.

The challenge

Challenged with creating an external business model for proprietary, reusable, packaging, the 3M Corporate Enterprise Development Division assembled an eight-member team of experts to formulate a solution. *PathFinder* Pragmatic Inquiry was used to help team members develop a cohesive vision that could yield practical, actionable results. The process yielded an eco-efficient service application that went beyond the product itself, and was implemented among component suppliers to Dell computers.

The complete story is best told in the words of the leader of the effort, Rick Salomone, Business Director for Corporate Enterprise Development, an organization within 3M established to facilitate the growth of new business by capitalizing on 3M proprietary processes for know-how and developing products outside the divisions that first created them.

While *PathFinder* Pragmatic Inquiry was originally designed to aid in strategic planning to ask the right questions, use the best thinking of each person on the team, and gain alignment around the best answer and action plan, it can also be used by individuals to do "strategic planning" in terms of their own career.

Here are his verbatim remarks, which show in detail how the five steps of the *PathFinder* Pragmatic Inquiry are followed. Then in a sequel, Rick tells how he used the *PathFinder* for his own personal inquiry.

"In the reusable packaging program that I headed, we took an existing solution (being used in the Scotch videotape business) to replace a corrugated box—a huge market—with a reusable, recyclable, refillable container. We looked at this container with six patents and asked, if it worked internally for 3M, could it work for businesses outside 3M? We had first asked Nahser and his associates at their advertising agency to develop a marketing campaign for our new business in reusable packaging. They asked us many questions that brought our diverse opinions to light and suggested that we go through a *PathFinder* Inquiry to gain alignment on our vision of the product offering and how best to market it."[137]

The process

Begin

"When the *PathFinder* Inquiry began, we thought that we were in the reusable packaging business. We assembled a team of eight people from various disciplines—logistics, marketing, environmental, supply chain, and finance—and found that we had eight different visions of the essence of our product or service offering. Our *PathFinder* Inquiry included the eight members of our reusable packaging team plus my boss at the time, Executive Vice President Harry Andrews who was involved in the entire process.

"Our preliminary pre-work assignment was to think about what question, when answered, would result in alignment of the group and enable us to present a unified voice to the market place as to what was unique and relevant and different about our business model.

"We were able to reach alignment because the *PathFinder* process allowed everyone to express themselves, to get all the different opinions and ideas out in a constructive way and not discount anybody's input. This was an extremely valuable part of the process."

Explore

"The high point of the *PathFinder* Inquiry was when we got all the data out on the table—seeing all the preliminary findings from different perspectives—which, in the case of our packaging team, were relevant data because we were all out in our different disciplines meeting with packaging people, environmental people, marketing people, supply-chain people, and a variety of customers on a target list that seemed to make the most sense when we started this business.

"Our findings took us in 15 different directions, and we felt overwhelmed at first. But as we moved through the process and understood what the market was telling us, the concept of sustainable development and eco-efficiency dominated. We realized that an environmental program alone would not succeed, in the United States at least, strictly on environmental merits but must contribute significantly to the bottom line. We had to make a financial argument as well as an environmental argument if we wanted major companies to get on board. That was the whole idea of eco-efficiency, not just creating a healthier environment for your company and for the world but delivering tangible financial results and improving profitability— a whole packaging solution of which the box is a part."

Interpret

"We started to see our final answer when we got into Internal Conversations where we created imaginary dialogs with senior executives in the company. One of them asked: 'Did you sell any boxes yet?' That caused us to question whether selling boxes was what we were trying to do. Were we trying to sell reusable boxes, competing against corrugated box companies? Were we a packaging company, a box company, a logistics company, an environmental company, a solutions company, a financial organization? We began to see that we provided a service that happened to include a box. The utility that our customers gained was not in the physical makeup of the box (e.g., that it has six patents and folds flat) but that it eliminates waste, thereby reducing costs; improves workflow in the plant; and removes hazards for people working with box cutters and similar tools."

Results

Decide-hypothesize

"*PathFinder* helped us define not only the essence of our product offering and service but also helped identify the real customer. We completely changed our thinking. In our work with Dell computers we had thought in terms of shipping PCs in reusable containers from Dell's Texas plant to end users. But at that point in the Inquiry, we realized that we had to capture the cost savings at the source. Dell assembles PCs but makes none of the components: 80% of their supplies come from seven component companies. If we could get Dell to require those major vendors to ship their components to Dell in reusable containers and if we could design a work flow and supply chain back and forth between the suppliers and Dell Computer, Dell could save a considerable amount of money and increase warehouse space occupied by cardboard boxes that first required assembly and then had to be broken down and hauled away for recycling. We changed our customer—from Dell to the component supplier."

Act

"We needed Dell's blessing to have the strength to go to the component suppliers. In the end it became more than a blessing; it became a Dell component specification. It was a unique moment for us when eight people and an EVP agreed on the essence of our product and service offering and who our customer was.

"The last question we worked on was how best to market our product? After the *PathFinder* Inquiry, Globe created the best, most relevant tag line and signature for the business (defined as eco-efficient packaging system)."

"What the Future Holds. What Holds the Future?"

"Those two lines defined the future—sustainable development, more regulation, and eco-efficiency. Clearly what holds the future is for corporations to continue to build profitable, sustainable growth.

"The final question in the *PathFinder* Inquiry was: How do we break through? We came up with the "Just prove it" concept and we had to have a financial model to prove the eco-efficiency of our product. We could not just sell the environmental response to sustainable development but had to prove to companies that our product could contribute to bottom line results.

"To our surprise, we ended up using one of our drawings from the Maps and Images exercise in our presentation to the 3M Board. While crudely drawn, it showed the essence of our thinking—both the question and the revised answer."

Sequel: personal use of the *PathFinder*

"One year later, I was entering my 20th year with 3M and struggling because my business values, how I conducted myself, how I took care of the customers that I served, and the personal values that I brought to the table, were not in alignment with those of my direct VPs and Executive VPs. This lack of alignment became a source of tension. I realized that the *PathFinder* that was so successful in a business setting could also be used to resolve my personal issue.

"I identified the question that I had to answer: What am I willing to sacrifice in terms of stability to take a chance and find an organization that meets more closely my needs as a businessperson and as an individual? I then used the same process of *PathFinder* Inquiry we had used for our strategic question—challenge assumptions, explore the evidence of my experience, interpret the evidence, decide, and take action. The Inquiry helped me clearly determine what my values are, how they had guided my career so far, and, based on my values and what I have learned, make decisions and take action on the next steps in my career."

Levi Strauss & Co.: values supporting our brands

The venerable 150-year-old company, Levi Strauss & Co (LS&Co.), originator of the iconic blue jean that is the most successful clothing product ever developed, ran into trouble in the late 1990s as sales fell from over $7 Billion in 1996, to slightly over $4 Billion in 1999.

The challenge

The cause according to many critics was that Levi Strauss focused more on employee-oriented values and being "socially responsible" than on serving their retail customers and consumers. These critics claimed that the reason why this happened was because of the leadership of Haas family members who, since the founding by Levi Strauss, had always taken the lead in socially responsible issues and practices. In an article in *Fortune* magazine, the writer went so far as to call Levi Strauss a "failed utopian management experience."[138]

A new CEO, Phil Marineau, the first non-family member to hold that position, was brought in to turn the company around in 1999. When asked about the over-emphasis on values and Levi's being "a failed utopian management experience," Phil replied often and loudly: "baloney." He went on to say that the values of LS&Co. are what support the Levi's and Dockers brands that are at the heart of the relationship the company has with its consumers.

Therefore, after a period of gaining control and stabilizing the company, he embarked on a "Values and Vision Supporting Our Brands" inquiry with the top senior executives of the company—members of the Worldwide Leadership Team (WLT). The inquiry was to help define and reaffirm the LS&Co. values driving the behavior, decisions, and actions of the company; then, based on those values, determine the core purpose and, based on that, the goals of the organization. (As mentioned in the Preface to the Second Edition, we owe a huge debt to the work of Jim Collins and his associates over many years to develop and test this typology of sustainable corporate structures.)[139] Since LS&Co. is 150 years old with a storied history of social responsibility and marketing success, the task was not to invent them anew, but to understand the values, core purpose, and goals and focus them on defining and driving business strategies.

As we were beginning to plan the work, I met the Project Leader, the vice president of Human Resources, for breakfast one morning. Immediately after we sat down and we confirmed the project was about values, his eyes narrowed and asked: "What is a value?" Whew! Knowing this was not a time for a lengthy lecture on moral philosophy and virtue ethics, I paused a moment waiting for clarity when several thoughts came to me and slowly formed into these words: "A value is any belief, principle or virtue held so deeply that it guides our behaviors, decisions and actions." He nodded, ordered, and we were on our way. (Later, at the suggestion of Michael Stebbins, of whom more later, I added "consciously or unconsciously.") This definition has formed the foundation of our *PathFinder* Pragmatic Inquiry work ever since.

We were ready then to ask the WLT members the following questions:

- Why are the "LS&Co. values supporting our brands" important?

- What "LS&Co. values supporting our brands" are most important today and in the future in supporting our business strategies?

- How do we put them into practice?

- What are our core purpose and goals based on these values?

- What decisions, strategies and actions by LS&Co. employees in general, and the WLT in particular, will be evidence of this?

The process

All members of the WLT were asked to reflect on their own values in business and how they had been formed and tested. The WLT then looked at the values of LS&Co. from the perspective of the marketplace—the values behind the iconic Levi's and Dockers brands. They then inquired into what society expected and what the company wanted to contribute to society. Lastly, they inquired into what employees expected today and how the values have been lived, formed, and tested by reflecting on the LS&Co. history of operations and decisions over the decades. Each step was crucial because there had to be understanding and alignment of all the perspectives in order for the WLT to lead the organization in having the values drive business performance.

The results

During first of three two-day retreats, the members of the WLT described their values and how they were formed and tested through their careers and why they were important. We saw much convergence as they all talked and presented what they held to be important.

Over the course of the next several months, the WLT inquired into what values were needed and expected by the organization, the market, and society. They looked at these expectations from the perspective of the broadest range of stakeholders and considered the long, rich history of LS&Co.'s involvement with these constituencies.

We then interpreted the evidence of the inquiry and saw that four values emerged: empathy, originality, integrity, and courage.

Based on these values, the core purpose of the organization became clear: "People love our clothes and trust our company. We will market the most appealing and widely worn casual clothing in the world." And from this emerged an aspirational goal that is unique to LS&Co.: "We will clothe the world!"

These statements were presented as the "LS&Co. Way," where the values, core purpose, and goals emerged from the story; the history of the company. LS&Co. now had a statement to guide its behavior, decisions, and actions.

The largest challenge facing LS&Co. at this time, and the cause of much of the sales decline, was the well-documented massive shift in consumer purchase patterns of clothing from department stores and chains to the so-called value channel such as Wal-Mart and Target. Prior to the *PathFinder* inquiry, the organization was divided on the merits of going to the value channel, risking a negative response from present distribution and the potential damage to the brand in the eyes of design- and style-conscious consumers. However, the decision to go to the value channel, when based on the values and vision, was enthusiastically embraced by all employees and was understood by the distribution customers and consumers as a way to reach the broad mass market that is the historic strength of who LS&Co. was and is as a company.

The development of the LS&Co. collaborative leadership principles and model

After the "LS&Co. Way"—its statement of values, core purpose and goals—was written, the WLT wanted to be sure the statement would drive business strategies and behaviors, decisions, and actions and not be empty words on a wall somewhere.

Since Pragmatic Inquiry had been used as the method to guide the original work, the members of the WLT wanted to explore whether it could also provide a guide for decision-making for the entire organization—a collaborative leadership model based on the five steps of *PathFinder* Pragmatic Inquiry:

- Begin
- Explore
- Interpret
- Hypothesize
- Act

A member of the CORPORANTES team, Michael Stebbins, director of the Gonzaga University Ethics Center and a Bernard Lonergan scholar, explained the Pragmatic Inquiry methodology in Lonergan terms:[140]

- Be attentive
- Be intelligent
- Be reasonable
- Be responsible
- Be in love

Since Phil Marineau was Jesuit trained, when he heard these five steps, he immediately sensed that Lonergan's language explained the decision-making process in very clear terms. So, the two methods of inquiry—Pragmatic Inquiry and Method in Theology—were combined:

- Be attentive
- Explore intelligently
- Interpret openly
- Decide responsibly
- Act with firm resolve

(We have seldom mentioned, however, that the end result of an inquiry is to "Be in love." A more popular term is "to be committed" or "passionate.")

Now, reread the LS&Co. values and notice that they are written in a particular order, following the Collaborative Leadership Model.

- Empathy: listen, be attentive to the other
- Originality: be creative, insightful, innovate
- Integrity: be responsible, true to yourself and to your values
- Courage: be resolved in action

The principles, and the behaviors that support them, were put into action through the Collaborative Leadership Model, built on the scientific method of constantly testing decisions and beliefs, treating them as hypotheses. Phil called this process of continuous, life-long learning "De-construct/Re-construct."

As we completed the inquiry, Bob Haas, then Chairman and great-great-grandnephew of Levi Strauss himself, reminded me LS&Co. had done a lot of work on corporate values over many years which focused on the way they ran their operations and how this impacted their employees and stakeholders, with many dramatic advances in corporate responsibility over the decades. But he noted that, by reflecting on key events in their over-150-year history, the unique value of this pragmatic inquiry was to uncover and recognize their values driving historic product innovation and marketing events, thereby validating those values to drive their strategies and support their brands in the future. A perfect example of "learning from the evidence of our experience."

Because of the success of the Inquiry, LS&Co. adopted the *PathFinder* Pragmatic Inquiry method as their Collaborative Leadership Model, renaming the five steps: Be Attentive, Explore Intelligently, Interpret Openly, Decide Responsibly and Act with Firm Resolve.

University of Notre Dame Executive Integral Leadership: What does it take to create exceptional, sustainable value?

The challenge

The University of Notre Dame, one of the leading Catholic universities in the world, has long had a tradition of teaching values, ethics, and social responsibility to its students. The challenge, of course, was for its business school to continue that tradition and apply it to the world of commerce. The latest in a long line of distinguished leaders and professors was Leo Burke, Associate Dean of Executive Education.

One of the reasons why Leo had accepted the post was to put into practice his many years of experience and learning as head of Executive Education at Motorola University working with senior executives, where he had developed a strong perspective on the need to develop executives, not just intellectually but emotionally, spiritually, and physically as well. He developed a program, bringing together all this learning, which he called Executive Integral Leadership. Based on the work of Ken Wilber, a renowned philosopher and psychologist, who developed what he called Integral Theory, Leo developed a week-long program that helped executives work on their "interior" as well as their "exterior" development, both individually and as a part of a group.

The process

An essential part of the program was to have the students experience this integral perspective by working on a leadership challenge issue that they faced. The *Path-Finder* Pragmatic Inquiry was used as a thread running through the course with the students reflecting on their question, making notes, and going through the various exercises. As an example: for Maps and Images the students visited the Smythe Museum at the University and were exposed to art and its importance in the expression of ideas and feelings. The students then worked on the Maps and Images section.

The results

The work is the result. Over 1,000 executives have gone through the Integral Leadership Program either as a stand-alone certificate course, or as part of an Executive MBA.

The ratings for the program have been exceptional and students find that the *PathFinder* within the context of Integral Leadership gives them the ability to rethink their question and come up with better solutions. Typical responses after engaging in the program are:

> "The *PathFinder* allowed me an in-depth look into the issue, the meaning of the problem and how to take the appropriate steps for the resolution of the problem."
>
> "The *PathFinder* was a great learning tool during residency week; however I am determined to utilize this resource going forward address-ing my work and personal problems when they arise."
>
> "It's been an excellent tool in helping me identify, dissect, and evalu-ate the components of a business issue that has been troubling me for the past few years. Although mine won't be an easy or fast fix, I'm certain the awareness the *PathFinder* journey has raised will be a positive first step in the long road to a permanent solution."
>
> "The *PathFinder* tool was extremely useful in guiding me through a process to examine past behaviors and biases that have not just prevented us from solving the problem, but have, in fact, fostered a negative envi-ronment in which the problem could grow."

Reflecting on his experience using the *PathFinder* in his program on Integral Leadership, Leo wryly commented: "It is quite a great journey. I am very impressed with the deceptive simplicity of the *Pathfinder* to really invite people—those blank pages have more utility to them than you first might think. It allows executives to explore ideas which they otherwise might not do."

Beta Gamma Sigma: What kind of leader *can* I be?

In 2001, when Carolyn Woo, then Dean of Notre Dame's Mendoza College of Business, was a member of the board of Beta Gamma Sigma (BGS) Honor Society—the business school equivalent of Phi Beta Kappa for schools of liberal arts and science—they were wrestling with the issue of how to provide more service to their honorees who are among the top business students in the country. They planned to start a Student Leadership Forum and invite accredited member colleges of the prestigious Association to Advance Collegiate Schools of Business International to send their top student to this Forum.

They talked about various ideas and Dean Woo suggested that they look at *Path-Finder* Pragmatic Inquiry, which they had just introduced successfully at Notre Dame in their Executive Integral Leadership program under her leadership with Leo Burke (see Notre Dame case above). When they asked her what that was, she replied simply: "*PathFinder* Pragmatic Inquiry is strategic planning for individuals as well as organizations." (By the way, this succinct definition linking pragmatism to strategy has set many skeptical business minds at ease, usually curtailing any need for deeper explanation of philosophy and moral reasoning.)

The process

The Student Leadership Forum introduces the students to many engaging and enlightening presentations and exercises (the Myers-Briggs profile is always a favorite) by leading executives and deans—mostly BGS graduates. Toward the end of the Forum, our CORPORANTES team, led by Alyssa Groom, conducts the *Path-Finder* Inquiry, often from noon to noon to give the students time to reflect overnight on their issues.

The results

To date, having worked with over 1,000 of America's brightest business students in over a dozen Student Leadership Forums, the results continue to affirm the earliest hopes of being able to awaken in students some clarity on the kinds of leaders they can be in different fields, driven by their values and vision. One always-successful exercise is the drawings (Maps and Images) of their hopes, concerns, and career path, which are always revealing. (See the website link for pictures and stories.[141]) Here are some of the typical comments that we have received over the years:

> "It is not often that I get time to reflect on my goals and where I see my life headed."
>
> "A complete and enlightening experience. I am leaving the conference a better leader."
>
> "This weekend was one of the most beneficial of my life. Doing Dr. Nahser's program really helped me focus in on where I am going in life."
>
> "I didn't expect that much, but this conference was life changing."
>
> "Conferences rarely provide the opportunity to allow creativity and intuitive thinking of participants. This was a truly rare outstanding exception."

Kellogg School of Management, Northwestern University: leadership and ethics

Kellogg School of Management is ranked regularly as one of the top business schools in the world, and is justly known for its response to student concerns and needs and its marketing perspective on strategy.

The challenge

In the fall of 2003, David Messick, Kaplan Professor of Ethics and Decision in Management at Kellogg, invited me to coteach "Leadership and Ethics" to 55 members of the Executive Management Program (EMP), Kellogg's senior executive MBA program. David's approach to the subject had proven highly successful over ten years. However, he had seen ample evidence over the years that the students in the EMP were contemplating issues and career changes—often dramatic changes—as the reason for undertaking the arduous program. Otherwise, why would they do it?

He had been looking for a methodology for the students to use to guide their decision-making and felt the *PathFinder* Pragmatic Inquiry might be helpful and proposed using it as a test.

In David's words to the students at the final "commencement class," he explained his reason behind his approach and for using the *PathFinder*:

> In this class we're talking about leadership and one of the things Warren Bennis talks about in his book *On Becoming a Leader'* is the need to be comfortable in your own skin and Ron's work helps a lot because it supports it ... We don't teach that well in a business school because it isn't part of the curriculum ... but it ought to.
>
> It takes courage to be a leader. And where that courage often comes from is that it takes courage and guts to be authentic. To know who you are and to be comfortable with whom you are and to be able to say to people, *"this is who I am and what I stand for"*[142]—and sometimes that takes real guts. But it is important to be part of a leadership course because it's really important.

The process

Leadership and Ethics was a five-week, ten-part course, one of a series of very successful courses David taught to EMP students. We presented the *PathFinder* in three of the ten classes: second, sixth and tenth.

The *PathFinder* work was titled Leadership Challenge Inquiry and began with "Begin" baseline pre-work (process described in Chapter 7 in "The CORPORANTES *PathFinder* Pragmatic Inquiry") to establish the baseline challenge and hypothesis to be tested during the course.

The results

The final paper, which was due two weeks after the conclusion of class, was optional, non-credit, and non-graded. Papers were submitted by 38 students outlining their results and experiences with the *PathFinder* in addressing their Leadership Challenge Inquiry. Several students remained in contact with Nahser and carried on working on their papers since they would be used in their work. A number of students asked not to turn in papers given the personal nature of their Inquiries. Others stated that they found the Inquiry to be too personally focused to be of value.

Here are some of the student comments:

"As part of the *PathFinder* Inquiry process, I learned a lot about who I am and the values that I hold closely. I have reflected on my boss's way of seeing the world and his associated strengths and shortcomings. I have deeply considered compromise and the risks and benefits, and finally I have come to envision a course of action that could just change health-care in America. Thanks for helping me see the opportunity."

"*PathFinder* allowed me to think about different aspects of the question and their relative importance. Especially, the risks associated with organizational and culture impact. My original answer would not change but the method of going about evaluating and processes for making the change will probably be altered."

"The *PathFinder* Inquiry allowed me to achieve the following learnings:

- Clarity of the intended question is key to understanding how to over-come it

- Going through the thought process outline in the Inquiry allows for inputs to flow into your thinking on an issue that may not otherwise come to mind

- Seeking input from different angles of thinking is imperative to suc-cessfully answering your question

- Using some of the framework with others you are involving allows the critical ideas to be received much more readily."

St. Mary's College: business as a calling/the calling of business

The challenge

Jack Ruhe, Professor of Management, St. Mary's College, Notre Dame, Indiana, one of the premier colleges in the country, had a long-standing interest in ethics leader-ship development. He was concerned about how to get students to reflect on the important ethical issues in their careers and even the direction a career should take. He wanted the students to look on their careers as a vocation or a calling. He used various teaching techniques to engage the students in reflection on their personal values but had been concerned that in their final papers what the students wrote in response to the assignment of ambitions, intentions, and goals were "sterile", rote answers to checklist questions with little passion indicated. He saw the *PathFinder* as a way to get deeper into the movement of their lives.

The process

Jack taught two courses: Personal Values and Corporate Culture; and Leadership Development. In Personal Values and Corporate Culture, he had the students consider their own career ambitions, but also the corporate culture of the various organizations they were thinking of joining. There was also a community service component where the students worked at a social service organization. During the course they were writing reflection papers from the various perspectives in the *PathFinder*.

The results

Jack was measuring over ten thousand students from various universities and colleges on the Maccoby Values Scale.[143] He found that with the *PathFinder* process increased statistically their sense of the importance of **compassion, independence,** and **courage** (critical of authority). Jack considered these three as essential for an ethical values-based career.

Time magazine: assigning a new sales strategy

The challenge

Time magazine is one of the world's great magazines, pioneering the newsweekly format. It has a strong editorial content and had been one of our most successful magazines in terms of advertising revenues. However, with the proliferation of news media, maintaining profit margins had been difficult. Jack Haire, the then new *Time* publisher, needed to address the issue and had some concerns.

The process

Jack explained to me over breakfast—as we watched the skaters at Rockefeller Center—that he had reviewed the kind of advertising clients *Time* was going after. They tended to be just interested in buying "tonnage"—advertising at the lowest price. Jack felt the sales force needed to focus on more creative, relationship-oriented clients, who would better fit with Time's editorial strengths.

He had a gut feel for what needed to be done but wasn't sure how to articulate it and prove the case for his 40 sales associates who were gathering for their annual sales meeting. In the course of the next 45 minutes, I explained to Jack the premise of the CORPORANTES *PathFinder* Notebook and explained how it might be exactly the way to help articulate his hypothesis and then test it against the evidence that he had seen.

Jack wrote instructional notes in half of the sections, paying particular attention to the Explore sections where he could gather his evidence to support or challenge the hypothesis that he had listed under Begin.

The results

Jack worked through the method of inquiry over the next several weeks, putting notes and ideas in the various sections that seemed appropriate. He was able to make clear what he had intuitively felt was the right answer. And most importantly, he was able to articulate his reasoning to his sales force.

The Nahser Agency: developing strategy and purpose through effective teamwork

My company is a mid-sized advertising agency based in Chicago, with a client base ranging from a $17 billion insurance company to a family-held toy manufacturer. We create advertising to help sell home equity loans, food, mufflers, shoes, and stereos. We will not advertise for certain products such as tobacco nor create messages that we feel do not "benefit the user and contribute to the well-being of society."

The Nahser Corporate Values state: "Our purpose is to create and implement outstanding ideas to help our clients' businesses grow, benefit the user, and contribute to the well-being of society." I thank Bill Smithburg, CEO of the Quaker Oats Company, for encouraging me to develop and publicly state these beliefs.

The challenge

Like most traditional ad agencies, our staff was organized by function: creative, account management, media, production, traffic, and administrative. In attempting to draw this picture, I realized that each of our clients, too, had its own "shape" and that to serve them we needed to match their structure and needs. I then saw that we could draw a picture of our relationship with each client, and then restructure the firm around client-based teams, in an effort to become more customer-focused. I also realized that each client had a basic task or tension or paradox in its business that defined much of its strategy. Our job was to understand that basic tension/paradox and create communications that would solve it.

I wanted to create viable, effective teams, based on a shared sense of mission and long-term strategic planning. To get us from where we were to where I hoped we would be, I would use the *PathFinder* process.

Predictably, this was my hardest sell, because there is a great truth in the adage that a prophet is without honor in his own company [sic]. My associates had heard me talk about this process from Progoff to Peirce and had seen me go off to classes, conferences, and day-long seminars for the past 12 years. Needless to say, they were skeptical that all this could really apply to advertising. Even though I often reminded them I was not studying the mysteries of Etruscan art, they still wanted to see how these studies would pay off in new business and making better ads. I did too.

After the success of Common Ground, I was sure that at least I had enough exercises, which formed the beginnings of the *PathFinder* process, to work with. The first Nahser management committee strategic planning meeting in 1990 was affectionately dubbed "Geneva I" after the beautiful lake north of Chicago where it was held. I had in the back of my mind, of course, the idea to conduct the meeting along the lines of what is now the *PathFinder* process. I went to each member of the Executive Committee and asked what they wanted to accomplish during the weekend meeting, and on the first morning the *PathFinder* process was constructed before my very eyes.

The process

The first person I talked to, Bob Cote, Media Director, said that as we were moving forward he wanted to be sure we answered the question: What are we to carry forward from our past and what do we jettison? This question was a perfect example of what is now asked in the Corporate Trail section of the *PathFinder*.

Next I talked to Bruce Marsh, Executive Vice President, who wondered what our founder, who had died in 1986, would think of all this analysis. (Our founder was famous for focusing on work, not analysis and endless meetings.) I suggested we should have a Conversation with the founder, and from the look in Bruce's eyes, I could tell he was not looking forward to a visitation from the other side of the veil. I assured him that we were going to write a Conversation with the founder in order to see what he might have to say to us about our upcoming Geneva Conference.

Tom Perlitz, Senior Vice President, said, "I've got a crazy idea. I've been in idea sessions where we actually become the product, and maybe we should think about the business that way." I suggested that we consider ourselves as the company, and perhaps have Conversations from that point of view. He thought that was an intriguing idea. And Don Burke, one of our more image-oriented members, unusual for a financial officer, suggested that it might be helpful if we even drew some pictures using symbols to describe what we were feeling.

Thus began the first of a series of annual meetings, the first held at Lake Geneva, then Chicago, and then back at the beautiful lake north of Chicago. Many of the staff came to these meetings dripping in skepticism, with (in the words of one senior manager) "BS antennae up high." When I asked them to have a Conversation with the agency, some came up with monologues, getting very little response from their inner voices. Others found the prospect of writing in a notebook unappealing. "Let's make the decisions we need to make first, then if we have time it might be good to do some reflective stuff." In short, I met all sorts of resistance, but I persisted.

The group stuck with it and in time they came to see the merits of the various parts of the *PathFinder* process. We all dug deeper in our thinking, and everyone came up with pieces of the truth that gave us better solutions on how to organize and run the teams, and to serve our clients better.

The results

Using the *PathFinder* process, Nahser developed a new corporate strategy: "Creating enduring relationships by going beyond expectations." In determining the important values and skills required of us, we came up with a set of resilient teams whose morale remained high even after restructuring brought some downsizing. We were able to determine the individual, complementary strengths of the members of the executive team, and figure out how to cut 15% of our overhead while maintaining the volume of our business. The process brought us an awareness of our blind spots and our strengths. It also helped us achieve and refine a statement of purpose that has served us well.

And at Geneva VII, we set out to develop a better method of inquiry to guide the development of our creative work; what we call a "creative brief." After a day and a half of writing in the *PathFinder*, we found ourselves returning over and over again to an idea that had surfaced early: tension. As we developed the concept we saw that tension inevitably found its way into our everyday process of working together. The issue was how to manage the right amount to foster better creative work; at one point we compared it to the necessary tension on a string to make music. But we further determined that our best work had developed out of solving a tension, dilemma, or seeming paradox that our clients faced. In one revealing image, we saw a river of information that needed to be dammed and put to creative use. We came up with a three-part, creative-strategy brief to capture the tension: (1) Investigate various aspects of the client's situation; (2) Determine what is the real problem—not the symptom—seen as the crux point of opportunity based on the tension, dilemma, or paradox the client faces; (3) Develop a clever communications plan to seize the opportunity by resolving the tension for the consumer. As our work on the creative strategy brief came to a conclusion, the wonderful symmetry slowly dawned on me—that we were using the *PathFinder* pragmatic method for corporate inquiry to create a pragmatic method of inquiry for our agency: explore, interpret, hypothesize, and act! A perfect reflection.

As we worked with the idea of tension it became clear to me that it was the basis for generating creativity because the tension or paradox creates doubt, which as we have seen begins an earnest pragmatic inquiry. Finding the point of tension, challenge, or problem in our client's situation begins our work in finding the answers and communicating the results to enlist the efforts of employees and customers alike.

As a result of over a decade of using the *PathFinder* in our own work, we recognized the paradox of change in our own industry and reconfigured our business to better reflect our findings. CORPORANTES, Inc. began offering the *PathFinder* Pragmatic Inquiry.

In our work as a strategy and communications firm, use of the *PathFinder* process gave us insights into the changing character of our clients' markets. Thanks to the wisdom we were able to access through the *PathFinder* exercises, we reconceptualized what it is we do as advertisers. In true Peircean fashion, we now see the business of marketing as a process of interpreting the signs of the facts and trends evident in the market, using all of our perspectives and experiences. And following Progoff, we consider how the products and services help people as they journey through life.

As a CEO, the *PathFinder* process helped me to reflect on both the personal growth of the people who work with me, and the corporate growth of my business. It has provided a way for me to see patterns in my personal and corporate life that were not visible before. It has helped me clarify my own vision for the business, and for the way we want to create advertising in serving our clients and society. As people have come and gone in our fast-paced business, it has helped me continue to develop and communicate this vision. It has helped us at the agency to become more open, and able to look at ourselves and each other in ways that we haven't done before, and most important we have all come to see the value in the statement: "We all have a piece of the truth." We have come to see that the *PathFinder* process can help us "uncover the truth we do not yet know, and the action we have yet to take."

Some general lessons

From my experience with the *PathFinder* process, in over a hundred applications in a variety of businesses and organizations, I have come to several general conclusions.

First, everyone has a piece of the truth: every employee can make a contribution toward seeing the big picture, but to do so, employees need a process that gives them a voice and a way to be heard.

Second, there is immeasurable value in quiet reflection, those times when we sit, notebook in lap, pen in hand, allowing the deep insights and wisdom of our inner voice to come through. By going more deeply into ourselves, we are paradoxically taken out of ourselves and connect with those around us in a more meaningful way.

We experience instinctively the movement between our beliefs and the facts that we confront outside ourselves, which corresponds to the movement between inductive and deductive thinking, so admirably developed by Peirce, which he called "abduction." (For a reminder of what abduction is, see Chapter 5). We are thus led to a greater appreciation for diversity and difference. Time and again, in my own company and in the many settings I have been called into, staff diversity has become a source of strength, not division, once the *PathFinder* process has been applied. People can feed off each other's insights and ideas in this supportive, nonjudgmental environment, and a dynamic synergy results: the whole group becomes much more than the sum of its parts.

Likewise, the organization comes to have a life of its own. There is intrinsic value in understanding the corporation's history, for this history informs both the present and the future. And the people who work for the business become much more effective when they recognize their place in the larger movement under way.[144]

Perhaps the most personally meaningful lesson I take away from my experiences with the *PathFinder* process is the value of listening as the basis for learning and building a viable organization.[145] I have come to realize that, if he or she is not an effective listener, a CEO can wreak havoc in a business. This is, in fact, what happened with John Hudiberg.

Back in Chapter 2 we left Hudiberg basking in the glow of winning the Deming Award for his firm, Florida Power & Light. No U.S. company had done this before, and it was possible because John Hudiberg experienced that unforgettable Sunday when his neighbors picketed his house. I mentioned in passing that he made one critical mistake, and it was this: Hudiberg failed to listen. While he had gone through an epiphany, and thereafter preached his gospel and imposed it on his subordinates, he never bothered to listen, or even to try to gauge the reactions others in the company were having to his total quality management edicts.

The result? His staff followed his orders, but the corporation began to unravel. In Hudiberg's frenzied drive to break apart, measure, and improve all the systems in the business, the company fragmented. People would understand what they needed to measure in their particular function (and he measured everything), but they lost sight of the larger picture of which they were a part. Hudiberg had become like the religious convert who enthusiastically begins shoveling the doctrine down everybody's throat. And so, shortly after he won the Deming Award, Hudiberg was asked by the Board of Directors to step down, and his successor had to dismantle the entire total quality management effort and put the company back together again.

This sequel to Hudiberg's story echoes the wisdom in the *PathFinder* process: that everyone has a piece of the truth, has to interpret the signs for him or herself, and deserves to be heard. Without these, no total quality management program will work, and no genuine teamwork is possible.

Reading the signs

- How does your organization bring people together to explore decisions?

- What habits, both good and bad, does your corporation have?

- What are your favorite examples of teamwork in sports, society, family, etc., and what are the underlying causes of their success?

- Have you worked with dreams and images as a way of finding clarity in a situation?

- What are your internal conversations? Are they monologues or dialogues? Who are they with?

- Did any of the case histories give insight into your situation?

- What is your "case history"?

Part V
Act: The path ahead

9
The creative community

We assume either that the individual must be left alone to create, as in the case of our entrepreneurs, or that the individuals must join the group and sacrifice their personal creativity. But when we get beyond the command-and-control, hierarchical business structure, we can get through and around the paradox of the individual within a group.

The truth we do not yet know

Over and over again, I have seen the difficulty we have in bringing together individual points of view and talent to create a better product. I have seen and heard all about the problems of groups, and how they pull down creativity to the lowest common denominator. Think of the derogatory ways in which group committee or bureaucracy efforts are often described. Reflecting on our general disdain for creative group effort, David Ogilvy, an advertising industry leader, said, "Search all the parks in your cities and you'll find no statues to committees."

As the previous chapters have attempted to show, we are coming to recognize that to learn about ourselves and pursue the "truth we do not yet know," we need to be in a group. What weakens dualistic thinking and individualism more than anything else is the honest feedback of a group, which is M. Scott Peck's argument for "developing community." We are beginning to realize that many of our efforts in group dynamics can be seen as ways to pull each of us from the deep belief that we can know ourselves just by looking within; and from the opinion that our image of reality can justifiably be whatever works for us. We are evolving a new sense of "pragmatism" at the same time that we are waking up to how much we need creative teamwork in our corporations to meet the challenges of global competition.

What are we really doing? And why?

Creative corporate communities can also help us get past the filters described in chapters 2 and 4. We can turn to the deepest beliefs we hold in our society to help us reclaim thinking about the creative community. The model can be based on some of the oldest religious traditions in our society. These too, like pragmatism, have been narrowed.

The issue seems to be not so much what we do or how we do it, but what we are really doing. And why we are doing it.

Luther McKinney, legal counsel at the Quaker Oats Company put it this way:

> One of these days, a time bomb is going to go off in this country. The time bomb is this and it is written into the corporate charters of every company: Why is the corporation permitted to exist? What is the corporation's purpose?

Part of that purpose must be to serve the society, and the other part must be the development of the employees, for that is the way toward creative community. The following incident made this clear to me.

Truth telling

What does it really mean to tell the truth? One day I paid a visit to Ken Goodpaster, who was then teaching a course on Ethics and Corporate Policy at Harvard Business School. I had experienced the case method at Northwestern and so was eager to see it in operation at Harvard, where it originated. The case that day, "Building Trust at Warner Gear," dealt with the union problems at Warner Gear's plant in Beloit, Wisconsin, where many years of bad faith had led to mistrust among the various labor and management groups. At this point in the history of the firm, the plant was going to have to make some changes in its manufacturing structure. The essential questions the case considered were: How should management present the facts to the union, if at all? What course of action should management take?

The students consistently argued against complete candor, predicting that the union would turn against management. The debate went on for 90 minutes as everyone looked for an angle: How to couch it? When to do it? What advantage would there be to the company in being honest? What advantage would there be to the union? What would management be giving away if they chose to disclose the whole story?

Finally, Ken Goodpaster admitted his surprise that not one of the students argued for openness as simply the right thing to do in itself. The students sat back in their chairs, and then took notes furiously, as if they had been presented with a novel idea. The class ended. Several students continued the discussion with Goodpaster after class, and I asked, "Why didn't any of you just come out and say you should tell the truth to the union?" One student replied, "Why would we do that? Why would it be in our interest to do that?" Another added, "It's not in our culture to do that." "What do you mean?" I asked. "Well," he said, "why do you do good, in our culture? You do good, not because it is good—the right thing to do—you do good to get to heaven."

That, for me, was a big aha! moment when I suddenly saw our instrumentalist ethics as alive and well. We never see things as right in and of themselves, but for some purpose.[146] Likewise in business: we look at something only in terms of its gain, of what it will do for us—the recurring theme of our utilitarianism.[147] In this ethical orientation, we see the foundation of relationships among people as one of exchange.

No wonder corporations, in downsizing, treat people like cogs in the machine of business. No wonder that insightful analysts such as Senge, Peters, Deming, Bellah, and Drucker call for business to develop foresight, giving a philosophy or vision of the corporation's purpose and values as the driving impulse that creates return to shareholders, meaningful work employees can believe in, fair paychecks, and worthwhile products for customers. Harvard Business School, obviously drawing from Whitehead's "Foresight" speech[148] has revised its MBA program vision: "We aspire to develop outstanding business leaders who contribute to the well-being of society." (Sounds like the Nahser values statement!) The old "social contract" that once led employees to feel some sense of loyalty to their employers has been abrogated, and something must be offered to counter the resulting evaporation of worker loyalty. No wonder the business literature now is full of lamentations that loyalty is dead in the workplace, where profits are placed before the welfare of the employees.[149] Where do we turn for our models?

An old model for today

Committed to finding ways to lead organizations in their efforts to change and communicate the results, I have been watching all these trends for years, trying to piece together some better way. Peirce's pragmatism is part of it. Josiah Royce's extension of Peirce into wider, more social, realms is another. But where, I asked myself, do we look for pragmatic working, successful models?

As I mentioned in Chapter 6, Royce took Peirce out of the science lab and into the religious community. Peirce's community of inquirers thus became the congregation of interpreters—the beloved community—joined together by their commitment to a shared idea, belief, and a common end. Through commitment they had sparked feelings of loyalty—and commitment is what draws people into community. The common end they all shared was something inspiring and uplifting—a vision or mission based on beliefs beyond mundane goals. Royce built his model around studying the early Pauline communities of prayer and faith that sprang up as the early Church communities were forming after Jesus' death and resurrection; a role which the monasteries were to fill later, as we shall see.

I knew Royce was on to something in taking Peirce beyond science, and I emulated him as I applied Peirce's ideas to business in the CORPORANTES *PathFinder* process. There is more to this task than just following a process, however, as I realized from my experience in Goodpaster's class. There is a deeper, wider, transcendent element to all this, which for want of a better word I'll call "religious."

While the origin of the word is, to say the least contested, it does come from the Latin *religio*. The problem is the root of *religio*. Cicero thought it came from *relegere*, to read again, in the sense that religion offered a body of laws that we read over and over for living. Lactantius and later Augustine preferred the meaning "bound to God" (*religati*), which appears in most of major dictionaries. Augustine also offered *re eligere*, "choose again," in that we recover what was lost.

The way I am using it here is the attempt, through Pragmatic Inquiry, to discern a connection/calling/binding of one's life together with whatever name we give to something larger than ourselves. In individual lives, as in business, certain truths integrate and bind together a corporate enterprise. In this time of moral confusion about the purpose of business, it is appropriate to consider what elements enable such integration with something larger than ourselves and how this integration might be achieved. Then it dawned on me that we do not have to reinvent the wheel. We have a model that corporations can use to foster the loyalty, ethical sensitivity, work ethic, and effective teamwork and personal development that are the trademarks of the religious life and of the successful organization.

This original model, from which our modern corporation evolved, was developed fourteen hundred years ago and is the oldest still-functioning organizational corporate schema in the Western world. Its basic document is also the oldest organizational development strategy statement still extant.[150] And it is not Japanese, although certain aspects of it resemble the Samurai warrior code! It is called the monastery

The corporation as a modern monastery

I refer to the Rule of St. Benedict,[151] which established the basic form of Western European cenobitic, or community-based, monasticism. St. Benedict closely associated work with prayer and study of scriptures. He wrote the Rule in the early 6th century to establish the association of work and prayer and community life. Monasticism as a model for late-20th-century business? Bear with me, as I interpret it and adapt it to our time and situation. I intend to show that monasticism is useful to business in more ways than just making money from whiskey-soaked date-nut bread, cheeses and recordings of Gregorian chant. Remember that the modern corporation can trace its roots back to the monasteries that sprang up after the fall of the Roman Empire.[152]

St. Benedict's name has come up before, in Chapter 4, where I referred to him as "one source for the notion that work might have a higher purpose."[153] Benedict closely associated work with prayer and study of scripture, and in his Rule—the "business plan" for his monastery at Monte Cassino—the day is planned around these three activities.

How is monasticism a model for today's corporation? Try Benedict's insights into the mind and heart of his monk-workers. No brother was allowed to loaf around, and no form of work was demeaned. No matter how menial it might seem, every activity was important. In fact, Benedict is often credited with making manual labor acceptable and honorable since previously it had always been seen as the lot of the lower or slave classes.

 The stress on work was just one feature of monastic life. Since monasticism is rather foreign to the experience of most people, I will describe some of its other features. The word "monastery" is derived from the words for "to be alone" and "a place" (Greek *monazein* and *terion*). Specifically, it refers to leaving society for a hermit's cell. On a deeper level, monastic life aims at achieving mystical oneness, which alone gives meaning. In their Western form, as developed by St. Benedict, monasteries were mostly communal because he had seen the dangers of the solitary pursuit of union with God. People came together in a shared endeavor, realizing they could do more with mutual aid than they could alone. The communal life was designed around a strict discipline of work and leading to the peak experience of contemplative alertness in order to read the signs of God's presence and purpose.[154]

This combination was, and in many ways is still, unique to give energy and purpose to organization life. Whitehead goes so far as to say that the Benedictines "saved for mankind the vanishing civilization of the ancient world by linking together knowledge, labor, and moral energy."[155] I mentioned constraints in monastic life. Monks lived under a set of limitations that arose out of a value system—a value system we have not lost. It was based on serving the highest good of both individual and society. In this value system, life was not to be spent in pursuit of material wealth, sensual pleasure, or selfish egotism, but in the quest for higher goods and a "binding" to God. Monks joining the monastery were required to take three vows, of poverty, chastity, and obedience, forswearing the three false gods of Mammon, flesh, and self.[156]

In the course of the Middle Ages, many of the best and the brightest chose to live in the monastic environment. Their efforts and relationships were organized. They had ranks such as abbot and prior, and various roles and responsibilities. They instituted rules and regulations that clarified to everyone just what was and was not appropriate behavior in a community based on the stance of humility. Each monastery had a relationship with the wider world beyond its walls. In fact, over time, many monasteries came to play a major economic role in their regions by producing wool, food, liqueurs, wines, and manufactured goods that the members sold to the laity. Monasteries also employed masons, carpenters, and artisans, and made use of many other trade occupations. No matter how menial it might seem, every activity was important. Benedict even addressed the question of the sale of monastery products and said: "The evil of avarice must have no part in establishing prices, which should therefore always be a *little lower* [my emphasis] than people outside the monastery are able to set, *so that in all things God may be glorified* [Benedict's emphasis]." Can you picture the reaction of weavers, cobblers, and merchants on a medieval Main Street hearing that a monastery was going up outside the town? The monastery had greeters at the door, hospitality at its heart, and quality products. Add his sharp eye to pricing, and St. Benedict was 1,500 years ahead of Sam Walton and Walmart. It seems the medieval monasteries had everything offered by the big category killer "big box" discounter of today, lacking only a big "Every day Low Prices" banner flying from the belfry.

With these values put into practice, at the height of their power in the early Middle Ages, the monasteries controlled the gross domestic product of Europe, which at that time, of course, was primarily agricultural. So powerful were they that even royalty wanted to become abbots for the wealth and power these positions held. Economic prosperity, however, was not the original point; monasteries had come into being for the wider purpose of service to God. So they all had a transcendent vision and mission that informed what they did. Finally, monastic life was run under a set of expected constraints that we might well consider making use of in our corporations, as we shall see.

Might the monastic vows apply to business today?

When I was first working on this idea of what monasticism can teach a corporation, I gave a copy of Benedict's Rule to the head of administration at our advertising agency to see what he would take from it. His first reaction was skeptical, but curious: "Are you trying to turn this place into a monastery?" I assured him I was not, but I told him that I did see some interesting parallels between monasteries and businesses, then and today. Businesspeople always get interested in monasteries when I tell them they had the major market share of GNP in the Middle Ages. When he had read the Rule, he came back to me with a look on his face that clearly expressed his reaction to the possibility that we might add poverty, chastity, and obedience to our statement of corporate values!

I am not proposing that we literally reinstitute the ancient Christian virtues. If we did, U.S. business or at least Nahser Advertising would quickly come to a standstill. But we can and should make its underlying spirit operative in the modern corporate context.

Poverty

For example, one can adopt for our business purposes a version of "poverty" in the sense of "moderation" and in keeping with the growing trend toward "voluntary simplicity." More and more people are coming to realize that Americans are overconsumers. We use far more than our fair share of the world's resources and produce a disproportionate amount of the pollution. Our environment, as well as our personal lives, would be much healthier if we cut back on our spending or "getting," as William Wordsworth called it. Would this be good for business? Certainly not, under the usual model in which "consumption leads to happiness."[157]

However, there are market indicators that show that U.S. consumers are becoming more conscious of the limits of materialism as we experience the stresses of international competition, the constraints of ecology, and the pursuit of quality relationships in our personal lives. For corporate personnel, this new sensibility finds expression in the movement now afoot to restrain the rise in executive pay scales, to restore a more just and equitable allocation of corporate monies among the staff. Keeping in mind the ideal of "poverty" might also help us to get beyond the "money society," the term used by Myron Magnet, a former member of the Board of Editors of *Fortune* magazine, to describe our contemporary reality in which money becomes the only way we have to measure our self-worth.[158]

Chastity

Similarly, chastity can be reappreciated for its reminder of our need for respect in our relationships. People are not machines, nor are our bodies mere pleasure devices. Like a monastery, a corporation is not a place for sexual harassment, sexual politics, or exploitative interactions of any kind. If we redefine chastity as "abstention from that which demeans, lessens or exploits the personhood of self or other," chastity is, in fact, a significant component of corporate ethics, yet rarely seen as such. Indeed, it refers us back to one of the cardinal virtues of Plato, temperance.

Obedience

The word "obedience" I reinterpret by going back to the Latin root, *ob* + *audire*, meaning to listen to, to relate toward or to be willing to give ear to another. Implied here is the humility to be willing to listen to another person. A stress on listening—which was what the vow of obedience meant—brings us back to a key element of the CORPORANTES *PathFinder* method: listening to each other. The corporate environment would be much healthier, for both its people and its profit margin, if there were more listening, more "obedience," in the sense of people being patient to give each other their ear.

Humility

One of the central sections in Benedict's Rule deals with humility. Interestingly enough, this theme involves 12 chapters, or sections, making it the first "twelve-step program." His message can be seen as the other side of the same coin of doubt. As a matter of fact, through the practice of pragmatism, we can observe ourselves from above. Humility does not mean to think less of oneself—not a popular idea in our individualistic society—but to be grounded, or to be aware of who one is. As we have said before, the best way to know this is in community, because we need another voice, another set of eyes, to make us aware.

Poverty, chastity, obedience, and humility, seen in their modern applications, may not be as irrelevant to U.S. business as one might think. Again, the work of Jim Collins, especially in the best-selling *Good to Great* points out the need for humility in what he calls "Level 5 Leadership."[159] In fact, envisioning the corporation as a contemporary form of monastic community brings us to what I will call the "creative community."

The corporation as creative community

The corporation is a "creative community" when it stresses a broad range of well-defined roles, including service to society. It treats its employees justly and stimulates their creativity in both individual and group settings. It respects human dignity and reaffirms the dignity of work. It practices and relies on listening, and fosters listening among its members, to achieve the effective teamwork on which just success today must be built.

"Community" today, of course, does not have to mean living together as medieval monks did; it can mean interacting and working together in an ongoing process that calls us out of our self-certainty, while valuing and cultivating our individually unique skills. The purpose is not to control others, but to give our gifts to them so that we live and create freely together. Community offers a place for stability, where we know what is valued and that things are to be worked out when the tough times come. People find strength in adversity through their bonds with each other.

Such a creative community also changes the filters I discussed in Chapter 4: the machine model, dualism, individualism, and ethical blindness. The corporation, as a creative community, is seen not as a machine but as a living organism. Its members recognize that everyone has a talent and piece of the truth. Rather than seeing only right or wrong, or black or white, a corporation must not lose sight of its "whole," within which a wide range of valid and useful perspectives coexist, making dualistic responses difficult or impossible. In such an environment everyone is encouraged to contribute, not as a "lone ranger," but as part of a whole. Ethical sensitivity then becomes central to the organization—in its vision, mission and daily operation.

Visit any Benedictine monastery and you will see prominently displayed on everything from walls to napkins the phrase *Ora et Labora*, "Pray and Work". While Benedict clearly valued work, he never actually said these words.[160] He had something else in mind, an unusual phrase: *conversatio morum*, conversation as a way of life or custom.[161] The word *conversatio* also means sexual intercourse. Benedict wanted, in the most graphic manner possible, to make the point that we had to be in intimate conversation with God, that "still, small voice" that spoke to the prophet Isaiah.[162]

Before you dismiss the idea of basing business on the deeply spiritual mode of the monastery, consider two points. First, consider what the "still, small voice" means to you. Some call it intuition, a gut feeling, or a hunch. Others call it conscience. You may not want to call it the voice of God, but we have all experienced it and recognize its creative value. Second, you might recall the most recent time when business embraced a religious idea and developed the wildly successful, if individualistic, Puritan work ethic.

So, despite the fact that the skeptical Harvard Business School students of Ken Goodpaster's class speak for many business practitioners, I remain committed to my journey of practicing Benedictine values of communication, *conversatio*, in a communications firm that tries to live as a creative community. And a still, small voice inside me says that, if we can test it and if it can work for us in our business of "creating and implementing outstanding ideas" in advertising, it can work anywhere.

The creative value of the still, small voice is the subject of our next chapter.

Reading the signs

- How does your organization serve the larger good?

- How might we become more of a creative community, borrowing from the monastic model?

- What aspects of the model might apply today?

- What was my last conversation—my last true conversation—in my organization?

- What characterized that conversation?

- Who would I like to have a conversation with?

10
The still, small voice within

The CORPORANTES *PathFinder* Lab Journal and Field Notebook are designed to help people discover the paths and stories of their own businesses and their careers within the various organizations where they have worked. It begins with a doubt or question they face: some fact that does not quite fit or some situation that causes them to think again about their basic assumptions and beliefs.

If we are lucky enough to have the time to reflect and listen, we hear new voices inside us, helping us make sense of what seems to be random or confusing. Our lives begin to look increasingly as if we are responding to a calling. And, we realize, the most important voice to listen to is the still, small voice within. We have seen this at work in the accounts in Chapter 8 of individuals in corporations who have attempted to listen to their inner voice to discern where their journeys should lead and what beliefs have guided them in their actions. We have just seen how Benedict based his Rule for the monastery on the vow of conversation. I have also seen this at work in my own company and in my teaching.

A changing social environment

For many years, I have taught in MBA programs at Stanford, Notre Dame, DePaul, Presidio, and Kellogg. For 12 years I had the opportunity, as Executive in Residence, to teach a course at DePaul entitled Marketing in a Changing Social Environment. I added a subhead in more recent versions of the course—Learning to Read the Signs—the better to reflect its Peircean orientation. This course developed out of my master's thesis in Religious Studies from Mundelein College, now part of Loyola University Chicago. The thesis was written to help answer the "why" question of business. (I had good ideas about the "what" and "how" questions after the MBA

from Kellogg.) In it I attempted to put together a program of study for business executives that would, in Whitehead's words, help them "think greatly of their function."
As the years have passed, the emphasis of the course has shifted from helping the
students discover what I had learned and thought important, to teaching a method
of inquiry—which is what pragmatism is. I became more interested, and found I
learned more, in seeing them learn how to find the truth for themselves.[163] And
every so often students provide me with clear evidence that they are catching on.

I recall one such incident vividly. It was at the end of the last session of the term,
when a student, an engineer by training, came up to me and said that he really
thought he had everything figured out now. Except, he had one little doubt that just
"sort of nagged" at him. I asked him what it was, and he told me a dilemma had
popped into his head: What would he do if someone pointed out to him that one of
his company's products was harmful to the environment? He said he had thought
about that for a long time, and then suddenly it dawned on him: that was why he
was working toward an MBA—so he could be a manager and delegate that problem
to some underling!

Then he gave me a wry smile to show he knew he would have more thinking
to do. I knew that for him the seed had been planted: the seed of inquiry. He had
grasped the essential point of the class: the importance of doubt and of listening.
How my student will deal with the dilemmas and issues in his life is what makes
up the story that each one of us finally tells. This shows us the practice of virtue
as Alasdair MacIntyre understands it, because his hypothesis is that "Generally a
stance on the virtues will be to adopt a stance on the narrative character of human
life." MacIntyre goes on to tell us why this is so:

> If a human life is understood as a progress through harms and dangers,
> moral and physical, which someone may encounter and overcome in bet-
> ter or worse ways and with a greater or lesser measure of success, the virtues
> will find their place as those qualities the possession and exercise of which
> generally tend to success in this enterprise and vices likewise as qualities
> which likewise tend to failure. Each human life will then embody a story
> whose shape and form will depend on what is counted as harm and danger,
> and upon how success and failure progresses and its opposite are under-
> stood and evaluated. To answer these questions, we will also explicitly and
> implicitly answer the question as to what the virtues and vices are.[164]

The idea of a story, or narrative, of each one of the lives in business certainly
came to be central to the CORPORANTES *PathFinder* Notebook. It is the attempt to
bring people to see their lives as part of a larger picture or story and to understand
the virtues and values driving their actions.

Pragmatism and advertising

Remember that all this began in my search for a better way to lead an organization
to change. In our pursuit to get the most bang for the least buck it might be efficient

to treat consumers as self-absorbed and anxious. But what is the effect of these messages in the larger scheme of things? Is such an approach uplifting for us and for society? Or is it part of the reason advertising has been so maligned by so many critics of contemporary culture, which they characterize as "materialistic"? In other words, we define ourselves by what we have. Acquisition becomes an end.

Advertising began as a part of the ancient and honored discipline of rhetoric, or persuasion. Over thousands of years, our job seems to have narrowed to supporting the acquisitive instinct for material goods. But as we enter a new era of limits brought on by social friction and ecological demands, we need to redefine the role of consumption. Can we create an advertising philosophy by which we can participate in creating the "great society" Whitehead hoped to see, where "men of business think highly of their function?"[165]

At the Nahser Agency, and subsequently at CORPORANTES, Inc., we believe a new paradigm is needed for marketing and its arm of persuasion based on a different image of what it means to be human.[166] We need a model of marketing built not on exchange alone, but on the principle of extended relationships with customers and employees, and with society and nature, within which exchange takes place.

The conventional criticisms of advertising are that it feeds on fears and insecurities and that it treats the individual as a consuming entity who needs advertising and products for self-definition, to be happy, and to feel fulfilled.[167] We reject such advertising as it is born out of the machine model—both the kind that tries to find the buttons to push on the consumer/machine, and the kind that accepts the less rigorous legal standard of "truth in advertising," which, by the way, exempts "puffery." We believe there is a much larger truth—that people buy and consume products to aid their own personal development, to express and reveal parts of themselves to others and, finally, to contribute in the development of their own lives and the lives of their community.[168]

Our goal, then, is to create "advertising that tells the truth" about the company and its products and how they affect personal being, to aid people with the narrative of their own lives and of the society in which they live. Our ethical stance, therefore, uses the twin standards of societal context and respect for the individual. We consider the products we sell in terms of how they are consumed, and whether they and their advertising, which is the visible sign of the product, help to foster a fuller sense of what it means to be human. Or, if a product imposes an identity on a person, as opposed to helping express and develop that identity, the product diminishes his or her wholeness. Christopher Lasch has pointed out that the healthy person would be bad for business: "The anxious person is the ideal consumer."[169]

By contrast, we start from the belief that the consumer is healthy now, and does not need the product as medicine to make him or her well. We also refuse to play on fears or weakness. In principle, we look on products as a way for the consumer to grow in respectful relationships with others. Therefore we like to think of the consumer as a customer, which implies "custom" or relationship rather than exchange. And we ask with them: What does this product or service actually do, and what is it doing to the environment?

Human beings at work

Development and implementation of the CORPORANTES *PathFinder* process to determine what is going on has helped me define and demonstrate what it is for me to be both a human being and head of Nahser as we go about our work of creating and producing advertising and seeing its moral dimension. Ultimately, one must be in dialogue (*conversatio* in Benedict's monastery) and ensure that the corporate environment in general nurtures development and growth, especially for employees. Stories like the following, told to me by our chief operating office at Nahser, Tom Perlitz, support our view.

A new employee was trying to understand just how we work at Nahser and was still puzzled. After several weeks on the job, she recognized that she went home each night feeling that people were not trying to knife her in the back—a most unusual feeling for her compared to her previous experience in the business world. My associate explained how we actively try to create an environment where people can feel safe and free to express themselves, and how this is part of Phase I of the deprogramming at Nahser, which he called "putting down your shield."[170] She was used to working in ad agencies where the focus was on exploiting the weaknesses in people to gain advantage. We are convinced that, when employees have a positive environment, a place to work where they feel safe to present their ideas and to work together, the advertising we produce is equally positive and nourishing.

One day we were working on creative strategy for Bang & Olufsen, Danish maker of beautiful hi-fi equipment. The creative strategy came to this basic position: "Buy a Bang & Olufsen product and feel good about yourself." When I asked the account person about this strategy, explaining this view of the healthy and weak consumer, he looked at me for a moment in disbelief and then said, somewhat patronizingly, "Ron, 95% of all creative strategies are based on this idea." In another instance, an account representative told a prospect that he was pleased that the product actually had a difference since "so much of advertising is designed to create a difference between parity products." That's when I realized our advertising approach turned the usual process of creating advertising on its head.

Therefore, in the spirit of pragmatism, we go on to confirm the truth of what we want them to believe about our product. We ask: "Would people who truly know the product enthusiastically agree with our statements about it?" We then create advertising to draw the attention to these central truths about the product experience. The brand—the sign for the product—becomes a believable picture of reality on which trust can be built.

Alan McNally, then CEO of Harris Bank referred to this trust-building as "right-sided." Being right-sided means being on the side of the customer and making product and service decisions accordingly. McNally's comment is similar to a Japanese executive's statement. He tried to explain to me the differences between Japanese and U.S. strategy approaches as he had experienced them in both the automotive and electronics markets. "You try to give the customer as little as you can and charge as much as you can, and we try the opposite."

Reclaiming pragmatism in business

If we succeed in our endeavor here, it is because we practice pragmatism. Not pragmatism in its ordinary U.S. definition, but the original, Peircean version.

My investigation has convinced me that our contemporary dilemma in U.S. business is not the result of our needing to be more pragmatic (as some have suggested), but of our having practiced the wrong version of pragmatism. The conventional version—"do whatever works"—is erroneous, and has gotten us into our present impasse, with its short-term, reactive, tactical thinking distorted by the filters of dualism, individualism, ethical blindness, and the machine model of business.

Telling our stories and being open to musement

Reclaiming Peircean Pragmatism holds a way out of the narrow and unprincipled "do whatever works" mindset that hobbles its use today. In its *PathFinder* form, it is a way for people to discover and tell their stories and exchange their beliefs, based on and discovered through their life experiences. Stories are one of the most powerful forms of reading the signs. Both listeners and storytellers benefit in this process. We benefited from our insights during a painful downsizing. Because we were clear on our vision and the qualities of the people needed within the organization, we were able to make better decisions, with broad participation and acceptance, even by those asked to leave.

Listeners get the chance to discover other people's reality, which creates deeper mutual understanding. Through the stories we share, we can also come to a better sense of the virtues that guide, or should guide, our behavior.[171] Tellers also benefit by being observers of their own lives and by bringing a sense of meaning and purpose to a corporate life they all share. By telling a story, an individual comes to see what he or she is becoming and where his or her life is heading. We can see more clearly the path, plot or plan for our lives through the stories we share. Through exchanging stories we come to realize our own story is a part of a much larger one, so that we are part of, and responding to, a larger calling. That is why I ended the Preface to the first edition of this book with what I consider one of Peirce's most important definitions of pragmatism: "This activity of thought (pragmatism) by which we are carried, not where we wish, but to a foreordained goal, is like the operation of destiny."[172] And the means by which we accomplish this thought, which I see as the beginning point of the scientific method, is what Peirce calls "musement":

> Enter your skiff of musement, push off into the lake of thought and leave the breath of heaven to swell your sail. With your eyes open, awake to

> what is about or within you and open conversation with yourself for such is all meditation.[173]

This important idea of musement[174] brings the intuitive to what too often is considered a very utilitarian form of logic. This has been particularly important in my work in advertising, where we rely so much on the intuitive, yet need to be guided also by more formal structured thinking so that we can work together in developing ad campaigns. By opening my associates up to this form of musement, I have found that we can look at our business beyond the more narrowly rational and manipulative model, in which we turn the consumer into a machine and try to find the right buttons to push.

To see how central stories are to our creation of reality, consider the facts and trends cited in Chapter 1. The point of these facts and trends is to enable us to discern the larger story of which they are signs.

One example is the well-known story of the U.S. automobile industry in the late 1960s and 1970s, when Japanese cars were just beginning to make an impact on the American market. American car-makers in Detroit remembered Japanese cars as the ones that could barely get up the hills in Los Angeles back in the 1950s. The auto executives were characterized by one caustic observer as

> sitting in their country clubs in Bloomfield Hills, outside of Detroit, and, after checking out the club parking lot … reassur[ing] each other that they had nothing to worry about from Japan, since it was clear Americans were still buying American cars, and a lot of big wagons in particular.

They talked only among themselves, exchanging stories so insular that they were blind to the larger reality happening all around them. They did not attend to signs, nor learn from exchange of views about what was happening. Their filters kept them from seeing what the Japanese saw—a need for high-quality, efficient cars.

As Levi Strauss CEO Philip Marineau put it: "The key to success in business, I think, is learning, listening, and leading." When he told me this, I thought for a moment and proposed a reordering to "listening, learning, and leading"—a perfect summary of our pragmatic method of inquiry.

In the decades of this century, we are challenged to listen to stories from many different sources—from employees, from competitors, from different cultures, from opponents of the market orientation, and from a wide array of consumers—all of whom are changing and have very different stories to tell. We are having to listen, to hear, and to *learn* from different stories.[175]

At the start of this chapter, I mentioned an experience at the end of my course at DePaul several years ago. Recalling the power of that story, I decided one year that we should end the course with a story. I chose one with all the stunning qualities of transformation that storytelling using dialogue (*conversatio*) can give us to discover the true business vocation. Since the class was taught at the Kellstadt Center at DePaul, I gathered two students together to form the "Kellstadt Center Players" and we put on a performance of Charles Dickens's *A Christmas Carol*. We recounted how Scrooge came home one night before Christmas and was visited in his room by the ghost of his partner, Jacob Marley. Trying to bring Scrooge to see the world in a new way, or through different filters, Marley told how "in life, my spirit never roved beyond the narrow limits of our money-changing hole," and how he did not "know that any Christian spirit working kindly in its little space, whatever it may be, will find its mortal life too short for its vast means of usefulness."

> "But you were always a good man of business, Jacob," faltered Scrooge, who now began to apply this to himself. "Business," cried the ghost wringing its hands again. "Mankind was my business, the common welfare was my business; charity, mercy, forbearance, and benevolence were, all, my business. The dealings of my trade were but a drop of water in the comprehensive ocean of my business."[176]

This compelling example of changing filters demonstrates how we need other perspectives, other voices, and other people to tell us about our own lives and what look for.

The organization as community

Alasdair MacIntyre concludes his assessment of the state of our world in what he calls the period "after virtue." He describes how, as the Roman Empire was declining, we entered into the Dark Ages:

> men and women of good will turned aside from the task of shoring up the Roman imperium and ... what they set themselves to achieve instead, often not recognized fully what they were doing, was the construction of new forms of community within which the moral life could be sustained so that both morality and civility might survive the coming ages of barbarism and darkness.[177]

He believes, as many do, that we are at a similar turning point in our own history. Interpreting signs like those at the start of my story convinces me that we are indeed going through massive change. What are we to do? MacIntyre continues:

> What matters at this stage is the construction of local forms of community within which civility and the intellectual and moral life can be sustained through the Dark Ages, which are already upon us ... We are waiting for another—doubtless very different—St. Benedict.[178]

My thesis is that organizations can and must, given their dominant influence, be one type of these communities.[179] We need to look beneath the turbulence and too-frequent wreckage of expense reduction thinly disguised as reengineering to the issues of quality, customer relationships, worker empowerment, team learning, and flatter structures, and to the broader purposes our corporations truly fulfill in society.

I have described the practice of pragmatism and how this method of logic and inquiry can help us to examine more accurately the evidence of change all around us, and so realize a different purpose for business. I agree with MacIntyre that we are waiting for another St. Benedict and that his monastic model for the corporation as expressed through the value of *conversatio*, telling stories, and listening to others, can help the modern corporation play its part in helping to profitably foster a just and compassionate society.

Conclusion

Now that we have come to the end of my story—how I came to write this book, and reclaim pragmatism through the CORPORANTES *PathFinder* process to help us read the signs—I would like to ask: What is your story? What have you seen? What have you heard? Where are you and your corporation on your journey? What paths have you taken? What truths and purposes have you discovered? What action will you and your associates take in the future? What is the focus of your attention? What do you value? Where is your organization going? Where are you going?

What was the spark that ignited your moments of doubt and caused you to question your assumptions, change filters, and read the signs differently? Whatever its particulars, I'll bet your story really got interesting when you confronted that doubt and began to listen to other voices, especially to the still, small voice within.

> You who are deaf, listen,
> You who are blind, look and see.
>   Isaiah 42:18

Reading the signs

- What is your story?

- What have you seen? What have you heard?

- Where are you and your organization on your journey? What paths have you taken?

- What beliefs, values, purposes, and goals have you discovered that are driving your behavior, decisions and actions?

- How is this affecting you and your work?

- What is the focus of you attention?

- Where is society going?

- Is our practice of living and producing sustainable?
- Where are your customers going?
- Where is your organization going?
- Where are you going?
- Who else is on the journey with you?
- How do you lead them?

Epilogue

The story of the UN-supported Principles for Responsible Management Education (PRME)

Jonas Haertle

Head, Principles for Responsible Management Education secretariat, UN Global Compact Office

At the end of this journey through the book, especially in light of the questions posed by the "still, small voice" in Chapter 10, I trust you will now be able—as was I when I was reading the first edition of this book—to stop people and begin a good conversation whenever you hear someone define pragmatism as "whatever works."

Some may think that business has been a little *too* pragmatic, a little *too* focused on results, a little *too* adept at the business function, and as a result, has failed to consider the broader social, economic and environmental challenges of the 21st century. But as you now know, this is precisely the point: Pragmatic Inquiry offers a method for corporate inquiry, discovery, interpretation, and, most importantly, responsible action to help organizations reclaim the trust and integrity of everyone among their stakeholders—especially employees and those they serve, that is customers or clients, etc. It is this vision of pragmatism reclaimed that can foster the process of dialogue … as well as to help create learning organizations built on dialogue between people. For the reflective business practitioner, reclaimed pragmatism offers a way to better understand the realities in which we live, a way to think critically about our own patterns of thought and belief, a way to improve how we think, a way to think more creatively, and a way for businesspeople to think together to make the best use of all perspectives and talents.

It is about putting values to work in addressing the major problems we face in the world and none is bigger than the environmental and social crises we face. The premise also is that every organization, whether commercial, civic, or government, needs to design strategies to address society's needs within the context of a thriving physical and social and economic environment, especially as rapid urbanization spreads throughout the world.

Given the vast scope of the challenges facing us, what better platform to begin thinking through these issues than the United Nations, which has been working in this area for decades. More recently, the UN created the UN Global Compact (in 2000) and Principles for Responsible Management Education (PRME—in 2007) to engage the business and the management-related academic sector respectively on these issues (see Georg Kell's comments in his 2013 Foreword). It is a remarkable story of development leading to a leverage point of management education, which many have concluded is the battleground where the issue must be fundamentally addressed: "theory of the firm" or why this is organization permitted to exist (as Robert Bellah states in his 1997 Foreword). Once we take that question seriously we realize that profit, indispensable though it is, cannot be the only answer, for every commercial, civic and government organization is involved with the whole of society; it meets basic social needs and it has basic social obligations. A healthy economy is only possible if it is part of a healthy society. And that is the simple, but profound logic behind the history of how the UN came to focus on management education.

Background: the role of government

On the global scale, governments have been wrestling with policies and practices that foster peace and economic justice going back to the League of Nations after World War I, if not well before. The idea of an international society or world federation goes back at least to Immanuel Kant's *Perpetual Peace: a Philosophical Sketch*.[180] The Declaration of Human Rights, created shortly after the founding of the United Nations in 1945 and passed by the General Assembly in 1948, was a major breakthrough in shared global governance. After decades of work, the UN Global Compact was launched in 2000, building from the work of many within the peace and human rights movement who recognized the invaluable contributions of corporations and nongovernmental organizations in the pursuit of peace and justice. The UN Global Compact quickly became the world's largest voluntary corporate citizenship initiative, bringing together labor, civil society, and governments with business organizations to advance the ten universal principles in the area of human rights, labor, environment, and anticorruption.

After the creation of the UN Global Compact, an obvious question followed: what is the role of management education in preparing managers to take a leadership role in these broader efforts for sustainable development? Responses to this question led to the establishment of the UN PRME initiative in 2007. The 2012 UN Rio+20 Summit marked 20 years since the first Earth Summit in 1992, and decades of development bringing together many different sectors of society. Held in Rio from June 12 to 22, three conferences all focused on the themes of sustainable development in "The Future We Want." The first of the three conferences, the PRME Global Forum, brought together 300 attendees from leading business schools around the world. It was followed by the UN Global Compact Corporate Sustainable Development Forum—"Innovation and Collaboration for the Future We Want"—with 3,000 corporate and nonprofit leaders attending. The summit concluded with the UN Conference on Sustainable Development with 30,000 attendees. In many ways, it represented a growing convergence among many sectors of society to focus on sustainable development as a common concern.

The first UN Rio Earth Summit in 1992 was followed by some significant disappointment; many concluded that it is virtually impossible for nearly 200 countries to come to any substantial agreement that has "teeth" when it comes to the daunting sustainability challenges of the 21st century. At the time of the 1992 Rio Earth Summit business leaders and business schools were hardly represented. Today, however, many CEOs see the potential for business schools to take real leadership in sustainable development.[181]

And that brings us to Rio+20 and the PRME 3rd Global Forum, using Pragmatic Inquiry methodology.

UN PRME 3rd Global Forum: The future we want

The challenge

The 3rd Global Forum for Responsible Management Education was entitled "The Future We Want," in keeping with the overall UN Rio+20 Conference theme of Sustainable Development—"The Future We Want." Held on June 14–15, 2012, it was the official platform for management-related higher education institutions at Rio+20 to discuss and decide how to accelerate action for a **healthier, more equitable and prosperous world for all**. It was clear that in order to succeed, critical action is required by all major actors in business, government, and society to build the foundation for a sustainable global economy, society, and biosphere. Business schools, management-related academic institutions, and universities have a unique role to train current and future generations to lead this process. However, as a global sector, management education must still make considerable change to be at the forefront of innovation and progress for sustainable development.

Guiding question(s)

Organized by the PRME Secretariat of the UN Global Compact Office, with the active support of PRME participant institutions, the PRME Steering Committee and strategic partners, the 3rd Global Forum provided a space to discuss and mobilize action around two fundamental questions:

1. What is the role of management and leadership education in society for the future we want?

2. How can the PRME initiative facilitate individual and systemic change within higher education as the community mobilizes action toward achieving the Rio+20 vision on sustainable development?

The process

Methodology

As in previous years, our goal was to maximize the interaction of participants at the Global Forum and to build an action-oriented program. The overall design of the two-day Forum followed the format of Sustainable Strategy Inquiry, which is based on Pragmatic Inquiry (see pragmaticinquiry.org). This approach required the active engagement of all participants and their openness to hands-on learning.

In preparation for the Global Forum, we asked participants to read the Participant Guide (See Appendix I) and think about preliminary responses to the questions that were going to be posed during the Forum itself—and specifically about the strategy challenges, barriers, and issues they face—and then write their preliminary answers. As a way of maximizing the value of the Forum, we asked them to be prepared to work with these strategy issues both within their own organizations (their business schools or department of management as appropriate), and as an initiative for PRME.

The five Pragmatic Inquiry Strategy questions to be answered beforehand:

Question 1: **Purpose/need.** What is the role of management and leadership education in society in achieving/attaining the future we want?

Question 2: **Barriers.** What major issues and challenges do you see in fulfilling that role?

Question 3: **Decisions.** What are the plans, ideas, and strategies to meet these challenges and opportunities for successful collective action to implement responsible management education?

Question 4: **Support.** What is the role of PRME in achieving responsible management education for the future we want? What assets, leverage points, partnerships, and capabilities can be tapped?

Question 5: **Action.** What are specific implementation/tactical steps?

With their preliminary answers as *assumptions* in hand, the goal was to have each participant challenge their assumptions and, at the conclusion of the Forum, to develop new strategies, based on what they had learned.

The results

While the official government outcomes of Rio+20 fell short of the expectations in light of the environmental and social challenges we face, many other stakeholder groups committed to far-reaching actions in support of the objectives of Rio+20, including higher education institutions (HEIs). At the close of the 3rd Global Forum, a series of measures to inject sustainability principles into management and business school curricula were announced through the *Rio Declaration on the Contribution of Higher Education Institutions and Management Schools to The Future We Want: A Roadmap for Management Education to 2020*, through which 300 leading business school and university representatives worldwide agreed on a number of concrete commitments to action, including to:

- Launch PRME Regional Chapters to better engage management education communities on a local level

- Form a leadership group to incentivize the most engaged PRME signatory schools to go further in their implementation of sustainability principles.

- Delist those signatories that fail to regularly share information on progress made in implementing PRME as an accountability mechanism

The Sustainable Strategy Inquiry method helped to structure the preparation as well as the deliberations at the Global Forum for an inclusive approach. The result was an outcomes declaration that was endorsed unanimously. Many participants lauded the inclusive nature of the approach as well as the arc of an inquiry that helped to incorporate the input by the widest group of stakeholders.

Appendix I shows the 3rd Global Forum Participant's Guide, marking the beginning of PRME using Pragmatic Inquiry. Appendix II compares two important management models developed by the UN Global Compact, with the Pragmatic Inquiry *PathFinder* Field Notebook in an effort to show how this work all comes together to develop, implement, and integrate strategies with the UN Global Compact Principles to help foster sustainable development.

Appendix I
UN PRME 3rd Global Forum Participant's Guide

3RD GLOBAL FORUM FOR RESPONSIBLE MANAGEMENT EDUCATION:
The Future We Want

PARTICIPANT GUIDE

Setting the Context: Developing the 3rd PRME Global Forum

The 3rd PRME Global Forum on 14-15 June 2012 will be the official platform for management-related Higher Education Institutions (HEIs) at **Rio+20** – the United Nations Conference on Sustainable Development – and the **UN Global Compact Corporate Sustainability Forum**.

Marking the 20th anniversary of the 1992 United Nations Conference on Environment and Development (UNCED) held in Rio de Janeiro, the Rio+20 Summit will bring the world together in Rio de Janeiro, Brazil, to discuss and decide how to accelerate action for a *healthier, more equitable and prosperous world for all*. **The Forum and Summit provide us with an opportunity to plan for the future we want.**

As Rio+20 will highlight, critical action is required from all major actors in business, government, and society to build the foundation for a sustainable *global economy, society, and biosphere*. Business schools, management-related academic institutions, and universities have a unique role to train current and future generations to lead this process. However, as a global sector, management education must make considerable change to be at the forefront of innovation and progress for sustainable development.

This guide is intended to facilitate your participation in the Global Forum. We ask that you carefully read and reflect on the first 6 pages of the document; an Appendix is also included that provides further information on the background discussions that led to the creation of this guide. View the Agenda online.

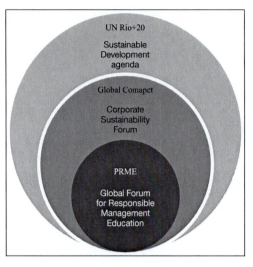

Figure 1: 3rd PRME Global Forum in the context of Rio+20

Global Forum Outline

Guiding Question(s)

Organized by the Principles for Responsible Management Education (PRME) Secretariat of the UN Global Compact Office, with the active support of PRME participant institutions, the PRME Steering Committee and strategic partners, the 3rd Global Forum (GF) will provide a space to discuss and mobilize action around two fundamental questions:

1. **What is the role of management and leadership education in society for the future we want?**

2. **How can the PRME initiative facilitate individual and systemic change within higher education as the community mobilizes action toward achieving the Rio+20 vision on sustainable development?**

Goals of the Global Forum

As the main meeting for the PRME community taking place every two years, the 3rd Global Forum for Responsible Management Education aims at taking stock of the PRME initiative, ensuring that the voice of signatories is heard as genuine owners of the initiative, generating traction and outreach, and providing overall direction to the initiative. The main goals of the 3rd Global Forum are to generate:

1. An agreed concrete plan of action on how to move forward for:

   - Individual schools to start and/or lead initiatives within their own organizations;

   - Groups of schools and their stakeholders to collaborate together on projects; and

   - PRME as an initiative to further enhance its value as a learning and action network.

2. A statement (1) highlighting the contributions and commitments of the management education sector for actions for sustainable development over the next decade, and (2) outlining support required from governments and industry to enable this action. The GF Outcomes Document will be presented to the Corporate Sustainability Forum (CSF), Rio+20, the Education for Sustainable Development agenda, and governments.

Methodology

As in previous years, our goal is to maximize the interaction of participants at the Global Forum and to build an action-oriented program. The overall design of the two-day GF agenda follows the format of "Sustainable Strategy Inquiry," which is based on "Pragmatic Inquiry" (see pragmaticinquiry.org). This approach requires the active engagement of all participants and their openness to hands-on learning.

In preparation for the Global Forum, we ask that you read this Participant Guide and think about preliminary responses to the questions that will be posed during the Forum itself – and specifically about the strategy challenges, barriers and issues you face; and your preliminary answers. As a way of maximizing the value of the Forum, be prepared to work with these strategy issues within your own organization (your business schools or department of management as appropriate), and for PRME as an initiative.

The Forum will be divided into **three 60-minute plenary sessions featuring expert panel discussions** conducted in "Question & Answer style. Each session will be followed by a **60-minute facilitated table discussion, with focused feedback to the plenary to ensure knowledge sharing among participants. Feedback is sought on concrete action plans** which you would like to initiate or continue at your school, within a partnership of schools and/or other partners, as well as for PRME as an initiative. A summary of the proposed action plans will be presented at the closing session (CSF session ID = SE8). There will be 30 tables with ten participants each and a table Discussion Leader. Participants will be randomly assigned to a table for Session I (SE2), with the opportunity to select focused table discussions in Sessions II (SE4) and III (SE6).

At the conclusions of the Forum, there will be time to compare and reflect on your beginning thoughts with what you have learned in the Forum – leading to new strategies and action plans for us all.

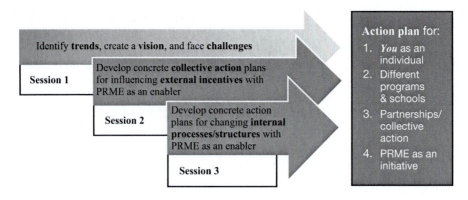

Figure 2: The Flow of Three Sessions

We appreciate your willingness to engage actively in the 3rd Global Forum and to work with colleagues of the PRME community to create the future we want!

SESSION I: BUSINESS CAPABILITIES FOR ACHIEVING SUSTAINABLE DEVELOPMENT (SE2)

Session description: *To set the stage, this session will examine current trends and potential pathways to achieve sustainable development. Global leaders will help identify top priorities for the next twenty years and make the case for urgent change and collaboration necessary to achieve the future we want. HEIs have a unique role to spearhead this process by providing thought leadership and training responsible leaders for the future we want.*

The main question of Session 1: How should sustainable development affect the management education sector?

- **Question 1**: What is the role of management and leadership education in society in achieving/attaining the future we want?

- **Question 2**: Given the envisioned (future) role of management education, what major issues and challenges do you see in implementing the answers/responses to Question 1?

1. <u>Role of management/leadership education</u>	2. <u>Major issues & challenges</u>

SESSION II: SETTING THE INCENTIVES FOR RESPONSIBLE MANAGEMENT EDUCATION (SE4)

Session description: Following the previous afternoon's discussion, and building on the insights from previous PRME meetings, Session II revolves around the external factors that encourage change within the global business/management school system and the challenges of managing those change processes. This session will look at some of the key drivers, including: accreditation and rankings; student demand; political /legislative change affecting curricula, and funding at the national level.

Building on the concrete outcomes from Session 1, participants will have the opportunity to select a focused table discussion on a specific external incentive, with the goal of identifying ideas for collective action, needed resources and support, and specific action steps that could enable this external incentive to become a driver for responsible management education.

The main questions of Session 2: What are the external incentives (e.g., accreditation, rankings of business schools), and how can they further support the values of sustainable development and responsible management education?

- **Question 1**: What are the possible collective actions to influence and to (further) align this external incentive (see explanation above) to implement responsible management education?

- **Question 2**: What assets, leverage points, and capabilities of PRME and other partnerships and actors (e.g. governments, companies, others) can be tapped?

- **Question 3**: What specific action steps should be taken to implement these solutions?

1. Your ideas for collective actions
2. Capabilities, assets & leverage points of PRME & other partners
3. Specific action steps

SESSION III: INNOVATION IN PRACTICE: INTEGRATING (CORPORATE) SUSTAINABILITY INTO EDUCATION, RESEARCH, BUSINESS MODEL AND CAMPUS LIFE (SE6)

Session description: Once an HEI starts to integrate the values of the UN Global Compact and PRME, challenges and opportunities arise around how to adapt its core business model, teaching methods, research, and campus practices. This session will highlight inspirational examples as well as resources and tools for successful implementation of the Principles.

Building on the outcomes from Session 1 & 2, participants will have the opportunity to select a focused table discussion on a specific dimension of individual school activity (e.g., faculty development, curriculum, research, pedagogy), with the goal of identifying ideas for individual school action, needed resources and support, and specific action steps that could enable this internal incentive to become a driver for responsible management education.

The main questions of Session 3: What are the challenges, opportunities, and successes by individual schools to (further) implement responsible management education? How can PRME help in this process?

- **Question 1**: What are the solutions/activities that individual schools have used (or can use) to implement responsible management education?

- **Question 2**: What assets, leverage points, and capabilities of PRME and other partnerships and actors (e.g. governments, companies, others) can be tapped?

- **Question 3**: What action plans are you prepared to take as an individual, in your organization, and what could PRME do to support your initiative?

1. Your ideas for & experience with individual schools
2. Capabilities, assets & leverage points of PRME and other partners
3. Specific action steps

Appendix II
UN models and Pragmatic Inquiry Model

Here is the description of two models and a blueprint developed by the UN Global Compact to help signatory organizations implement the principles. These models are intended to help organizations **align** and **implement** their strategies with the UN Global Compact Principles.

In Appendix III you will find a reproduction of the *PathFinder* Pragmatic Inquiry Method and the *PathFinder* Field Notebook. We offer Pragmatic Inquiry as a **method for creating and developing** sustainable management strategies.

UN Global Compact Management Model

The first model was launched in June 2010 entitled the UN Global Compact Management Model.[182] It was designed to help Global Compact signatories align their operations and strategies with both the letter and spirit of the Global Compact's ten universally accepted principles.[183]

> "While the UN Global Compact has evolved in countless ways over the past decade, there has been one unshakable and non-negotiable constant, and that is the aim of translating the core ten principles into value-enhancing management practices," said Georg Kell, Executive Director of the UN Global Compact. "It is our hope that through the application of the new Management Model, our signatories will attain ever-higher levels of performance and, in the process, generate real and lasting value for their business, stakeholders, and society at large."
>
> The UN Global Compact Management Model, developed with input and feedback from more than 50 business participants of the Global

Compact, incorporates six time-proven management steps: commit, assess, define, implement, measure, and communicate.

The Management Model has broad applications for all companies, regardless of scale, industry, geographic location, or sustainability maturity. The guide is particularly helpful for new signatories as they begin to engage in the Global Compact. For companies that have more experience with the Global Compact, the Management Model provides example "Leadership Practices" to serve as both inspiration for further improvement and aspiration as these companies set and work toward long-term goals.

"This Management Model represents, in our view, the very best management thinking with respect to translating the UN Global Compact's principles into practice, but, as a public good, it offers value to any company committed to corporate sustainability," added Kell.[184]

Environmental Stewardship Strategy

Environmental issues—be they related to climate change, water scarcity, or other natural-resource and ecological challenges—are growing in scale and complexity.

Figure AII.1 **UN Global Compact Management Model**

Source: UN Global Compact and Deloitte, *UN Global Compact Management Model: Framework for Implementation* (New York: UN Global Compact, 2010): 6

What is also increasingly clear is that traditional corporate environmental management approaches—based largely on compliance and narrow risk assessments—will not be sufficient to successfully navigate and address these 21st-century challenges.

In order to assist companies in preparing for this increasingly challenging landscape, and to give further expression to the UN Global Compact's three core environmental principles, the UN Global Compact Office brought together a group of committed participants and—in partnership with Duke University—developed during the 2009–2010 period a next-generation Environmental Stewardship Strategy and related Resource (taking the form of both a website and CD-ROM).

This Environmental Stewardship Strategy is designed to help companies—at the highest levels of the organization—develop a truly holistic and comprehensive strategy. And, importantly, it recognizes the growing linkages among various environmental issues as well as their connections to social and development priorities. As well, this Environmental Stewardship Strategy incorporates and leverages the UN Global Compact's Caring for Climate and CEO Water Mandate initiatives.[185]

The second step in this model is called "Declare," which is described as follows:

> Environmental stewardship leaders develop strategies that incorporate clear statements of environmental goals related to every aspect of the organization. The declaration of environmental goals inoculates the

Figure AII.2 **UN Global Compact Environmental Stewardship Strategy**

Source: nicholasinstitute.duke.edu/globalcompact

organization with strategic environmental stewardship ambition and provides benchmarks for the organization to aspire to far into both the short-term and the future. It is important to communicate these goals to all stakeholders external to, within and across the organization. Stakeholder involvement is essential to meeting short- and long-term goals.[186]

To help leading organizations further their development, the Blueprint for Corporate Sustainability Leadership was developed.

Blueprint for Corporate Sustainability Leadership

As a further effort to help signatories of the Global Compact further their development, the Blueprint Corporate Sustainability Leadership model was developed:

> for achieving higher levels of performance and generating enhanced value through the UN Global Compact. It allows companies and their stakeholder network to assess progress with respect to their commitment, strategy and implementation and to communicate effectively as they ascend the learning and performance curve.[187]

Figure AII.3 **Blueprint for corporate sustainability leadership**

Source: UN Global Compact *Blueprint for Corporate Sustainability Leadership* (New York, UN Global Compact, 2010): 4

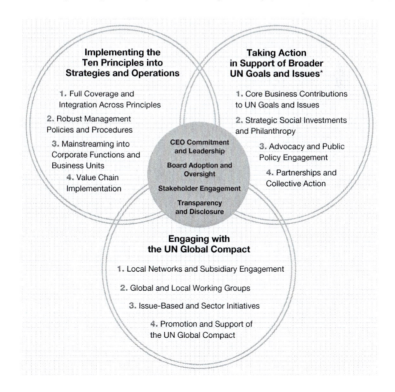

PathFinder Pragmatic Inquiry Method

You have read all about pragmatism in this book, so you know the major points about it as a method of inquiry. We believe that it complements the UN models that focus on aligning and implementing the Global Compact Principles and Principles for Responsible Management Education. We offer Pragmatic Inquiry as a critical self-reflective way to face challenges; articulate assumptions; and create, develop, and test values-driven strategies. And, most importantly, to learn from experience ... and begin again.

Figure AII.4 *PathFinder* Pragmatic Inquiry

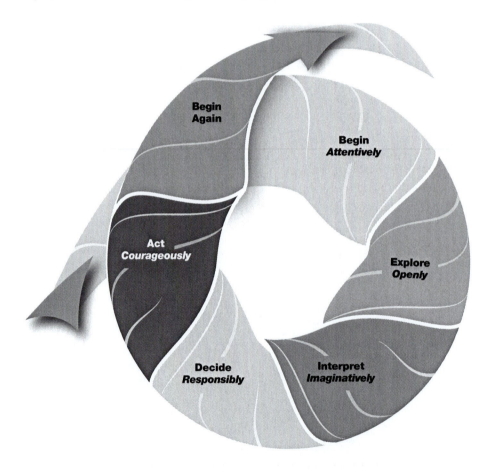

In Appendix III you will find the *PathFinder* Lab Journal: Field Notebook. We use this as a quick introductory overview of the method, and, for experienced pragmatic inquirers, a specific project sketch book.

Appendix III

The *PathFinder* Lab Journal Field Notebook

A PDF download of this Notebook is available at www.greenleaf-publishing.com/signs

The *PathFinder* Lab Journal

Field Notebook

Corporantes, Inc

Own Who You Are®

CORPORANTES is the PathFinder that helps us
uncover the truth we do not yet know,
leading to the action we have yet to take.

Pragmatic Inquiry®

A method of reflection to ignite your values and vision
to drive personal and organizational sustainable performance.

Our Values and Our Vision are what guide us as we choose and confront the
problems, opportunities, issues, trends, challenges and competitive situations
that face us.

Values Statement

"A Value is any belief, principle or virtue held so deeply
(consciously or unconsciously)
that it guides our Behaviors, Decisions and Actions."

RON NAHSER

A *Behavior* is an Action that gives evidence of a *Value*.

Vision Statement

A *Core Purpose* defines the fundamental reason for an organization's existence
from a market perspective — the needs it meets ("What business are you in?").
It is based on and grows out of the *Values*.

A long-term aspirational *Goal* is not quantifiable, is highly intuitive and is
used to motivate and inspire. It is based on and grows out of the *Core Purpose*
(Includes a Vivid Description–what it will look like when we achieve our *Goal*.)

CORPORANTES, Inc. • P.O. Box 6629 • Evanston, IL 60204-6629 • 312.845.5000
www.OwnWhoYouAre.com   LabInfo@ownwhoyouare.com

Igniting Your Values & Vision to Drive Sustainable Organization Performance

Leadership Challenge Inquiry —
"What's *Really* Going On —
and What Can I do About It?"

What is your question?

The purpose of your Inquiry is for you to address a strategic issue, idea, challenge, opportunity, or problem that you and your organization face. For example, consider the larger context of the dramatic evidence of climate change, energy issues, and the increasing scarcity of resources all societies face in our efforts to build a sustainable world for us and for future generations. Every part of our often inequitable carbon constrained, consumer economy — how we live together and exchange the things we need and value — has to be re-thought and re-designed. And the process of facing these enormous challenges starts with each of us.

The premise of your Inquiry is to help define the problems you see, needs you think you can address, and then develop ideas to meet those needs. During your Inquiry, you will test those ideas, based on the evidence of your experience and learning. The outcome of the Inquiry will be to decide on the best course of action for you and your organization to take to test the Ideas; after all, that is the reason for its existence.

A major weakness of traditional problem solving approaches is the lack of awareness around the assumptions (unstated contexts or paradigms) underlying the issue — or even what the real issues are, which always involve overcoming barriers in meeting some need. This lack of awareness stems from a decision making process that fails to take into account the larger and longer-term context, align the competing views and different data around unclear questions and assumptions. This is as true for individuals as it is for groups.

And most importantly, strategy decisions need to be based on the Values, Core Purpose and Goals — the Vision — of the individual and the organization:

"Own who you are"

— the expression of your character, culture and your brand.

The *PathFinder*, as the name implies, helps participants come to a decision leading to action, based on the evidence of their experience. Alignment can be achieved through data evaluation from different perspectives and a rigorous and open interpretation of the data where "everyone holds a piece of the truth."

We will look in depth at the three elements which are too seldom examined in most decision-making processes and overlooked in the day-to-day pressure of business:

1. Your Values and Beliefs which guide your behavior, decisions and actions.

2. Your Core Purpose — "what business are you in."

3. Your Goals — what is the result, the aim, of accomplishing your purpose.

During the course of your Pragmatic Inquiry, you will have the opportunity to think about the issues that are important to you, answer your questions, determine needs to be met, develop ideas and implement a plan of action.

The result will be a clear plan and strategy with compelling reasoning — told with your true voice often as a story — to support it and engage others in the Path Ahead. It will be based on work you believe in — "Own Who You Are," your "calling," and your unique marketable value as a leader. You will also have followed the advice of one of our greatest strategists and leaders:

*"If we could first know **where** we are, and **whither** we are tending,*
*we could then better judge **what** to do, and **how** to do it."*

ABRAHAM LINCOLN, "A HOUSE DIVIDED," JUNE 16, 1858

Baseline Exercises — write your answers in the *Begin Attentively* section of the Notebook

1. As you move forward, what question, issue, doubt, problem, opportunity do you and your organization face? What needs can you meet? Why is it important? What is the impact of your project?

2. Challenge/question **Cq**: What questions, doubts or barriers do you face in developing and implementing your Project — The Pragmatic Inquiry begins with a Challenge/question, which prepares you to examine your experience and challenge the assumptions, values, vision and hypotheses driving your Project.

3. What is your preliminary answer now? (Hint: Write quickly your best guess, hunch, or thoughts.)

4. What are your personal values, beliefs, goals, etc. and how are they impacting and driving your question and your answer?

5. Based on your answer, what action will you take? What action are you taking now?

During your Inquiry, you will probably revise your answers, and even your question as you get deeper into the work. At the end of the Inquiry, you will revisit your Baseline Work and compare it with your final work to see what you have learned and where you are headed now.

Kinds of Inquiry Questions

Every inquiry begins with a question, idea, problem, barrier, need, issue, doubt, opportunity or challenge and a tentative answer that will drive the Inquiry. Here are questions that have begun Inquiries in the past.

• What are the Values of the Organization? Why are they important?

• What is the Core Purpose and Goal of the Organization — what is our reason for existence? What business are we in?

• What are our Social and Environmental Responsibilities?

• What is our view of the future?

• Who are our customers?

• What needs in society do or can we meet?

• What are our core competencies? Are they relevant & differentiating?

• Is our strategy sustainable?

• What investments should we make?

• How do we innovate and renew?

• What Values and Visions are driving my behavior, decisions and actions?

• What are my personal and career goals?

Learning To Read The Signs — Why Practice Pragmatic Inquiry

Each day of our lives, we are confronted with facts, problems, barriers, conversations, situations, ideas, issues, opportunities and challenges that demand our attention. This is especially true now, in light of the overwhelming evidence of potentially catastrophic climate change which is threatening to overshadow the perennial economic, business, social and political concerns.

Usually we react to this daily flood of information and events almost automatically by fitting them into our existing patterns and habits of thinking and behaving. (And if the facts and events don't fit into our patterns of belief, we tend to ignore them.) That's because we assume we know what's going on — what the facts and events mean — and based on these assumptions, we decide what to do. But the information and events are no more than signs, clues, evidence or symptoms and our interpretations of them may not be the best choice, especially since our complex environment is always changing!

The importance of a question...and a baseline answer.

Learning begins when some fact, idea, incident, barrier, or opportunity comes along that forces us to stop and begin to question or doubt what we know or challenge what we value. We now state what we know and value as assumptions which are treated as an hypothesis to be tested. We begin to re-think our experiences, our plans and what we know and value, and then search for new explanations. We are, in effect, reinterpreting the meaning of our experiences into new belief patterns.

This is where the method of inquiry outlined in this Notebook can be so helpful — by challenging our assumptions and providing a time-honored and well-tested practice that can help us interpret the signs in new ways. The result of the inquiry may range from a small adjustment in plans to a complete change in direction.

The method of Inquiry is based on Pragmatism; so-called "Classic American Philosophy." It is an original American insight that the meaning of ideas is determined by their consequences — by what action results from the ideas. This takes us far beyond the usual stance of *"do whatever works"* to a stance of putting ideas and beliefs to the test in action. It offers the thoughtful business practitioner and student a simple, efficient way to inquire into and act on the pressing questions they have on which they must decide and act.

Pragmatic Inquiry concerns itself with consequences. In the case of igniting values and vision, issues to be addressed are ones which deal with turning the problems and issues into needs that you can address.

"Education is / not the filling of a pail, / but the igniting of a fire."

WILLIAM BUTLER YATES

How To Practice Pragmatic Inquiry

Pragmatic Inquiry provides a practical method of reflection for personal and corporate success for which the *PathFinder* serves as a guide. It offers a flexible framework of exercises to help you — individually or as a group — look at a situation, problem, opportunity or idea from several angles to put it in a more realistic context. With this better picture, better investment decisions can be made.

By adapting the stance of a Pragmatic Inquirer, you avoid the two traps of either staying with an idea, position or strategy too long, or reactively changing it without any basis of values, purpose or goal. Also, too often, leaders implement partial solutions or simple strategies for complex business challenges when a comprehensive, integrated approach based on values and vision is necessary.

Central to this inquiry is to treat your career and the organization as living entities with values, a vision, character, talent, a service to provide, a goal to reach, a path to follow and a story to tell. As with any journey, there are questions: What is the purpose? Why do you believe in it? What is the destination? What is the best path? How to prepare? What investments need to be made? Who to travel with? When to go? How do you measure progress? How do you measure success?

Inquiry mindsets

Each step in your inquiry requires a different cognitive and emotional stance. Based on our experience with thousands of executives and students, here's the habits of thought required.

The *Begin* phase — attentive, humility, asking tough questions, not knowing the answer and being open to learn.

The *Explore* phase — being open, observant and attentive, especially to data you might not like or usually overlook. Be prepared to have your thinking diverge.

The *Interpret* phase — imaginative, intuitive where you are "connecting the dots" from the *Explore* phase and using your eyes and ears and heart.

The *Decide* phase — responsible, thinking, using the head, logic.

And the crucial step of *Action* — the courage to ignite your values and vision in the face of obstacles that are sure to arise.

Finally, *Begin Again* — as evidence comes in and the context changes, new challenges arise, and the Inquiry begins again.

Keep notes on an ongoing basis.

Be open to surprises, capture vague impressions, feelings and memories–as well as hard data–and look for patterns and connections over time. Be willing to test your hypotheses and entertain new explanations and ideas in which you don't now believe.

Remember that most cases of discovery have involved moments of insight and intuition that were non-linear and unexpected!

> *"I write to discover what I think."*
> Daniel
> Boorstin

Begin Attentively Instructions

Begin Your Inquiry with Questions, an Idea or Need and a Baseline Answer.

Questions

1. As you move forward, what question, issue, doubt, problem, opportunity do you and your organization face? What needs can you meet? Why is it important? What is the impact of your project?
2. Challenge/question $\boxed{\text{Cq}}$: What questions, doubts or barriers do you face in developing and implementing your Project.

Baseline Answer

3. What are your preliminary answers now? (Hint: Write quickly your best guess, hunch, or thoughts.)
4. What are your personal and organizational values and vision and how are they impacting your answer? (Note: Your values and vision are what focused your attention on your question in the first place.)

Baseline Action

5. What actions are you and your organization planning to take or are taking now? How do purpose and mission shape the actions you're taking?

During the inquiry, note if your question is changing, becoming clearer, etc.

Put daily thoughts and experiences in the Daily Log that don't fit elsewhere.

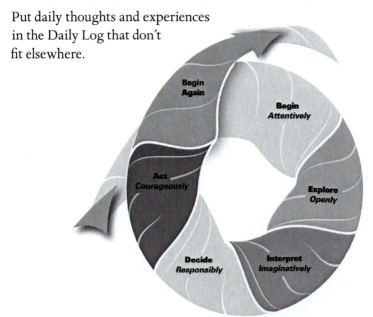

1. Begin

1. Begin

Explore Openly Instructions

All strategic questions involve three relationships:

- You personally and professionally

- Your organization/industry/profession

- The markets you and they serve (including customers, consumers, citizens, prospects and competition in general)

Identify these three elements narrowly or broadly.

These relationships exist within the larger society/community and the environment, without which we could not exist! (Please read this sentence again.)

Strategic Stakeholder Networks

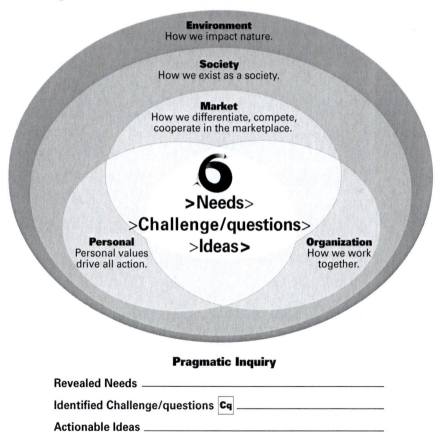

Environment
How we impact nature.

Society
How we exist as a society.

Market
How we differentiate, compete, cooperate in the marketplace.

6

>Needs>
>Challenge/questions>
>Ideas>

Personal
Personal values
drive all action.

Organization
How we work
together.

Pragmatic Inquiry

Revealed Needs _____

Identified Challenge/questions Cq _____

Actionable Ideas _____

2. Explore

2. Explore

Interpret Imaginatively Instructions

External Conversations: What are the conversations going on in your Stakeholder Network?

Compare your ideas with other Stakeholders. Who do you need to talk with?

Habits: What are known and unknown Stakeholder practices, patterns of culture, beliefs, barriers, strategies or tactics which lead or limit your progress?

Internal Conversations: Explore your inner voice through what you think others might say.

Maps and Images. What does your Project and Challenge/question **Cq** look, feel and sound like now. What will it look like when it is successful?

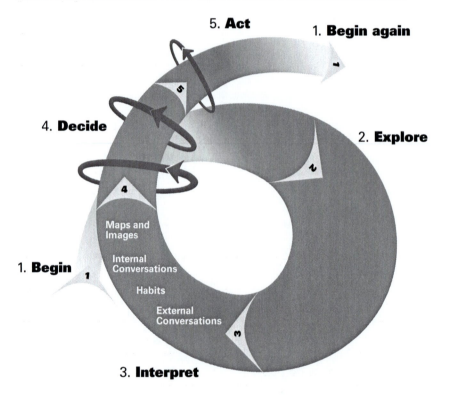

3. Interpret

3. Interpret

Decide Responsibly-**Hypothesize Instructions — Continue To Explore**

What questions are coming to you?

What answers are coming to you?

What values, beliefs, core purpose, goals etc. are becoming clear?

Conclude:

1. What is your Challenge/question **Cq** now?

2. Why is it important; its impact?

3. What is the answer to your Challenge/question **Cq** now?
   What is the need you are meeting?
   What is your idea to meet that need?

4. What values, beliefs, knowledge, assumptions, core purpose, and goals is your concluding answer based on?

Compare your conclusion with your *Begin* Baseline work.

What have you learned?
The purpose of the inquiry is to challenge assumptions, your initial thoughts. Compare your Begin and Concluding *Questions, Answers and Action.*

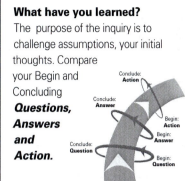

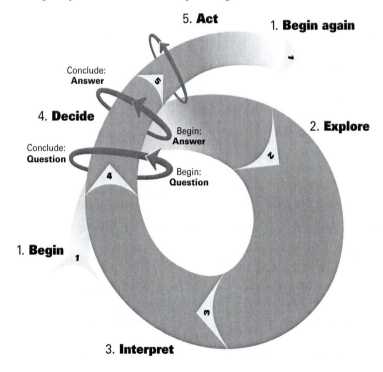

5. **Act**

1. **Begin again**

Conclude: **Answer**

4. **Decide**

Conclude: **Question**

Begin: **Answer**

Begin: **Question**

2. **Explore**

1. **Begin**

3. **Interpret**

4. Decide-Hypothesize

4. Decide-Hypothesize

Act Courageously

Continue to Explore

What new ideas may be developing for action plans?

Conclude

Put your **Hypothesis** to the test in action:

What will you/your organization do now?

What investments will you make?

How will you involve and lead others?

Will your actions be sustainable?

How will you measure results?

Measurement

Every decision has consequences and these can and must be measured. This is not "whatever works," but is a foundational test of how the decision enters reality and creates results, both intended and unintended.

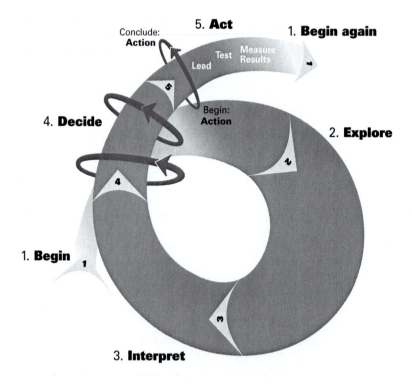

5. Act

5. Act

Conclusion — What is learned

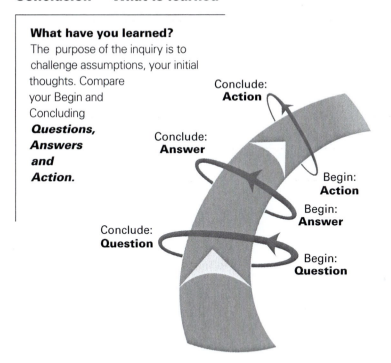

What have you learned?

The purpose of the inquiry is to challenge assumptions, your initial thoughts. Compare your Begin and Concluding ***Questions, Answers and Action.***

Conclude:
Action

Conclude:
Answer

Conclude:
Question

Begin:
Action

Begin:
Answer

Begin:
Question

If the goal of life is some version of "Know Thyself" ("Own Who You Are") and take action on that, then this reflection is the full measure of the success of the Inquiry.

Here is where you see, feel and understand through your own evidence, written in your own hand, what is different. You may now see more objectively what truth you have uncovered.

It is especially instructive and impactful for you to read carefully your Baseline and compare where you are now and what your interpretation of the "evidence of experience" means to you. See how your question and answers have changed. And see the differences in your management practices.

As John Dewey has said:

> "The aim of education is not to put theory into practice,
>
> but to make practice understandable."

Conclusion

Conclusion

Begin Attentively Again

Here is where the word "Hypothesis" is most important. The decision is held tentatively as results come in. Then, just as in the past, a chapter ends and another chapter of Inquiry begins again.

What are your Challenges/questions **Cq** /etc.?

What needs will you meet?

What are your ideas?

1. Begin again

1. Begin again

Selected bibliography

Adams, John D. (ed.) *Transforming Work* (Alexandria VA: Miles River Press, 1984).

Addams, Jane, *Democracy and Social Ethics* (New York: Macmillian Company, 1911).

Aristotle, *Nicomachean Ethics,* edited by Richard McKeon (New York: Random House, 1941).

Bellah, Robert N., Richard Madsen, William M. Sullivan, Ann Swidler, and Steven M. Tipton, *The Good Society* (New York: Alfred A. Knopf, 1991).

——, *Habits of the Heart: Individualism and Commitment in American Life* (Berkeley, CA: University of California Press, 1985).

Benedict, *The Rule of St. Benedict,* edited by Timothy Fry (Collegeville MN: The Liturgical Press, 1981).

Berdyaev, Nicholas, *The Bourgeois Mind* (Freeport, NY: Books for Libraries Press, 1965).

——, *Fate of Man in the Modern World* (Ann Arbor, MI: Ann Arbor Paperbacks, 1961).

——, *The Realm of Spirit and the Realm of Caesar* (New York: Harper & Brothers, 1952).

Bohm, David, *Thought as a System* (New York: Routledge Press, 1994).

Boswell, Jonathan, *Community and Economy* (New York: Routledge Press, 1990).

Braudel, Fernand, *Afterthoughts on Material Civilization and Capitalism* (Baltimore: Johns Hopkins University Press, 1977).

Castro, Janice, "The Simple Life," *Time,* April 8, 1991.

Chappell, Tom, *The Soul of Business* (New York: Bantam Books, 1993).

Church, George J., "We're Number 1 and It Hurts," *Time,* October 24, 1994.

Coles, Robert, *The Call of Stories* (Boston: Houghton Mifflin Company, 1989).

Collins, James C., *Good to Great* (London: Random House Books, 2001).

Collins, James C., and William C. Lazier, *Beyond Entrepreneurship* (Englewood Cliffs, NJ: Prentice Hall, 1992).

Collins, James C., and Jerry I. Porras, *Built to Last* (London: Random House Business, 1998).

Columbia College, "Karl Marx, 'The Manifesto of the Communist Party,'" in *An Introduction to Contemporary Civilization in the West, II* (New York: Columbia University Press, 1961).

Coplon, Jeff, "The Age of Jackson," *New York Times* Magazine Section, May 17, 1992.

Davis, John P., *Corporations: Origin and Development* (New York: G.P. Putnam's Sons, 1905).

de Mello, Anthony S.J., *Awareness.* New York: (Doubleday, 1990).

Dewey, John, *How We Think* (republished Amherst NY: Prometheus Books, 1991; original published 1910).

——, *How We Think: A Restatement of the Relation of Reflective Thinking to the Educative Process* (New York, D.C. Heath and Company, 1933).

——, *Logic: The Theory of Inquiry* (Carbondale, IL: Southern Illinois University Press, 1991).

——, *The Philosophy of John Dewey*, edited by John J. McDermott (Chicago: University of Chicago Press, 1981).

Dickens, Charles, *A Christmas Carol* (London: Chapman and Hall, 1848).

Drucker, Peter, "The Age of Social Transformation," *Atlantic Monthly*, November, 1994.

——, *Concept of the Corporation* (New York: The John Day Company, 1946).

——, *The End of Economic Man* (New York: The John Day Company, 1939).

——, *Management* (New York: Harper & Row, 1973).

——, *Post-Capitalist Society* (New York: Harper Business, 1993).

Eckhart, "Sermon Thirty-two: Driving Merchant Mentalities from Our Souls: Economics and Compassion," in Matthew Fox, *Passion for Creation: The Earth-honoring Spirituality of Meister Eckhart* (Rochester, VT: Inner Traditions, 2000).

Eco, Umberto, and Thomas A. Sebeok, *The Sign Of Three* (Bloomington, IN: Indiana University Press, 1983).

Fisch, Max H., *Peirce, Semeiotic, and Pragmatism* (Bloomington, IN: Indiana University Press, 1986).

Fox, Matthew, "Meister Eckhart and Karl Marx: The Mystic as Political Theologian," in Richard Woods (ed.), *Understanding Mysticism* (Garden City, NY: Image Books, 1980): 541-63.

Frankl, Viktor E., *Man's Search for Meaning* (New York: Washington Square Press, 1985).

Freidman, Milton, "The Social Responsibility of Business is to Increase its Profits," Harvard Business School Reprint from *New York Times* Magazine, September 13, 1970.

Frings, Manfred, *Philosophy of Predictions and Capitalism* (Dordrecht: Martinus Nijhoff, 1987).

Haack, Susan, *Evidence and Inquiry* (Oxford, UK: Blackwell, 1998).

——, *Manifesto of a Passionate Moderate* (Chicago, IL: University of Chicago Press, 1998).

Harman, Willis, *Global Mind Change* (Indianapolis, IN: Knowledge Systems, Inc., 1988).

Harman, Willis, and John Hormann, *Creative Work* (Indianapolis, IN: Knowledge Systems, Inc., 1990).

Haughey, John C., *Where is Knowing Going?* (Washington, D.C.: Georgetown University Press, 2009).

Hawken, Paul, *The Ecology of Commerce* (New York, NY: HarperCollins, 1993).

Hegel, G.W.F., *Lectures on the Philosophy of History* (Berkeley, CA: University of California Press, 1984).

——, *Philosophy of Right*, translated by T.M. Knox (London: Oxford University Press, 1967).

Heidegger, Martin. *Discourse on Thinking* (New York: Harper & Row, 1966).

Hobbes, Thomas, *Leviathan* (New York: Pelican Books, 1968).

Hudiberg, John J., *Conversations for the 90s: The Total Quality Management Story*, (Harris Trust and Savings Bank, 1991).

Hume, David, *An Enquiry Concerning Human Understanding* (Chicago: Encyclopedia Britannica, 1984).

Illanes, Jose Luis, *On the Theology of Work* (New Rochelle, NY: Scepter Press, 1982).

James, William, *The Will to Believe* (Cambridge, MA: Harvard University Press, 1979).

——, *Writings 1902–1910* (New York: Library of America, 1987).

——, "Philosophical Conceptions and Practical Results," *University Chronicle* 1.4, September (1898).

John Paul II, *Crossing the Threshold of Hope* (New York: Alfred A. Knopf, 1994).

Ketner, Kenneth L., *Reasoning and the Logic of Things* (Cambridge, MA: Harvard University Press, 1992).

Kiechell, Walter, III, "How We Will Work in the Year 2000," *Fortune*, May 17, 1993.

——, "The Organization that Learns," *Fortune*, March 12, 1990.

King, Thomas M., *Jung's Four and Some Philosophers* (Notre Dame, IN: University of Notre Dame Press, 1999).

Kotler, Philip, "Philip Kotler Explores the New Marketing Paradigm," *Marketing Science Institute*, Spring 1991.

Kuhn, James W., and Donald W. Shriver, Jr., *Beyond Success* (New York: Oxford University Press, 1991).

Lapham, Lewis H., "An American Feast," *Wall Street Journal*, May 13, 1987.

Lakoff, George, *Thinking Points: Communicating our American Values and Vision* (New York: Farrar, Strauss, Giroux, 2006).

Lakoff, George, and Mark Johnson, *Metaphors We Live By* (Chicago: University of Chicago Press, 1980).

——, *Philosophy in the Flesh* (New York: Basic Books, 1999).

Levitt, Theodore, *The Marketing Imagination* (New York: The Free Press, 1983).

——, "Marketing Myopia," (Modern Marketing Strategy, Cambridge, MA: Harvard University Press, 1964).

Levy, Sidney J., *Marketplace Behavior* (New York: Amacom, 1978).

Locke, John, "*An Essay Concerning Human Understanding,*" *Encyclopedia Britannica* (Chicago: Encyclopedia Britannica, Inc., 1984).

Lonergan, Bernard, *Method in Theology* (Toronto: University of Toronto Press, 1990).

MacIntyre, Alasdair. *After Virtue* (Notre Dame, IN: University of Notre Dame Press, 1981).

Magnet, Myron, "The Money Society," *Fortune*, July 6, 1987.

Maynard, Herman Bryant, Jr., and Susan E. Mehrtens, *The Fourth Wave* (San Francisco: Berrett-Koehler, 1993).

Menand, Louis, *The Metaphysical Club* (New York: Farrar, Straus & Groux, 2001).

Merton, Louis (Thomas), "Conversatio Morum," *Cistertian Studies*, 1966: 130-44.

Miller, Mark Crispin, "Advertising and Our Discontents," *Adweek*, December 1994.

Mulvaney, Robert J., and Philip M. Zeltner (eds.), *Pragmatism* (Columbia, SC: University of South Carolina Press, 1981).

National Conference of Catholic Bishops, *Economic Justice for All* (Washington: United States Catholic Conference, 1986).

Parikh, Jagdish, *Intuition* (Oxford: Blackwell Business, 1994).

Peck, M. Scott, *The Different Drum* (New York: Simon & Schuster, Inc., 1987).

——, *A World Waiting to be Born* (New York: Bantam Books, 1993).

Peirce, Charles S., *Collected Papers of Charles Sanders Peirce*, vols. 1–6, edited by Charles Hartshorne and Paul Weiss, (Cambridge, MA: Harvard University Press, 1931–35).

——, *Collected Papers of Charles Sanders Peirce*, vols. 6 and 7, edited by Arthur W. Burks, (Cambridge, MA: Harvard University Press, 1958).

——, *The Essential Peirce*, edited by Nathan Houser and Christian Kloesel (Bloomington, IN: Indiana University Press, 1992).

——, *Peirce on Signs*, edited by James Hoopes (Chapel Hill, NC: University of North Carolina Press, 1982).

——, *Philosophical Writings of Peirce*, edited by Justus Buchler (New York: Dover Publications, 1955).

Percy, Walker, "The Divided Creature," *Wilson Quarterly* 13 (1989).

Peters, Tom, *Liberation Management* (New York: Alfred A. Knopf, 1992).

——, "Rediscovery of Ethics Spawns Too-Easy Answers," *Chicago Tribune*, September 18, 1989.

——, *Thriving on Chaos* (New York: Alfred A. Knopf, 1987).

Pink, Daniel, *To Sell is Human* (New York: Riverhead Books, 2012).

——, *A Whole New Mind* (New York: Berkeley Publishing Group, 2006).

Piper, Thomas R., "Creation of the Ethics Module," Unpublished Speech, 1990.

Piper, Thomas R., Mary C. Gentile, Sharon Daloz Parks, and John H. McArthur, *Can Ethics be Taught?* (Boston: Harvard Business School, 1993).

Plato, *The Collected Dialogues of Plato,* edited by Edith Hamilton and Huntington Cairns (Princeton, NJ: Princeton University Press, 1961).

Prahalad, C.K., and Gary Hamel, "The Core Competence of the Corporation," *Harvard Business Review,* May-June, 1990: 79-91.

Progoff, Ira, *At a Journal Workshop* (Los Angeles: Jeremy P. Tarcher, Inc., 1992).

——, *Depth Psychology and Modern Man* (New York: McGraw-Hill, 1959).

——, *The Dynamics of Hope* (New York: Dialogue House Library, 1985).

——, *The Symbolic and the Real* (New York: McGraw-Hill, 1963).

Ray, Michael, *The Highest Goal* (San Francisco: Berrett-Koehler Publishers, 2004).

Ray, Michael, and Rochelle Myers, *Creativity in Business* (New York: Doubleday, 1986).

Ray, Michael, and Alan Rinzler (eds.) *The New Paradigm in Business* (New York: G.P. Putnam's Sons, 1993).

Rochberg-Halton, Eugene, *Meaning and Modernity* (Chicago: The University of Chicago Press, 1986).

Rose, Frank, "A New Generation for Business," *Fortune Magazine,* October 8, 1990.

Royce, Josiah, *The Basic Writings of Josiah Royce,* edited by John J. McDermott (2 volumes; Chicago: University of Chicago Press, 1969).

——, *The Philosophy of Loyalty* (New York: McMillan, 1908).

——, *The Problem of Christianity* (Chicago: University of Chicago Press, 1968).

Scheffler, Israel, *Four Pragmatists* (New York: Routledge & Kegan Paul, 1986).

Scheler, Max, *Ressentiment* (New York: Schocken Books, 1960).

Schumacher, E.F., *A Guide for the Perplexed* (New York: Perennial Library, 1977).

Seigfried, Charlene Haddock (ed.), *Feminist Interpretations of John Dewey* (University Park, PA: Pennsylvania State University Press, 2002).

——, *Pragmatism and Feminism: Reweaving the Social Fabric* (Chicago: University of Chicago Press, 1968).

Senge, Peter M., *The Fifth Discipline* (New York: Doubleday Currency, 1990).

Senge, Peter M., Nelda Cambron-Mccabe, Timothy Lucas, Bryan Smith, and Janis Dutton, Schools that Learn (New York: Doubleday Currency, 2000).

Senge, Peter M., Betty Flowers, C. Otto Scharmer, and Joseph Jaworski, Presence (Cambridge, MA: Society for Organizational Learning, 2004).

Senge, Peter M., Art Kleiner, Charlotte Roberts, Rick Ross, and Bryan Smith, Fifth Discipline Fieldbook (New York: Doubleday Currency, 1994).

Senge, Peter M., Art Kleiner, Charlotte Roberts, George Roth, Rick Ross, and Bryan Smith, The Dance of Change. (New York. Doubleday Currency, 1999).

Sherman, Stratford, "Leaders Need to Heed the Voice Within," *Fortune Magazine,* August 22, 1994.

Smith Adam, *Theory of Moral Sentiment* (Boston: Wells & Lily, 1817).

——, *The Wealth of Nations,* edited by Edwin Cannan (Chicago: University of Chicago Press, 1976).

Stark, Andrew, "What's the Matter with Business Ethics?". *Harvard Business Review,* May– June 1993).

Stevens, Edward, *Business Ethics* (New York: Paulist Press, 1979).

Stewart, Thomas A., "Welcome to the Revolution," *Fortune Magazine,* December 13, 1993.

Taylor, Frederick Winslow, *Scientific Management* (New York: Harper & Brothers, 1911).

Thompson, Craig J., William B. Locander, and Howard R. Pollio, "Putting Consumer Experience Back into Consumer Research: The Philosophy and Method of Existential-Phenomenology," *Journal of Consumer Research* 16.2 (1989).

Thorbeck, John, "The Turnaround Value of Values," *Harvard Business Review,* January– February 1991.

Tocqueville, Alexis de, *Democracy in America* (Garden City, NY: Anchor Books, 1969).

Werhane, Patricia, *Moral Imagination and Management Decision-Making* (New York: Oxford University Press, 1999).

West, B. Kenneth, *Does the Corporation Have a Soul?"* (Chicago: Harris Bankcorp, 1987).

West, Cornel, *The American Evasion of Philosophy* (Madison, WI: University of Wisconsin Press, 1989).

White, Morton, *The Age of Analysis* (New York: Mentor Books, 1955).

Whitehead, Alfred North, *Adventures of Ideas* (New York: The Free Press, 1967).

——, *Aims of Education,* (New York: MacMillan, 1961).

——, *Symbolism* (New York: Fordham University Press, 1927).

Williams, Oliver F., and John W. Houck, *Full Value* (San Francisco: Harper & Row, 1978).

——, *A Virtuous Life in Business* (Lantham, MD: Rowman & Littlefield, 1992).

Wills, Garry, "What Makes a Good Leader?" *Atlantic Monthly*, April 1994.

Wojtyla, Karol, *The Acting Person* (Dortrecht, Holland: D. Reidel, 1969).

Wood, Robert Chapman, "A Lesson Learned and a Lesson Forgotten," *Forbes*, February 6, 1989: 70-78.

Woodward, Kenneth L., "On the Road Again," *Newsweek*, November 28, 1994.

Yankelovich, Daniel, *New Rules* (New York: Random House, 1981).

Zaleski, Carol, "The Spiritual Lives of Women," *New York Times*, February 9, 1992.

Zoglin, Richard, "Beyond Your Wildest Dreams," *Time*, Fall 1992.

Notes

Preface

1 United Nations Environment Programme, *Keeping Track of Our Changing Environment: From Rio to Rio+20 (1992–2012)* (Nairobi: UNEP, 2011, www.unep.org/geo/pdfs/Keeping_Track.pdf, accessed January 22, 2013).

2 James C. Collins and William C. Lazier, *Beyond Entrepreneurship* (Englewood Cliffs, NJ: Prentice Hall, 1992); Collins and Jerry I. Porras, *Built to Last* (London: Random House Business, 1998); Collins, *Good to Great* (London: Random House Books, 2001).

3 James C. Collins, "Level 5 Leadership," *Harvard Business Review*, July-August 2005: 2 (Reprint R0507M)

4 F. Byron (Ron) Nahser, *Journeys to Oxford: Nine Pragmatic Inquiries into the Practice of Values in Business and Education* (New York: Global Scholarly Publications, 2009).

5 One of my favorite comments, not often heard I must admit, was from an executive who had been a philosophy major in undergraduate. She said: "I didn't want Chapter 4 to end." Based on her comments and others who wanted a more complete explanation of pragmatism, including the noted moral philosopher Alasdair MacIntyre who was unhappy that, while liking the overall argument, the Peirce treatment was far too brief and could lead to substantial misunderstanding, it has therefore been expanded, and now you can decide.

Chapter 1

6 Paul Hawken, *The Ecology of Commerce* (New York: HarperCollins, 1993): 22.

7 Cornelia Dean, "Executive on a Mission: Saving the Planet," *New York Times*, May 22, 2007, www.nytimes.com/2007/05/22/science/earth/22ander.html?_r=1&scp=1&sq=RayAndersonspear&st=cse, accessed January 22, 2013.

8 UN Environmental Program www.unep.org; WorldWatch Institute www.worldwatch.org.

9 The International Union for Conservation of Nature, "Red List of Threatened Species," cmsdata.iucn.org/downloads/species_extinction_05_2007.pdf, accessed January 22, 2013.

10 Elroy Bos, "Threats to Species Accelerate," in Worldwatch Institute, Elroy Bos, Katie Carrus and Michael Browne (eds.), *Vital Signs 2007–2008: The Trends That Are Shaping Our Future* (New York: W.W. Norton, 2007): 96-97.

11 www.ipcc.ch/pdf/technical-papers/ccw/Chapter1.pdf.

12 Janet L. Sawin, "Wind Power Still Soaring," in Worldwatch Institute, Elroy Bos, Katie Carrus and Michael Browne (eds.), *Vital Signs 2007–2008: The Trends That Are Shaping Our Future* (New York: W.W. Norton, 2007): 36.

13 Hawken quoted in Ernst von Weizsacher, Amory B. Lovins and L. Hunter Lovins, *Factor Four: Doubling Wealth, Halving Resource Use. The New Report to the Club of Rome* (London: Earthscan, 1998): xx.

14 Susan S. Lang, "Slow, insidious soil erosion threatens human health and welfare as well as the environment," Chronicle Online, March 20, 2006, www.news.cornell.edu/stories/march06/soil.erosion.threat.ssl.html, accessed February 12, 2013.

15 Krista Hozyash, "How our food system is destroying the nation's most important fishery," Grist, February 11, 2010, grist.org/article/2010-02-08-who-owns-the-dead-zone, accessed February 12, 2013.

16 World Health Organization, "Obesity and Overweight", Fact sheet no. 311, May 2012, www.who.int/mediacentre/factsheets/fs311/en/index.html, accessed January 22, 2013.

17 www.washingtonpost.com/blogs/worldviews/files/2012/12/gun-own-totals.jpg, accessed February 12, 2013.

18 Lester R. Brown, "Designing Cities for People: The Return of Bicycles," in *Plan B 4.0: Mobilizing to Save Civilization* (Washington, DC: Earth Policy Institute, 2009; Chapter 6 available at www.earthpolicy.org/books/pb4/PB4ch6_ss4, accessed February 20, 2013).

19 United Nations Environment Programme, *Keeping Track of Our Changing Environment*: 11.

20 Jarvis, Brooke, "Can a Farm State Feed Itself?" *Yes! Magazine*, September 4, 2009, www.yesmagazine.org/new-economy/eating-in, accessed January 29, 2013.

21 www.pawpaw.net/forms/Water Series Part 2 $5.00 FiJi Water.pdf, accessed January 29, 2013.

22 www.worldwatch.org/node/5475.

23 United Nations Environment Programme, *Keeping Track of Our Changing Environment*: 14.

24 Chris Flavin and Gary Gardner, "China, India, and the New World Order," in Worldwatch Institute, *State of the World 2006* (New York: W.W. Norton, 2006): 5.

25 United Nations Environment Programme, *Keeping Track of Our Changing Environment*: 13.

26 Alana Herro, "Literacy Improves Worldwide," *Vital Signs 2007-2008* (New York: W.W. Norton, 2007): 96-97.

27 Courtney Berner, "Language Diversity Declining," *Vital Signs 2006-2007* (New York: W.W. Norton, 2006): 112-113.

28 Peter Stair, "Obesity Reaches Epidemic Levels," *Vital Signs 2006-2007* (New York: W.W. Norton, 2006): 120-121.

29 National Center for Public Policy and Higher Education, Policy Alert, "The U.S. Workforce is Becoming More Diverse," November 2005, www.highereducation.org/reports/pa_decline/decline-f1.shtml, accessed January 29, 2013.

30 Lesley Wroughton, "More People Living Below Poverty Line: World Bank," Reuters, August 26, 2008, www.reuters.com/article/2008/08/26/idUSN26384266, accessed February 12, 2013.

31 Ling Li, "Bottled Water Consumption Jumps," *Vital Signs 2007-2008* (New York: W.W. Norton, 2007): 102-103.

32 Congressional Budget Office, "Trends in the Distribution of Household Income Between 1979 and 2007: highlights," www.cbo.gov/publication/42729, October 2011, accessed February 20, 2013.

33 Lawrence Mishel, CEO-to-Worker Pay Imbalance Grows," Economic Policy Institute, June 21, 2006, www.epi.org/economic_snapshots/entry/webfeatures_snapshots_2006 0621, accessed January 29, 2013.

34 Gary Gardner, "Socially Responsible Investment Grows Rapidly," *Vital Signs 2007-2008* (New York: W.W. Norton, 2007): 96-97.

35 Alessandra Delgado, "Informal Economy Thrives in Cities," *Vital Signs 2007-2008* (New York: W.W. Norton, 2007): 114-115.

36 Flavin and Gardner, "China, India, and the New World Order,": 5.

37 Ibid.: 5.

38 Ibid.: 12.

39 Ibid.: 5.

40 David Brooks, "Carpe Diem Nation," *New York Times* February 11, 2013, www.nytimes.com/2013/02/12/opinion/brooks-carpe-diem-nation.html?ref=davidbrooks&_r=0, accessed February 20, 2013.

41 Bank for International Settlements, December 2008.

42 International Monetary Fund, October 2008.

43 en.wikipedia.org/wiki/File:U.S._Household_Debt_Relative_to_Disposable_Income_and_GDP.png, accessed February 12, 2013.

44 Alexis deTocqueville, *Democracy in America* (Garden City, New York: Anchor Books, 1969): 430.

45 The common definition of *philosophy* is "the love of wisdom," drawn from the Greek word *sophia*, ordinarily translated as "wisdom." It originally meant the study of the laws and causes underlying reality or nature. This specific activity later became called *phusis* or physics. Plato dramatically states the need for philosophy in his view of the human condition that people are like men in a cave, chained, facing a wall and looking at images projected from behind them which they consider to be real (*The Republic*, in *Plato: The Collected Dialogues*, edited by Edith Hamilton and Huntington Cairns [Princeton, NJ: Princeton University Press, 1961]: 747-52). To Alfred North Whitehead, "Philosophy is not a mere collection of noble sentiments …philosophy is at once general and concrete, critical and appreciative of direct intuition … its gifts are insight and foresight and a sense of the worth of life, in short, that sense of importance which nerves all civilized effort" (Chapter 6, "Foresight"' Lecture delivered at the Harvard Business School, in *Adventures of Ideas* [New York: The Free Press, 1967]: 98).

Charles Peirce has stated his philosophy this way: "yet my attitude is always that of a dweller in a laboratory, eager only to learn what I did not yet know." And indeed the first step in developing his philosophy was to "acknowledge you do not satisfactorily know already" (*Philosophical Writings of Peirce*, ed. Justus Buchler [New York: Dover Publications, 1955]:1-4). Josiah Royce says: "Interpretation is, once for all, the main business of philosophy," (Josiah Royce, *Problem of Christianity* [Chicago: University of Chicago Press, 1968]: 297).

We will hear more from these four philosophers later.

46 Semanticists are fond of reminding us that "the map is not the territory."

Chapter 2

47 Conversation with John J. Hudiberg, held in November 1990 in *Conversations for the 90s: The Total Quality Management Story* (Harris Trust and Savings Bank, 1991).

48 An example of this from pre-Socratic times is the old Heraclitean paradox of "the one and the many": the contrariness between the individual and the community.

49 Thomas R. Piper, "Creation of the Ethics Module." Delivered in a memo in 1990 circulated among a close circle of alumni. He goes on to say that the "MBA education seems to have failed in its most important responsibility: to generate excitement about careers and the opportunity for making a difference … [W]ithout realizing it, we gradually reduced our attention to issues of responsibility and purpose."

50 One executive, when I questioned his stretching of a particular sales point, responded: "If I wanted to be that good, I would have become a priest."

51 Another Hericletian paradox: this tension came to be known as the basic question of the "one and the many."

52 Daniel Goleman, *Emotional Intelligence* (New York: Bantam, 1995).

53 This phrase, which Bellah *et al.* use as the title of their book *Habits of the Heart* (Berkeley, CA: University of California Press, 1985), analyzing the paradox of individualism and commitment in America, comes from Tocqueville, whom we will discuss in Chapter 3.

54 Milton Friedman, "The Social Responsibility of Business is to Increase its Profits," Harvard Business School Reprint from *New York Times Magazine*, September 13, 1970: 32-33.

55 Robert Heath, *Seducing the subconscious: the psychology of emotional influence in advertising* (Chichester, UK; Malden, MA: Wiley-Blackwell, 2012).

56 Bob Levenson and Bill Bernbach, *Bill Bernbach's Book: A History of Advertising That Changed the History of Advertising* (New York: Villard Books, 1987).

Chapter 3

57 As a Northwestern/Kellogg School of Management graduate, I do not tire of pointing this out to my friends from these schools. Kellogg emphasizes marketing, which always needs to consider the impact of consumers. Perhaps this explains Kellogg's more relational focus.

58 Charles Protzman and Homer M. Sarasohn, "CCS: Industrial Management," Microfilm from the Harvard Business School Archives, 1949.

59 Ibid.

60 Peter Drucker, *Management* (New York: Harper & Row, 1973): 810.

61 Ibid.

62 Thomas A. Stewart, "Welcome to the Revolution," *Fortune Magazine*, December 13, 1993: 66.

63 Originally published as *The Principles of Scientific Management,* collected in Frederick Winslow Taylor, "Testimony Before the Special House Committee" *Scientific Management* (New York: Harper & Brothers, 1947): 26, 27.

64 Ibid: 196.

65 Robert Chapman Wood, "A Lesson Learned and a Lesson Forgotten," *Forbes*, February 6, 1989: 70-78. After talking about the impact of Sarasohn and Protzman's course on Japanese management thinking, Mr. Wood concludes the article by saying: "Capturing their employees imaginations—getting them to expend their energies for something less tangible than a paycheck—s the greatest challenge that managers face today. With help from a couple of young Americans more than four decades ago, the Japanese have excelled at this challenge. Now it is America's turn again."

66 Frederick Winslow Taylor, "Testimony Before the Special House Committee" *Scientific Management* (New York: Harper & Brothers, 1947): 146.

67 Ibid.: 146.

68 This idea has been expressed most forcefully by Max Scheler. He objects to looking on man as a tool, and offers the view of an organism in nature as a better model. He states that it is a mistake to "superimpose our method of understanding (tools), which is adapted to dead matter, on the factual process of the genesis of life " Max Scheler, *Ressentiment* (New York: Schocken Books): 168-69.

69 Peter Senge, "Team Learning: Dialogue and Discussion," in *The Fifth Discipline* (New York: Doubleday, 1990): 238-49.

70 Mark Crispin Miller, "Advertising and our Discontents," *Adweek*, December 1984: 36.

71 Philip Kotler, "Philip Kotler Explores the New Marketing Paradigm," *Marketing Science Institute*, Spring 1991: 1. To students of theology, this will sound like a faint echo of Martin Buber's famous formulation of "I–Thou" as opposed to "I–It," where the other is treated as an object. Of course, this is familiar to students of Kant in treating people as ends in themselves, as opposed to means to ends. Pope John Paul II said: "the path (of the philosophy of religion) passes not so much through being and existence as through people and their meeting each other, through the 'I' and the 'Thou'. This is a fundamental dimension of man's existence, which is always a coexistence," John Paul II, *Crossing the Threshold of Hope* (New York: Alfred A. Knopf, 1994): 36.

72 Dr. Kotler's quote is: "Marketing serves as the link between society's needs and its patterns of industrial response. It is at the heart of marketing." Philip Kotler, *Marketing Management* (Englewood Cliffs, NJ: Prentice-Hall, 10th edn., 2000).

73 M. Scott Peck, "Stages of Community Making," in *The Different Drum* (New York: Simon & Schuster, 1987): 86-106.

Chapter 4

74 Alfred North Whitehead, "Foresight", in *Adventures of Ideas*: 98.

75 Ibid.: 97-98.

76 www.businessweek.com/stories/1992-04-05/can-ethics-be-taught-harvard-gives-it-the-old-college-try; images.businessweek.com/ss/10/08/0816_harvard_virtual_tour/13.htm, accessed February 12, 2013.

77 Alasdair MacIntyre, *After Virtue* (Notre Dame, IN: University of Notre Dame Press, 1981): 104-105.

78 I am reminded of a story that Professor Sidney Levy of Northwestern University introduced me to, of how the ritual of diamond engagement rings through association with romance was developed by De Beers and its advertising agency several decades ago. Students, especially female students, who are engaged to be married, are shocked to find this out. They feel "manipulated." Professor Levy always is amused by this and wonders if they think the urge for diamonds as a sign of life-long commitment is something genetic. (The story can be found in Edward Jay Epstein, *The Diamond Invention* (London: Hutchinson, 1982,): Chapter 13 .

79 Adam Smith, *The Wealth of Nations* (Chicago: Encyclopedia Britannica, 1984): 340. Incidentally, this thought appears in the section of the work entitled, "Of the Expense of the Institutions for the Education of Youth"!

80 Karl Marx and Frederick Engels, *The Manifesto of the Communist Party* (Chicago: Charles H. Kerr. 1906): 23.

81 Here again, we can turn to Plato who in the *Gorgias* states through Socrates that he believed that the old stories and myths of creation were true (in Plato, *The Collected Dialogues*).

82 St. Augustine, *City of God*, Book XVIII. Chap. 2.

83 Thomas Hobbes, *Leviathan* (New York: Pelican Books, 1968): 160-88.

84 "John Locke, 'Of the State of Nature,' in *An Essay Concerning Human Understanding*" *Encyclopedia Britannica* (Chicago: Encyclopedia Britannica, Inc., 1984): 105.

85 Smith, *The Wealth of Nations*: 7.

86 Ibid.: 14.

87 Ibid.: 128.

88 He presents a different, more optimistic view of businesspeople in Adam Smith, *Theory of Moral Sentiment* (Boston: Wells & Lily, 1817): 27ff.

89 "David Hume, *An Enquiry Concerning Human Understanding*" (Chicago: Encyclopedia Britannica, Inc., 1984): 508.

90 Tocqueville, *Democracy in America*, Vol. 2: 104.

91 Many writers, particularly the Russian thinker Nicholas Berdyaev, have commented on how the bourgeois as "an organizer and business-man and organization 'kills organic life'," (Nicholas Berdyaev, *The Bourgeois Mind* [Freeport, NY: Books for Libraries Press, 1965]: 22). Berdyaev elsewhere says, "Community is a spiritual quality of persons, they being together in a brotherhood of men and it never means some sort of reality which is above men, or which can order them about. Community leaves judgment and consciousness in the depths of man's heart. Consciousness may be at once personal and communal, community is a quality of personal consciousness which cannot be closed up or isolated," in *The Realm of Spirit and the Realm of Caesar* (New York: Harper & Brothers, 1952): 123. Berdyaev ultimately calls for man's spiritual and moral development to keep pace with technical development in order to reestablish man's relationship to God.

92 McKinney is echoing the question of Protzman and Sarasohn. See Chapter 3.

93 Hume, *An Enquiry Concerning Human Understanding*: 508.

Chapter 5

94 As Walker Percy has said, "Most people have never heard of him, but they will" ("The Divided Creature," *Wilson Quarterly* XIII, 1989: 80).

95 He has been described this way: "For most of his life Peirce was treated as a skeleton in a Cambridge closet, a brilliant unemployable who had to be befriended by saintly people like William James; he was thought to be incapable of making himself intelligible or attractive to Victorian academic audiences." Morton White, *The Age of Analysis* (New York: Mentor Books, 1955): 140.

96 For a fascinating history of the Metaphysical Club in Cambridge, see Louis Menand's *The Metaphysical Club* (New York: Farrar, Straus & Groux, 2001). However, I disagree with Menand's key statement about pragmatism: "Pragmatism explains everying about ideas except why a person would be willing to die for one" (page 375). From what I have said and will about the pursuit of the truth, it should be clear that I believe pragmatism does lead to ideas that one would be willing to dedicate one's life to and for.

97 James paraphrased from Peirce's "How to Make Our Ideas Clear," *Popular Science Monthly*, January 1878. It is ironic that James chose to distort Peirce's pragmatism based on ideas from an article with that as its title!

98 William James, "Philosophical Conceptions and Practical Results," An address delivered before the Philosophical Union at Berkeley, California, August 26, 1898, in *William James, Writings 1878–1899* (New York: Literary Classics, 1992): 1077-97.

99 William James, "Pragmatism's Conception of Truth," in *Writings 1902–1910* (New York: Literary Classics, 1992): 573.

100 *The Collected Papers of Charles Sanders Peirce*, Vols. 1–6, ed. Charles Hartshone and Paul Weiss, 1933–35, Vols. 6,7 ed. Arthur Burks, 1958 (Cambridge, MA: Harvard University Press): Vol. 5: 2.

101 To show the difference between this utilitarian method of thinking of James and Peirce's pursuit of Objective Logic, consider the following quote by Peirce: "But to avoid any possible misapprehension, I am bound honestly to declare that I do not hold forth the slightest promise that I have any philosophical wares to offer you which will make you either better men, or more successful men." Kenneth L. Ketner, *Reasoning and the Logic of Things* (Cambridge, MA: Harvard University Press, 1992): 108.

102 William James, *The Will to Believe* (Cambridge, MA: Harvard University Press, 1979): xxii.

103 *The Philosophical Writings of Peirce*: 255.

104 Ibid.: 99.

105 An extreme example of maintaining that rational interpretation of entities and of the events of the world is Nietzsche's famous statement that: "Truth is error." He meant that we live by errors of interpretation but deceive ourselves by calling them truth. By contrast, for Peirce there is always the truth that one does not yet know. Nietzsche also said that "Power is truth," another way of saying "perception is reality," if you are powerful enough!

106 "The Fixation of Belief," in *Philosophical Writings of Peirce*: 5-22. This is the first paper in the series "Illustrations of the Logic of Science," *Popular Science Monthly* 12, January 1877.

107 "The Fixation of Belief," in *Philosophical Writings of Peirce*: 5.

108 Ibid.: 4.

109 Ibid.: 10.

110 Ibid.: 6.

111 Peirce said that a hypothesis can be stated this way: "If thus and so were true all along, then it would not be surprising that thus and so happened." Peirce often referred to mathematical equations as examples of hypotheses.

Chapter 6

112 Royce, *The Problem of Christianity*: 276-77.

113 Josiah Royce, *The Philosophy of Loyalty* (New York: McMillan Co., 1908): 16-17. Royce says the issue of loyalty as central to his philosophy: "In loyalty, when loyalty is properly defined, is the fulfillment of the whole moral law." "Loyalty shall mean, according to this preliminary definition: the willing and practical and thorough going devotion of a person to a cause." Further, Royce helps us with questions he poses in *The Philosophy of Loyalty* with his definition of philosophy: "It [philosophy] does desire to add its thoughtfulness to the intensity of life's great concerns and to enlighten us regarding what aims life has always really intended to pursue ... the religiously disposed man begins by learning that the chief end of his existence is to come into harmony with God's will" (*The Basic Writings of Josiah Royce*, vol. 2, ed. John J. McDermott [Chicago: University of Chicago Press, 1969]: 1020).

114 *The Basic Writings of Josiah Royce*: 277.

115 Ibid.: 306. Peter Senge says virtually the same thing, quoting David Bohm, where he says: "In dialogue people become observers of their own thinking," ("Team Learning: Dialogue and Discussion," in *The Fifth Discipline*: 242).

116 John Dewey states in his capstone work, *Logic: The Theory of Inquiry* (Carbondale, IL: Southern Illinois University Press, 1991) that "The word "Pragmatism" does not, I think, occur in the text. Perhaps the word lends itself to misconception ... But in the proper interpretation of "pragmatic," namely the function of consequences as necessary tests of the validity of propositions, *provided* these consequences are operationally instituted and are as such to resolve the specific problems evoking the operations, the text that follows is thoroughly pragmatic" (pages 4 and 5).

117 John Dewey, *Experience and Education*. (New York: Touchstone, 1997): 87.

118 Dewey, John, Logic: The Theory of Inquiry: 3.

119 After James had read Peirce's proposed lecture notes for his Harvard lectures in 1898, James pleaded, "I am sorry you are sticking so to formal logic. I know our graduate school here, and so does Royce, and we both agree that there are only 3 men who could possibly follow your graphs and relatives. Now be a good boy and think a more popular plan out. I don't want the audience to dwindle to 3 or 4" (Ketner, *Reasoning and the Logic of Things*: 25).

120 See particularly: John Dewey, *Logic: The Theory of Inquiry*. Dewey credits Peirce with focusing attention on "the principle of the continuum of inquiry" (page 3).

121 Peter Drucker, *Post-Capitalist Society* (New York: HarperBusiness, 1993): 9.

122 Senge, *The Basic Writings of Josiah Royce*: 241.

123 Ibid.

124 Prahalad, C.K. and Gary Hamel. "The Core Competence of the Corporation," *Harvard Business Review*, May–June 1990.

125 We can take comfort that in paradox and "fear of God, which is the beginning of wisdom" are the way to freedom from fear, as John Paul II says in conclusion of *Crossing the Threshold of Hope*: 228.

126 *How We Think* was a summarization of his studies in logic for educators. In 1933 John Dewey revised *How We Think*, originally published in 1910, based on the experience of 20 years of experience and discussion. He added the subtitle: "A Restatement of the Relation of Reflective Thinking to the Educative Process." But the major statement of his logical theory is *Logic: The Theory of Inquiry* published in 1938 when Dewey was nearly 80 years old. We will say more about Dewey's logic in Chapter 7.

Chapter 7

127 Ira Progoff, *At a Journal Workshop* (Los Angeles: Jeremy P. Tarcher, Inc., 1992).

128 See B. Kenneth West, *Does the Corporation have a Soul?* (Chicago: Harris Bankcorp., 1987)

129 Progoff felt that individuals could guide their own development using dialogue as the process Carl Jung called the "active imagination." Progoff studied with Jung for many years. See: August J. Cwik, "Active Imagination: Synthesis in Analysis," in Murray Stein, ed., *Jungian Analysis* (Peru, IL: Open Court Publishing, 1997): 136-69.

130 *The Essential Peirce*, edited by Nathan Houser and Christian Kloesel, Vol. 1 (*Bloomington*, IN: Indiana University Press, 1992): 350.

131 This is a vast field. What is affirming is that so many disciplines are recognizing the need to think differently, using all our faculties. Several approaches that I have found very helpful are mentioned in the Bibliography: see particularly Thomas King, Howard Gardner, Daniel Pink, David Boehm, Willis Harman, Patricia Werhane and David Senge. Martin Heidegger, known for big thoughts on phenomenology, made a simple distinction between "calculative and meditative thinking."

132 James C. Collins, "Level 5 Leadership".

133 John Dewey, *Education and Experienc*.

134 Max Scheler refers to this idea of the process of "becoming": through our actions we shape ourselves. That is another way of adding the dimension of investigation to Peirce's pragmatism, as the pursuit of the truth we do not yet know. (See Manfred Frings, *Philosophy of Prediction and Capitalism* [Dordrecht: Martinus Nijhoff Publishers, 1987].)

135 William James, *Writings 1902–1910* (New York: Library of America, 1987): 574.

Chapter 8

136 Core competence: this important focus in business is being led by Prahalad and Hamel, as articulated particularly in their article "The Core Competence of the Corporation", *Harvard Business Review*, May–June 1990: 79-91.

137 Interview with Rick Salomone, Business Director, 3M Corporate Enterprise Development, in 1998.

138 Nina Munk, "How Levi's Trashed a Great American Brand," *Fortune*, April 12, 1999.

139 The work of Jim Collins and his associates has been very important, starting with the often overlooked first book, *Beyond Entrepreneurship* (James C. Collins and William C. Lazier, *Beyond Entrepreneurship* [Englewood Cliffs, NJ: Prentice Hall, 1992]). This first laid out the typology of values, core purpose, and goals. Jim later commented that he knew all were important but wasn't sure which was more important (James C. Collins and Jerry I. Porras, *Built to Last* [London: Random House Business, 1998]). We have found that in our work, values come first, then core purpose based on those values, and then, what is the goal of the core purpose work. This incidentally solves a long-standing problem that you must first determine your ground (values) and then what you will do (core purpose) and where this will take you (goal).

140 Bernard Lonergan, *Method In Theology* (Toronto: University of Toronto Press, 1990). Lonergan is often referred to as the most significant philosophical thinker of the 20th century. He is best known for his book *Insight: A Study of Human Understanding.* I am indebted to several Lonergan scholars in addition to Mike Stebbins. Most prominently is Fr. John Haughey of Loyola University, a long-standing friend who has clarified and reinforced the religious foundations that discernment of a calling and pragmatic inquiry share.

141 www.betagammasigma.org/studentforum.htm.

142 This is what we call "Own who you are."

143 F. Byron (Ron) Nahser and J0hn (Jack) Ruhe, "Putting American Pragmatism to Work in the Classroom," *Journal of Business Ethics* 34.3/4: 317-30.

144 Jane Addams, the Nobel Prize winner who founded Hull House in Chicago to address the plight of the working class, said: "If a workingman is to have a conception of his value at all, he must see industry in its unity and entirety; he must have a conception that will include not only himself and his immediate family and community, but the industrial organization as a whole." Jane Addams, "Educational Methods," in *Democracy and Social Ethics* (New York: Macmillian Company, 1911): 213.

145 I saw that the important skill in both Peirce and Progoff was to be able to listen and see objectively.

Chapter 9

146 Aristotle in his discussion of the ethics of purpose in the *Nicomachean Ethics* (edited by Richard McKeon [New York: Random House, 1941]) asserts that all action is designed for some purpose. While we can't blame Aristotle for our focus on a misdirected teleology, his ethic may have led us to a utilitarian narrowness of purpose as indicated by the Goodpaster story.

147 Max Scheler has pointed out how different people can look at a table: the carpenter considers its qualities, the homemaker its use for serving, and the businessman its potential for profit (see Manfred Frings, *Philosophy of Prediction and Capitalism* [Dordrecht: Martinus Nijhoff Publishers, 1987]: 100-109).

148 Whitehead, "Foresight", in *Adventures of Ideas.*

149 See, e.g., George J. Church, "We're Number 1 and It Hurts," *Time*, October 24, 1994: 50-56. "The price of beating overseas competition has been bitterly high: wave after wave of downsizing layoffs, wage increases limited or foregone, replacement of full-time workers by part-time or temporary hired hands."

150 I often refer to Benedict's Rule as a marketing strategy because it essentially talks about how to develop and serve the needs of "customers."

151 *The Rule of St. Benedict*, ed. Timothy Fry (Collegeville, MN: The Liturgical Press, 1981).

152 After all, the monks are celibate and no property is owned in private. The property had to be owned by the community, or a corporate "sole" since an individual could not inherit it. See John P. Davis, *Corporations: Origins and Development* (New York: G.P. Putnam's Sons, 1905).

153 An example of Aristotelian teleology properly used—one which Royce would heartily approve.

154 Br. David Stendal-Rast, O.S.B, and F.K. David, "Monasticism," in *Encyclopedia Americana*, 1995.

155 Alfred North Whitehead, *Aims of Education* (New York: MacMillan Company, 1961): 68.

156 The three vows were originally stability, fidelity to monastic life, and obedience (*The Rule of St. Benedict*: 269). These evolved during the Middle Ages into the more familiar vows of poverty, chastity and obedience. Benedict's first vow of stability can have great application and meaning for business today, considering our obsession with the short-term. The original three vows also can be interpreted as a model for meditation: sit, converse with God, and obey.

157 This word "happiness" has been the subject of mountains of definitions over the centuries. One of the best I have come across is Martha Nussbaum's translation of the Greek *eudaimonia,* which "means something like 'living a good life for a human being'," in contrast to "happiness" in what she calls the misleading view that gives "supreme value to psychological states rather than to activities," Martha Nussbaum, *The Fragility of Goodness* (New York: Cambridge University Press, 1986): 6. The only modification I would make in this era of sustainability is to broaden the definition to include all living beings.

158 As we mentioned before, this would be an example of Scheler's sense of how we define ourselves through our actions. John Paul II, in his book based on Max Scheler's philosophy, says: "the performance itself of the action by the person is of value. If we call this value 'personalistic,' it is because the person performing the action *also fulfills himself in it,* that is, acquires a personal feature" Cardinal Karol Wojtyla, *The Acting Person* (Dortrecht, Holland: D. Reidel Publishing Company, 1969): 265.

159 James C. Collins, *Good to Great* (London: Random House Books, 2001) Collins says that the "Level 5" leader manages the paradox of resolve and challenging assumptions. He describes the virtue of humility, as well as the essence of Pragmatic Inquiry. He says that he doesn't know how to teach humility, nor do I, but I do say, along with Dewey, that we can make the practice understandable and then teach how to practice it.

160 "Ora et Labora" was actually coined in the 19th century by a German abbot, Maurus Wolter. One Benedictine monk has called it "our trademark," another parallel with the modern corporation near and dear to my advertising heart. I thank Fr. Terrence Kardong, o.s.b., for sharing his unpublished paper, "Work is Prayer: Not!" and leading me to the article by M.D. Meeuws, "Ora et Labora: devise benedictine?" *Collectanea Cisterciensia* 54 (1992): 193-214.

161 The word *conversatio* was dropped from copies of the Rule of St. Benedict early on and never appears in the other most widely used rule, *The Rule of the Master*, which was written just before Benedict's *Rule*. The word was used instead to mean conversion. Many modern scholars conclude that much was lost by this substitution. The actual phrase *conversatio morum*, the nominative and genitive cases, indicates a close intertwining of conversation and way of life to suggest conversation **of** or **as** a way of life that is difficult to capture in English. See Louis (Thomas) Merton, "Conversatio Morum," *Cisterian Studies*, 1966: 130-144.

162 Ibid.

Chapter 10

163 I reluctantly came to this conclusion because, as any beginning teacher knows, the tendency to preach is very strong. The shift from preaching to listening also relates to a basic shift from a selling to a marketing strategy—listening to the customer—which makes for better advertising.

164 MacIntyre, *After Virtue*: 135. Alfred North Whitehead said virtually the same thing, applied to a larger setting: "Every epoch has its character determined by the way its populations react to the material events which they encounter. This reaction is determined by their basic beliefs–by their hopes, their fears, their judgements of what is worthwhile" (Whitehead, "Foresight" in *Adventures in Ideas*: 99).

165 Whitehead, "Foresight" in *Adventures in Ideas*: 98. Incidentally, the Harvard Business School, in a preliminary confidential discussion draft written in response to one of our once-a-decade financial crashes, began their MBA Program vision with this statement: "We aspire to develop outstanding business leaders who contribute to the well being of society." I am happy to see that our statement, written a dozen years earlier, paraphrases the same idea. On our statement of purpose: "Our purpose is to create and implement outstanding ideas to help our clients' businesses grow, benefit the user, and contribute to the well being of society."

166 Of course we aren't the only ones searching. You know the question has reached critical mass when it makes the cover of *Newsweek*, November 28, 1994: "The Search for the Sacred. America's Quest for Spiritual Meaning." See particularly "On the Road Again," by Kenneth L. Woodward, who concludes: "In the traditions of the West, every serious sojourner arrives at the still point of an abiding Presence, who sustains the seeker and justifies the search" (p. 62).

167 In such a view, products and services take on a meaning far beyond their utility and importance in how they relate to personal being. This criticism may explain why advertising practitioners are always ranked second to last (just above car salesmen) when asked, How would you rate the honesty and ethical standards of people in these different professions? (out of two dozen occupations.) July 19-21, *1993 Gallup Poll Monthly*, July 1993.

168 Scheler refers to these as vital values as opposed to utility values, or noble versus useful: "Noble standing for those qualities that constitute the value life in living organisms" (Scheler, in Manfred Frings, *Philosophy of Prediction and Capitalism*: 155). We also look for these values in employees whom we bring into the firm (see Chapter 3).

169 Mark Crispin Miller, "Advertising and Our Discontents," interview with Christopher Lasch, *AdWeek* (December 1984): 36.

170 One employee, after hearing this, said that Phase II should be "putting down your sword."

171 Robert Coles, a Harvard psychiatrist interested in storytelling, has used literature as a way to teach an ethical stance to life for several decades. See, for example, Robert Coles, *The Call of Stories* (Boston: Houghton Mifflin Company, 1989). We have lost something valuable as we have shifted in recent times from the study of literature that reveals virtues and vice in human life, to an emphasis on entertainment in our books, movies, television and other media.

172 William James, of whom we have been critical at times, does share the same spirit as Peirce in terms of the role of philosophy. He says: "No particular results then so far, but only an attitude of orientation, is what the pragmatic method means. The attitude of looking away from first things, principles, "categories," supposed necessities; and looking towards last things, fruits, consequences, facts" (from William James, *Writings 1902– 1910*, Lecture II).

173 *Peirce on Signs*, ed. James Hoopes (Chapel Hill, NC: University of North Carolina Press, 1982): 264.

174 Plato says much the same thing in the *Phaedrus*, Number 270, (in *The Collected Dialogues of Plato*). where Socrates says, "Every great art must be supplemented by leisurely discussion, by stargazing, if you will, about the nature of things."

175 The reason to listen to different stories is that, just like facts, they all have a piece of the truth. Plato, at the end of the *Gorgias*, Number 523, (in *The Collected Dialogues of Plato*) about to recount to Callicles a story about Zeus, Poseidon and Pluto dividing the kingdom among themselves, says to Callicles: "Give ear then, as they say, to a very fine story which you, I suppose, will consider fiction, but I consider fact, for what I am going to tell you I shall recount as the actual truth." One of the core examples of this comes from the most basic stories of the Judeo-Christian tradition: the story of Creation and the story of the life of Christ. In each case, the story is told more than once. In the Book of Genesis, Chapter 1 tells the legalist version of Creation—the seven days, etc. In Chapter 2, the Yahwist, or creative, version, God creates Adam first, breathing into Adam's nostrils to create life. The story of Jesus is told in the Bible *four* times. All give us different points of view, all true.

176 Charles Dickens, *A Christmas Carol* (London: Chapman and Hall, 1848): 33.

177 MacIntyre, *After Virtue*: 244.

178 Ibid.: 245.

179 Max Scheler's writings lead us to think beyond the machine or tool model of the individual in business to the universal community of the "Kingdom on God," Scheler's ultimate model (in Manfred Frings, *Philosophy of Prediction and Capitalism*: 108). Scheler says, "Whenever a 'community' exists, we find that the *fundamental forms* of communal life were endowed with a value far *superior* to all individual interests, to all subjective opinions and intentions" (Ibid.: 167). According to Scheler, every human person possesses a nature which is "just as originally a matter of being, the being and acting 'together' as a matter of existing 'for himself': a communal nature which is spiritually as well as biologically determined from the start." Jonathan Boswell, *Community and the Economy* (New York: Routledge Press, 1990): 36.

Epilogue

180 Immanuel Kant. *Kant's Principles of Politics, Including his Essay on Perpetual Peace: A Contribution to Political Science*, trans. W Hastie. (Edinburgh: T. & T. Clark, 1891.

181 Buono, Anthony, Jean-Christophe Carteron, and Matthew Gitsham, "Schools Need to Champion a Sustainability Mindset," *Financial Times*, June 11, 2012, www.ft.com/intl/cms/s/2/e748533a-aa41-11e1-8b9d-00144feabdc0.html - axzz1zZvGumtI, accessed January 29, 2013.

Appendix II

182 UN Global Compact and Deloitte, *UN Global Compact Management Model: Framework for Implementation* (New York: UN Global Compact, 2010, www.unglobalcompact.org/docs/news_events/9.1_news_archives/2010_06_17/UN_Global_Compact_Management_Model.pdf, accessed January 27, 2013).

183 www.unglobalcompact.org/aboutthegc/thetenprinciples/index.html, accessed January 27, 2013.

184 www.unglobalcompact.org/news/37-06-17-2010, accessed January 27, 2013.

185 nicholasinstitute.duke.edu/globalcompact, accessed January 27, 2013.

186 www.nicholasinstitute.duke.edu/globalcompact/?q=declare, accessed January 27, 2013.

187 UN Global Compact, *Blueprint for Corporate Sustainability Leadership* (New York, UN Global Compact, 2010, www.unglobalcompact.org/docs/news_events/8.1/Blueprint.pdf, accessed January 27, 2013): 4.

About the author

F. Byron (Ron) Nahser, Ph.D. Managing Director for CORPORANTES, Inc., an outgrowth of The Nahser Agency/Advertising, Dr. Nahser is currently a Senior Wicklander Fellow and Director, Urban Sustainable Management Programs at DePaul University's Institute for Business and Professional Ethics; and also Provost Emeritus of Presidio School of Management, San Francisco (offering the first accredited MBA in Sustainable Management). He lectures and consults with business and academic audiences in the U.S. and internationally on business values, vision, marketing strategy, branding, social responsibility and integrative sustainable management.

The author of *Learning to Read the Signs: Reclaiming Pragmatism in Business* and *Journeys to Oxford: Nine Pragmatic Inquiries into the Practice of Values in Business and Education,* he has developed a values-driven strategy method known as PathFinder Pragmatic Inquiry® which has been used by more than 100 organizations and thousands of participants.

He is also a Fellow of the World Business Academy, Curator of the Willis Harman Archive, the Founding Partner of the Oxford Leadership Academy in U.S.A., and Strategic Advisor to the UN Principles for Responsible Management Education (PRME) Secretariat.

Dr. Nahser earned a BA degree from the University of Notre Dame, an MBA degree from Northwestern University's Kellogg School of Management, an MA degree in Religious Studies from Loyola/Mundelein College and the Ph.D. in American Business Philosophy from DePaul University.

Index